A GUIDE TO SQL

Tenth Edition

Mark Shellman
Gaston College

Hassan Afyouni, *Ed.D.*
e-conn Chief Information Officer

Philip J. Pratt
Grand Valley State University

Mary Z. Last

CENGAGE

Australia • Brazil • Mexico • Singapore • United Kingdom • United States

CENGAGE

A Guide to SQL, Tenth Edition
Mark Shellman, Hassan Afyouni,
Philip J. Pratt, and Mary Z. Last

SVP, Higher Education Product
   Management: Erin Joyner

VP, Product Management: Thais Alencar

Product Team Manager: Kristin McNary

Associate Product Manager: Danielle Klahr

Product Assistants: Anna Goulart and
   Tom Benedetto

Director, Learning Design: Rebecca von Gillern

Senior Manager, Learning Design: Leigh Hefferon

Learning Designer: Emily Pope

Vice President, Marketing – Science,
   Technology, & Math: Jason Sakos

Marketing Director: Michele McTighe

Marketing Manager: Cassie Cloutier

Product Specialist: Mackenzie Paine

Director, Content Creation: Juliet Steiner

Senior Manager, Content Creation: Patty Stephan

Content Manager: Michele Stulga

Developmental Editor: Joy Dark

Director, Digital Production Services: Krista
   Kellman

Digital Delivery Lead: Jim Vaughey

IP Analyst: Ashley Maynard

IP Project Manager: Carly Belcher

Manufacturing Planner: Ron Montgomery

Production Service/Composition: SPi Global

Design Director: Jack Pendleton

Text Designer: Lizz Anderson

Cover Designer: Joe Devine,Red Hangar Design

Cover image: © vs148/ShutterStock.com

> For product information and technology assistance,
> contact us at Cengage Customer & Sales Support,
> 1-800-354-9706 or **support.cengage.com**.
>
> For permission to use material from this text or product,
> submit all requests online at
> **www.cengage.com/permissions**.

Library of Congress Control Number: 2020911488

ISBN: 978-0-357-36168-9

Cengage
200 Pier 4 Boulevard
Boston, MA 02210
USA

Cengage is a leading provider of customized learning solutions
with employees residing in nearly 40 different countries and
sales in more than 125 countries around the world. Find your
local representative at **www.cengage.com**.

Cengage products are represented in Canada by Nelson
Education, Ltd.

To learn more about Cengage platforms and services,
register or access your online learning solution, or
purchase materials for your course, visit **www.cengage.com**.

Printed at CLDPC, USA, 04-24

TABLE OF CONTENTS

PREFACE

Structured Query Language (or SQL, which is pronounced "se-quel," or "ess-cue-ell") is a popular computer language that is used by diverse groups such as home computer users, small businesses owners, end users in large organizations, and programmers. Although this text uses the MySQL Community Server 8.0.18 implementation as a vehicle for teaching SQL, its module material, examples, and exercises can be completed using any SQL implementation.

A Guide to SQL, Tenth Edition is written for a wide range of teaching levels, from students taking introductory computer science classes to those students in advanced information systems classes. This text can be used for a stand-alone course on SQL or in conjunction with a database concepts text where students are required to learn SQL.

The modules in this text should be covered in order. Students should complete the end-of-module exercises and the examples within the modules for maximum learning. Because the content of Module 8 assumes that the reader has had instruction or experience in at least one programming language, the instructor should determine whether students will understand its concepts. Students without a programming background might have difficulty understanding the topic of embedded SQL. Instructors can easily omit Module 8 from the text in situations where students are not comfortable with programming examples.

The Tenth Edition builds on the success of previous editions by presenting basic SQL commands in the context of a business that uses SQL to manage orders, items, customers, and sales reps. Like in previous editions, this edition uses MySQL 8.0, Oracle 19c, and MS SQL Server 2019 as the vehicle to present SQL commands. This edition also shows Oracle and SQL Server commands when they differ from the MySQL version. Differences for Oracle and SQL Server users are featured in "User" notes, which make it easy for students to identify differences for the SQL implementation they are using. Students can download the Oracle 19c Enterprise/Standard Edition or the Oracle 19c Express Edition from the Oracle Web site for free and use it to complete this text without having to purchase or install the full Oracle program.

The Tenth Edition includes an entire module on database design, showing students how to create an appropriate design that satisfies a given set of requirements, and includes coverage of the important topics of stored procedures and triggers. The text also contains updated case problems that feature pet supplier and student accommodation companies.

DISTINGUISHING FEATURES

Use of Examples

Starting in Module 3, each module contains multiple examples that use SQL to solve a problem. Following each example, students will read about the commands that are used to solve the stated problem, and then they will see the SQL commands used to arrive at the solution. For most students, learning through examples is the most effective way to master material. For this reason, instructors should encourage students to read the modules at the computer and input the commands shown in the figures.

Case Studies

A running case study—KimTay Pet Supplies—is presented in all the examples within the modules and in the first set of exercises at the end of each module. Although the database is small in order to be manageable, the examples and exercises for the KimTay Pet Supplies database simulate what a real business can accomplish using SQL commands. Using the same case study as examples within the module and in the end-of-module exercises ensures a high level of continuity to reinforce learning.

A second case study—the StayWell Student Accommodation database—is used in a second set of exercises at the end of each module. This case study gives students a chance to venture out "on their own" without the direct guidance of examples from the text.

Question and Answer Sections

A special type of exercise, called a Q&A, is used throughout the text. These exercises drive students to consider special issues and understand important questions before continuing with their study. The answer to each Q&A appears after the question. Students are encouraged to formulate their own answers before reading the ones provided in the text to ensure that they understand new material before proceeding.

User Notes for Oracle and SQL Server Users

When an SQL command has a different use or format in Oracle or SQL Server, it appears in a User note. When you encounter a User note for the SQL implementation you are using, be sure to read its contents. You might also review the User notes for other SQL implementations so you are aware of the differences that occur from one implementation of SQL to another.

Helpful Hints

Helpful Hint boxes call out fundamental information and provide useful tips for the successful implementation of SQL. Students should pay careful attention to the advice within Helpful Hint boxes and are encouraged to review the hints as they are practicing SQL skills.

Review Material

A Summary and Key Terms list appear at the end of each module, followed by Review Questions that test students' recall of the important points in the module and occasionally test their ability to apply what they have learned. Critical Thinking questions that reinforce problem-solving and analytical skills are included for review questions and hands-on exercises. Each module also contains exercises related to the KimTay Pet Supplies and StayWell Student Accommodation databases.

Appendices

Three appendices appear at the end of this text. Appendix A is an SQL reference that describes the purpose and syntax for the major SQL commands featured in the text. Students can use Appendix A to identify how and when to use important commands quickly. The SQL reference appendix contains references to specific pages in the text where the command is discussed to make it easy for students to find additional information when they need to refer back to the section in the text where the topic is covered.

Appendix B includes a "How Do I" reference, which lets students cross-reference the appropriate section in Appendix A by searching for the answer to a question. Appendix C is the 10 Commandments of Writing Queries. This appendix presents summarized steps and rules for composing an SQL statement.

Instructor Support

The Tenth Edition includes a package of proven supplements for instructors and students. The Instructor's Resources offer a detailed electronic Instructor's Manual, figure files, Microsoft® PowerPoint® presentations, and the Cognero Test Bank. The Instructor's Manual includes suggestions and strategies for using this text as well as answers to Review Questions and solutions to the end-of-module exercises. Figure files allow instructors to create their own presentations using figures appearing in the text. Instructors can also take advantage of lecture presentations provided on PowerPoint slides; these presentations follow each module's coverage precisely, include module figures, and can be customized.

The Instructor's Resources include the KimTay Pet Supplies and StayWell Student Accommodation cases script files to create the tables and data in these databases in MySQL, Oracle, and SQL Server. These files are provided so instructors have the choice of assigning exercises in which students create the databases used in this text and load them with data, or they can provide the MySQL, Oracle, or SQL Server script files to students to automate and simplify these tasks.

ORGANIZATION OF THE TEXT

The text contains eight modules and three appendices, which are described in the following sections.

Module 1: Introduction to KimTay Pet Supplies and StayWell Student Accommodation Database

Module 1 introduces the two database cases that are used throughout the text: KimTay Pet Supplies and StayWell Student Accommodation. Many Q&A exercises are provided throughout the module to ensure that students understand how to manipulate the database on paper before they begin working in SQL.

Module 2: Database Design Fundamentals

Module 2 covers important concepts and terminology associated with relational databases, functional dependence, and primary keys, followed by a method for designing a database to satisfy a given set of requirements. It also illustrates the normalization process for finding and correcting a variety of potential problems in database designs. Finally, it shows how to represent database designs graphically using entity-relationship diagrams.

Module 3: Creating Tables

In Module 3, students begin using a DBMS by creating and running SQL commands to create tables, use data types, and add rows to tables. Module 3 also discusses the role of and use of nulls.

Module 4: Single-Table Queries

Module 4 is the first of two modules on using SQL commands to query a database. The queries in Module 4 all involve single tables. Included in this module are discussions of simple and compound conditions; computed columns; the SQL BETWEEN, LIKE, and IN operators; using SQL aggregate functions; nesting queries; grouping data; and retrieving columns with null values.

Module 5: Multiple-Table Queries

Module 5 completes the discussion of querying a database by demonstrating queries that join more than one table. Included in this module are discussions of the SQL IN and EXISTS operators, nested subqueries, using aliases, joining a table to itself, SQL set operations, and the use of the ALL and ANY operators. The module also includes coverage of various types of joins.

Module 6: Updating Data

In Module 6, students learn how to use the SQL COMMIT, ROLLBACK, UPDATE, INSERT, and DELETE commands to update table data. Students also learn how to create a new table from an existing table and how to change the structure of a table. The module also includes coverage of transactions, including both their purpose and implementation.

Module 7: Database Administration

Module 7 covers the database administration features of SQL, including the use of views; granting and revoking database privileges to users; creating, dropping, and using an index; using and obtaining information from the system catalog; and using integrity constraints to control data entry.

Module 8: SQL Functions, Procedures, and Triggers

Module 8 begins with a discussion of some important SQL functions that act on single rows. Students also learn how to use PL/SQL and T-SQL to cover the process of embedding SQL commands in another language. Included in this module are discussions of using embedded SQL to insert new rows and change and delete existing rows. Also included is a discussion of how to retrieve single rows using embedded SQL commands and how to use cursors to retrieve multiple rows. The module concludes with a discussion of triggers.

Appendix A: SQL Reference

Appendix A includes a command reference for all the major SQL clauses and operators that are featured in the modules. Students can use Appendix A as a quick reference when constructing commands. Each command includes a short description, a table that shows the required and optional clauses and operators, and an example and its results. It also contains a reference to the pages in the text where the command is covered.

Appendix B: How Do I Reference

Appendix B provides students with an opportunity to ask a question, such as "How do I delete rows?" and to identify the appropriate section in Appendix A to use to find the answer. Appendix B is extremely valuable when students know what task they want to accomplish but cannot remember the exact SQL command they need.

Appendix C: The 10 Commandments of Writing Queries

Appendix C provides students with a one-page guide (cheat sheet) on the Dos and Don'ts of writing query statements. The 10 commandments in Appendix C covers all the SQL rules presented in this text.

GENERAL NOTES TO THE STUDENT

For details on running script files in Oracle or SQL Server, check with your instructor. You can also refer to Module 3 in the text for information about creating and using scripts.

For information about downloading MySQL and Oracle 19c software, please visit the Oracle Web site. For information about SQL Server Express, please visit the Microsoft Web site.

Embedded Questions

In many places, you'll find Q&A sections to ensure that you understand some crucial material before you proceed. In some cases, the questions are designed to give you the chance to consider some special concept in advance of its actual presentation. In all cases, the answer to each question appears immediately after the question. You can simply read the question and its answer, but you will benefit from taking time to determine the answer to the question before checking your answer against the one given in the text.

End-of-Module Material

The end-of-module material consists of a Summary, a Key Terms list, Review Questions, Critical Thinking questions, and exercises for the KimTay Pet Supplies and StayWell Student Accommodation databases. The Summary briefly describes the material covered in the module. The Review Questions require you to recall and apply the important material in the module. The KimTay Pet Supplies and StayWell Student Accommodation exercises test your knowledge of the module material; your instructor will assign one or more of these exercises for you to complete. Critical-thinking questions that reinforce problem-solving and analytical skills are included for review questions and hands-on exercises.

Mark Shellman, Gaston College

Dr. Mark Shellman is an instructor and the Chair of the Information Technology Department at Gaston College in Dallas, North Carolina. Dr. Mark, as his students refer to him, prides himself on being student-centered and loves learning himself. His favorite subjects in the information technology realm include databases and programming languages. Dr. Mark has been teaching information technology for more than thirty years and has co-authored several texts in the New Perspectives Series on Microsoft® Access databases.

Hassan Afyouni, e-conn (Chief Information Officer)

Dr. Hassan Afyouni has been working in the information technology field for more than thirty years. He is a database expert, Oracle® specialist, an enterprise architect, technical advisor, and educator. He has been an instructor for several colleges and universities in Canada, the United States, and Lebanon. He is a respected author of several leading books in the database field.

Philip J. Pratt, Grand Valley State University

Philip J. Pratt is Professor Emeritus of Mathematics and Computer Science at Grand Valley State University, where he taught for 33 years. His teaching interests include database management, systems analysis, complex analysis, and discrete mathematics. He has authored more than 75 textbooks and has co-authored three levels of Microsoft® Office Access books for the popular Shelly Cashman Series, in addition to the popular A GUIDE TO SQL.

Mary Z. Last

Mary Z. Last has taught computer information systems since 1984. She retired from the University of Mary Hardin-Baylor, Belton, Texas, where she was an associate professor and the Director of the Center for Effectiveness in Learning and Teaching. Ms. Last is actively involved in the Computing Educator's Oral History Project that encourages young women to pursue careers in math and science. She has been a contributing author to the Shelly Cashman Series since 1992. She also authors many instructor resources for leading database texts.

ACKNOWLEDGMENTS

From Mark Shellman:

I would first like to dedicate this text to the memory of parents, Mickey and Shelba Shellman, that passed away during the writing of this text. No child has ever been more loved and supported in their life than I. I would also like to thank my wife Donna Sue, and children, Taylor and Kimberly, for their support and patience during this project. Last, but certainly not least, I would like to thank the entire development team of Amy Savino, Michele Stulga, and Joy Dark, along with my co-author Hassan Afyouni. Thank you all from the bottom of my heart for all of your support and caring during this project. It means more than you will ever know. You are truly the best!

From Hassan Afyouni:

I dedicate this text to my beautiful and patient wife, Rouba, for her everlasting love and support. I devote every letter of this text to my precious children, Aya, Wissam, Sammy, and Luna.

Special thanks to my co-author Mark Shellman and Cengage development team Amy Savino, Michele Stulga, Joy Dark, and to the whole production team. Also, thanks to Jennifer Bowes for giving me the opportunity to work on this project.

1

INTRODUCTION TO KIMTAY PET SUPPLIES AND STAYWELL STUDENT ACCOMMODATION DATABASES

OBJECTIVES

- Introduce KimTay Pet Supplies, a company whose database is used to manage a pet supplies business. The KimTay database is used as the basis for many of the examples throughout the text.
- Introduce StayWell, a Seattle-based company whose database is used to manage accommodation for university students on behalf of property owners. The StayWell database is used as an additional case that runs throughout the text.

INTRODUCTION

In this module, you examine the database requirements of KimTay Pet Supplies—a company that is used in the examples throughout the text. Then, you examine the database requirements for StayWell, whose database is featured in the exercises that appear at the end of each module.

WHAT IS A DATABASE?

Throughout this text, you will work with databases for two organizations: KimTay Pet Supplies and StayWell. A **database** is a structure that contains different categories of information and the relationships between these categories. For example, the KimTay Pet Supplies database contains information about categories such as sales representatives (sales reps), customers, invoices, and items. The StayWell database contains information about the offices that manage the accommodation, the owners of the accommodation, the residents, and the services (such as cleaning and maintenance) offered for the properties.

Each database also contains relationships between categories. For example, the KimTay Pet Supplies database contains information that relates sales reps to the customers they represent and customers to the invoices they have placed. The StayWell database contains information that relates the two main company offices to the properties that they manage, the owners, the different services to the service request, and to the resident renting a property.

As you work through the modules in this text, you will learn more about these databases and how to view and update the information they contain. As you read each module, you will see examples from the KimTay Pet Supplies database. At the end of each module, your instructor might assign the exercises for the KimTay Pet Supplies or StayWell databases.

THE KIMTAY PET SUPPLIES DATABASE

The management of KimTay Pet Supplies (a supplier of pet supplies, food, and accessories located in Cody, Wyoming) has determined that the company's recent growth no longer makes it feasible to maintain customer, invoice, and inventory data using its manual systems. In addition, KimTay Pet Supplies wants to build an Internet presence. With the data stored in a database, management will be able to ensure that the data is up-to-date and more accurate than in the current manual systems. In addition, managers will be able to obtain answers to their questions concerning the data in the database easily and quickly, with the option of producing a variety of useful reports.

Management has determined that KimTay Pet Supplies must maintain the following information about its sales reps, customers, and inventory in the new database:

- The sales rep ID, first name, last name, full address, cell phone number, total commission, and commission rate for each sales rep
- The customer ID, first name, last name, full address, e-mail address, current balance, and credit limit for each customer, as well as the ID of the sales rep who represents the customer
- The item ID, description, number of units on hand, category, storage location, and unit price for each item in inventory

KimTay Pet Supplies also must store information about invoices. Figure 1-1 shows a sample invoice.

The sample invoice shown in Figure 1-1 has three sections:

- The heading (top) of the invoice contains the company name and contact information; the invoice number and date; the customer's ID, name, and full address; and the sales rep's ID and full name.
- The body of the invoice contains one or more invoice lines, some-times called line items. Each invoice line contains an item ID, an item description, the number of units of the item ordered, and the quoted price for the item. Each invoice line also contains a total, usually called an extension, which is the result of multiplying the number ordered by the quoted price.
- Finally, the footing (bottom) of the invoice contains the invoice total.

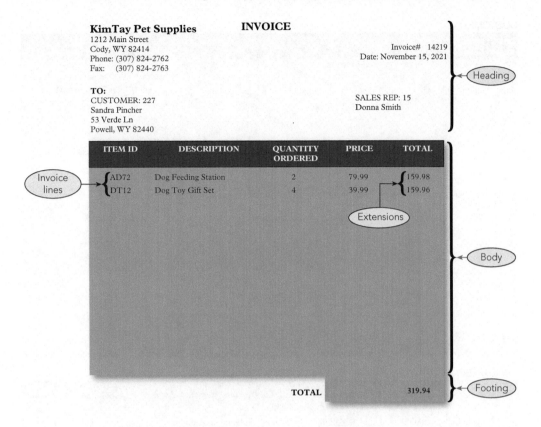

FIGURE 1-1 Sample invoice

KimTay Pet Supplies also must store the following items in the database for each customer's invoice:

- The invoice number, the date the invoice was placed, and the ID of the customer that placed the invoice. The customer's name, full address, and the ID of the sales rep who represents the customer are stored with the customer information. The name of the sales rep is stored with the sales rep information.
- The invoice number, the item ID, the quantity ordered, and the quoted price for each invoice line. The item description is stored with the information about items. The result of multiplying the number of units ordered by the quoted price is not stored because the database can calculate it when needed.

The overall invoice total is not stored. Instead, the database calculates the total whenever an invoice is printed or displayed on the screen.

Figure 1-2 shows sample data for KimTay Pet Supplies.

CUSTOMER

CUST_ID	FIRST_NAME	LAST_NAME	ADDRESS	CITY	STATE	POSTAL	EMAIL	BALANCE	CREDIT_LIMIT	REP_ID
126	Joey	Smith	17 Fourth St	Cody	WY	82414	jsmith17@example.com	$80.68	$500.00	05
182	Billy	Rufton	21 Simple Cir	Garland	WY	82435	billyruff@example.com	$43.13	$750.00	10
227	Sandra	Pincher	53 Verde Ln	Powell	WY	82440	spinch2@example.com	$156.38	$500.00	15
294	Samantha	Smith	14 Rock Ln	Ralston	WY	82440	ssmith5@example.com	$58.60	$500.00	10
314	Tom	Rascal	1 Rascal Farm Rd	Cody	WY	82414	trascal3@example.com	$17.25	$250.00	15
375	Melanie	Jackson	42 Blackwater Way	Elk Butte	WY	82433	mjackson5@example.com	$252.25	$250.00	05
435	James	Gonzalez	16 Rockway Rd	Wapiti	WY	82450	jgonzo@example.com	$230.40	$1,000.00	15
492	Elmer	Jackson	22 Jackson Farm Rd	Garland	WY	82435	ejackson4@example.com	$45.20	$500.00	10
543	Angie	Hendricks	27 Locklear Ln	Powell	WY	82440	ahendricks7@example.com	$315.00	$750.00	05
616	Sally	Cruz	199 18th Ave	Ralston	WY	82440	scruz5@example.com	$8.33	$500.00	15
721	Leslie	Smith	123 Sheepland Rd	Elk Butte	WY	82433	lsmith12@example.com	$166.65	$1,000.00	10
795	Randy	Blacksmith	75 Stream Rd	Cody	WY	82414	rblacksmith6@example.com	$61.50	$500.00	05

SALES_REP

REP_ID	FIRST_NAME	LAST_NAME	ADDRESS	CITY	STATE	POSTAL	CELL_PHONE	COMMISSION	RATE
05	Susan	Garcia	42 Mountain Ln	Cody	WY	82414	307-824-1245	$12,743.16	0.04
10	Richard	Miller	87 Pikes Dr	Ralston	WY	82440	307-406-4321	$20,872.11	0.06
15	Donna	Smith	312 Oak Rd	Powell	WY	82440	307-982-8401	$14,912.92	0.04
20	Daniel	Jackson	19 Lookout Dr	Elk Butte	WY	82433	307-883-9481	$0.00	0.04

ITEM

ITEM_ID	DESCRIPTION	ON_HAND	CATEGORY	LOCATION	PRICE
AD72	Dog Feeding Station	12	DOG	B	$79.99
BC33	Feathers Bird Cage (12×24×18)	10	BRD	B	$79.99
CA75	Enclosed Cat Litter Station	15	CAT	C	$39.99
DT12	Dog Toy Gift Set	27	DOG	B	$39.99
FM23	Fly Mask with Ears	41	HOR	C	$24.95
FS39	Folding Saddle Stand	12	HOR	C	$39.99
FS42	Aquarium (55 Gallon)	5	FSH	A	$124.99
KH81	Wild Bird Food (25 lb)	24	BRD	C	$19.99
LD14	Locking Small Dog Door	14	DOG	A	$49.99
LP73	Large Pet Carrier	23	DOG	B	$59.99
PF19	Pump & Filter Kit	5	FSH	A	$74.99
QB92	Quilted Stable Blanket	32	HOR	C	$119.99
SP91	Small Pet Carrier	18	CAT	B	$39.99
UF39	Underground Fence System	7	DOG	A	$199.99
WB49	Insulated Water Bucket	34	HOR	C	$79.99

FIGURE 1-2   Sample data for KimTay Pet Supplies

INVOICES

INVOICE_NUM	INVOICE_DATE	CUST_ID
14216	11/15/2021	125
14219	11/15/2021	227
14222	11/16/2021	294
14224	11/16/2021	182
14228	11/18/2021	435
14231	11/18/2021	125
14233	11/18/2021	435
14237	11/19/2021	616

INVOICE_LINE

INVOICE_NUM	ITEM_ID	QUANTITY	QUOTED_PRICE
14216	CA75	3	$37.99
14219	AD72	2	$79.99
14219	DT12	4	$39.99
14222	LD14	1	$47.99
14224	KH81	4	$18.99
14228	FS42	1	$124.99
14228	PF19	1	$74.99
14231	UF39	2	$189.99
14233	KH81	1	$19.99
14233	QB92	4	$109.95
14233	WB49	4	$74.95
14237	LP73	3	$54.95

FIGURE 1-2 Sample data for KimTay Pet Supplies (Continued)

In the SALES_REP table, you see that there are four reps, whose ID values are 05, 10, 15, and 20. The name of sales rep 05 is Susan Garcia. Her street address is 42 Mountain Ln. She lives in Cody, WY, and her postal code is 82414. Her cell phone number is 307-824-1245. Her total commission is $12,743.16, and her commission rate is 0.04 (four percent).

In the CUSTOMER table, 12 KimTay Pet Supplies customers are identified with the ID values of 126, 182, 227, 294, 314, 375, 435, 492, 543, 616, 721, and 795. The name of customer number 126 is Joey Smith. This customer's address is 17 Fourth St in Cody, WY, with a postal code of 82414. The e-mail address of the customer is jsmith17@ example.com. The customer's current balance is $80.68, and their credit limit is $500.00. The value 05 in the REP_ID column indicates that Joey Smith is represented by sales rep 05 (Susan Garcia).

In the table named ITEM, you see that there are 15 items, whose item ID values are AD72, BC33, CA75, DT12, FM23, FS39, FS42, KH81, LD14, LP73, PF19, QB92, SP91, UF39, and WB49. Item AD72 is a Dog Feeding Station, and KimTay Pet Supplies has 12 units of this item on hand. The Dog Feeding Station item is in the DOG category, and it is located in area B. The price of the Dog Feeding Station is $79.99. Other categories are BRD (bird), CAT, FSH (fish), and HOR (horse).

In the table named INVOICES, you see that there are eight invoices which are identified with the numbers 14216, 14219, 14222, 14224, 14228, 14231, 14233, and 14237. Invoice number 14216 was placed on November 15, 2021, by customer 125 (Joey Smith).

The table named INVOICE_LINE might seem strange at first glance. Why do you need a separate table for the invoice lines? Could they be included in the INVOICES table? The answer is technically yes. You could structure the table named INVOICES as shown in Figure 1-3. Notice that this table contains the same invoices as shown in Figure 1-2, with the same dates and customer ID numbers. In addition, each table row in Figure 1-3 contains all the invoice lines for a given invoice. Examining the second row, for example, you see that invoice 14219 has two invoice lines. One of the invoice lines is for 2 units of item AD72 at $79.99 each, and the other invoice line is for 4 units of item DT12 at $39.99 each.

Q & A

Question: How is the information from Figure 1-2 represented in Figure 1-3?
Answer: Examine the INVOICE_LINE table shown in Figure 1-2 and note the second and third rows. The second row indicates that there is an invoice line on invoice 14219 for 2 units of item AD72 at $79.99 each. The third row indicates that there is an invoice line on invoice 14219 for 4 units of item DT12 at $39.99 each. Thus, the information that you find in Figure 1-3 is represented in Figure 1-2 in two separate rows rather than in one row.

It might seem inefficient to use two rows to store information that could be represented in one row. There is a problem, however, with the arrangement shown in Figure 1-3—the table is more complicated. In Figure 1-2, there is a single entry at each

INVOICES

INVOICE_NUM	INVOICE_DATE	CUST_ID	ITEM_ID	QUANTITY	QUOTED_PRICE
14216	11/15/2021	125	CA75	3	$37.99
14219	11/15/2021	227	AD72	2	$79.99
			DT12	4	$39.99
14222	11/16/2021	294	LD14	1	$47.99
14224	11/16/2021	182	KH81	4	$18.99
14228	11/18/2021	435	FS42	1	$124.99
			PF19	1	$74.99
14231	11/18/2021	125	UF39	2	$189.99
14233	11/18/2021	435	KH81	1	$19.99
			QB92	4	$109.95
			WB49	4	$74.95
14237	11/19/2021	616	LP73	3	$54.95

FIGURE 1-3   Alternative INVOICES table structure

location in the table. In Figure 1-3, some of the individual positions within the table contain multiple entries, making it difficult to track the information between columns. In the row for invoice number 14219, for example, it is crucial to know that the AD72 corresponds to the 2 in the QUANTITY column (not to the 4) and that it corresponds to the $79.99 in the QUOTED_PRICE column (not to the $39.99). In addition, a more complex table raises practical issues, such as the following:

- How much room do you allow for these multiple entries?
- What happens when an invoice has more invoice lines than you have allowed room for?
- For a given item, how do you determine which invoices contain invoice lines for that item?

Although none of these problems is unsolvable, they do add a level of complexity that is not present in the arrangement shown in Figure 1-2. In Figure 1-2, there are no multiple entries to worry about, it does not matter how many invoice lines exist for any invoice, and finding every invoice that contains an invoice line for a given item is easy (just look for all invoice lines with the given item number in the ITEM_ID column). In general, this simpler structure is preferable, and that is why invoice lines appear in a separate table.

To test your understanding of the KimTay Pet Supplies data, use Figure 1-2 to answer the following questions.

Q & A

Question: What are the customer ID values of the customers represented by Susan Garcia?
Answer: 125, 375, 543, and 795. (Look up the REP_ID value of Susan Garcia in the SALES_REP table and obtain the value 05. Then find all customers in the CUSTOMER table that have the value 05 in the REP_ID field.)

Q & A

Question: What is the name of the customer that placed invoice 14222, and what is the name of the sales rep who represents the customer?
Answer: Samantha Smith is the customer, and Richard Miller is the sales rep. (Look up the CUST_ID value in the INVOICES table for invoice 14222 and obtain the ID value 294. Then find the customer in the CUSTOMER table with the CUST_ID value of 294. Using the REP_ID value, which is 10, find the name of the sales rep in the SALES_REP table.)

Q & A

Question: List all items that appear in invoice 14228. For each item, give the description, quantity ordered, and quoted price.
Answer: Item ID: FS42; description: Aquarium (55 Gallon); quantity ordered: 1; and quoted price: $124.99. Also, item ID: PF19; description: Pump & Filter Kit; quantity ordered: 1; and quoted price: $74.99. (Look up each INVOICE_LINE table row on which the invoice number is 14228. Each of these rows contains an item ID, quantity ordered, and quoted price. Use the item ID to look up the corresponding item description in the ITEM table.)

Q & A

Question: Why is the QUOTED_PRICE column in the INVOICE_LINE table? Can't you just use the item ID and look up the price in the ITEM table?
Answer: If the QUOTED_PRICE column did not appear in the INVOICE_LINE table, you would need to obtain the price for an item on an invoice line by looking up the price in the ITEM table. Although this approach is reasonable, it prevents KimTay Pet Supplies from charging different prices to different customers for the same item. Because KimTay Pet Supplies wants the flexibility to quote and charge different prices to different customers, the QUOTED_PRICE column is included in the INVOICE_LINE table. If you examine the INVOICE_LINE table, you will see cases in which the quoted price matches the actual price in the ITEM table, and cases in which it differs. For example, in invoice number 14216, Joey Smith bought three Enclosed Cat Litter Stations, and KimTay Pet Supplies charged only $37.99 each, not the regular price of $39.99.

STAYWELL STUDENT ACCOMMODATION DATABASE

StayWell finds and manages accommodation for owners of student accommodation in the Seattle area. The company rents out and helps to maintain 1–5-bedroom properties located in two main areas in the city, Columbia City and Georgetown. This is done on behalf of property owners based both in the local area and throughout the United States. Each location is administrated by a different office, StayWell-Columbia City and StayWell-Georgetown.

StayWell wishes to expand its business. The current model relies on advertisements in student and university publications in print and online, but prospective owners and renters need to contact the offices and speak to an administrator on all matters relating to renting of properties. The office organizes maintenance services for a fee, which is also currently done via email or direct communication.

StayWell has decided that the best way to increase efficiency and move toward an e-commerce-based business model is to store all the data about the properties, owners, tenants and services in databases. This will mean that the information can be easily accessed. StayWell hopes that these databases can then be used in future projects such as mobile apps and online booking systems.

The data is split into several tables as described below.

The OFFICE table shown in Figure 1-4 shows the office number, office location, address, area, city, state, and ZIP code.

OFFICE

OFFICE_NUM	OFFICE_NAME	ADDRESS	AREA	CITY	STATE	ZIP_CODE
1	StayWell-Columbia City	1135 N. Wells Avenue	Columbia City	Seattle	WA	98118
2	StayWell-Georgetown	986 S. Madison Rd	Georgetown	Seattle	WA	98108

FIGURE 1-4 Sample data for StayWell offices

StayWell is split into two offices to better manage the properties. This management includes communicating with owners about the status and upkeep of their properties. They also facilitate the payment from the properties, meaning that the owners get regular income without having to collect rent in arrears. Offices also advertise properties and place students in appropriate properties, facilitating initial visits and taking deposits. Lastly the office administers the maintenance of the properties, communicating with residents, owners, and maintenance services. This is discussed later.

StayWell stores information about the owners of each property in the OWNER table, as seen in Figure 1-5. Each owner is identified by a unique owner number that consists of two uppercase letters followed by a three-digit number. For each owner, the table also includes the last name, first name, address, city, state, and ZIP code. Notice the owners are from across the United States. Although some apartments may be owned by a couple or a family, only the primary contact is given.

Each property at each location is identified by a property ID, as seen in Figure 1-6. Each property also includes the office number that manages the property, address, floor size, the number of bedrooms, the number of floors, monthly rent per property, and the owner number. The property ID is an integer unique for each property.

OWNER

OWNER_NUM	LAST_NAME	FIRST_NAME	ADDRESS	CITY	STATE	ZIP_CODE
MO100	Moore	Elle-May	8006 W. Newport Ave.	Reno	NV	89508
PA101	Patel	Makesh	7337 Sheffield St.	Seattle	WA	98119
AK102	Aksoy	Ceyda	411 Griffin Rd.	Seattle	WA	98131
CO103	Cole	Meerab	9486 Circle Ave.	Olympia	WA	98506
KO104	Kowalczyk	Jakub	7431 S. Bishop St.	Bellingham	WA	98226
SI105	Sims	Haydon	527 Primrose Rd.	Portland	OR	97203
BU106	Burke	Ernest	613 Old Pleasant St.	Twin Falls	ID	83303
RE107	Redman	Seth	7681 Fordham St.	Seattle	WA	98119
LO108	Lopez	Janine	9856 Pumpkin Hill Ln.	Everett	WA	98213
BI109	Bianchi	Nicole	7990 Willow Dr.	New York	NY	10005
JO110	Jones	Ammarah	730 Military Ave.	Seattle	WA	98126

FIGURE 1-5   Sample data for the owners of StayWell properties

PROPERTY

PROPERTY_ID	OFFICE_NUM	ADDRESS	SQR_FT	BDRMS	FLOORS	MONTHLY_RENT	OWNER_NUM
1	1	30 West Thomas Rd.	1,600	3	1	1,400	BU106
2	1	782 Queen Ln.	2,100	4	2	1,900	AK102
3	1	9800 Sunbeam Ave.	1,005	2	1	1,200	BI109
4	1	105 North Illinois Rd.	1,750	3	1	1,650	KO104
5	1	887 Vine Rd.	1,125	2	1	1,160	SI105
6	1	8 Laurel Dr.	2,125	4	2	2,050	MO100
7	2	447 Goldfield St.	1,675	3	2	1,700	CO103
8	2	594 Leatherwood Dr.	2,700	5	2	2,750	KO104
9	2	504 Windsor Ave.	700	2	1	1,050	PA101
10	2	891 Alton Dr.	1,300	3	1	1,600	LO108
11	2	9531 Sherwood Rd.	1,075	2	1	1,100	JO110
12	2	2 Bow Ridge Ave.	1,400	3	2	1,700	RE107

FIGURE 1-6   Sample data for StayWell properties

It might at first seem reasonable to include property IDs in the OWNER table, as it would only add one more column. However, if you look at the tables, you notice that there are more properties than owners because some owners have more than one property managed by StayWell. If the OWNER table included the property codes, this would require some entries to have more than one property ID. This would either require multiple property columns or require single rows to contain multiple data entries, creating issues in cross-referencing.

StayWell provides maintenance services across the properties in the two areas; this is shown in Figure 1-7. The SERVICE_CATEGORY table includes details of these services. The CATEGORY_NUM provides a unique number for the service, and CATEGORY_DESCRIPTION shows what the service is.

SERVICE_CATEGORY

CATEGORY_NUM	CATEGORY_DESCRIPTION
1	Plumbing
2	Heating
3	Painting
4	Electrical systems
5	Carpentry
6	Furniture replacement

FIGURE 1-7   Sample category data for StayWell maintenance services

The SERVICE_REQUEST, as shown in Figure 1-8, table shows requests that residents have put into the offices for maintenance. Each row contains a unique service ID number, the property ID, and the category relating to Figure 1-7. For example, the first line shows the unique service ID, followed by the property ID, which is 11. Looking at the PROPERTY table, we can see that this is 9531 Sherwood Rd, and by referencing the office number we can see that this is managed by StayWell-Georgetown. The table includes details of the request, along with the current status. The estimated time to complete the service is included, plus the actual amount of time and the date of the action to be taken, where applicable.

The RESIDENTS database, as shown in Figure 1-9, includes details about the residents living in each property. The RESIDENT column includes the first name and last name for each of the residents, along with a resident ID. The PROPERTY_ID is the unique identification number of the property in which they are staying.

SERVICE_REQUEST

SERVICE_ ID	PROPERTY_ ID	CATEGORY_ NUMBER	OFFICE_ NUM	DESCRIPTION	STATUS	EST_ HOURS	SPENT_ HOURS	NEXT_ SERVICE_DATE
1	11	2	2	The second bedroom upstairs is not heating up at night.	Problem has been confirmed. Central heating engineer has been scheduled.	2	1	11/01/2019
2	1	4	1	A new strip light is needed for the kitchen.	Scheduled	1	0	10/02/2019
3	6	5	1	The bathroom door does not close properly.	Service rep has confirmed issue. Scheduled to be refitted.	3	1	11/09/2019
4	2	4	1	New outlet has been requested for the first upstairs bedroom. (There is currently no outlet).	Scheduled	1	0	10/02/2019
5	8	3	2	New paint job requested for the common area (lounge).	Open	10	0	
6	4	1	1	Shower is dripping when not in use.	Problem confirmed. Plumber has been scheduled.	4	2	10/07/2019
7	2	2	1	Heating unit in the entrance smells like it's burning.	Service rep confirmed the issue to be dust in the heating unit. To be cleaned.	1	0	10/09/2019
8	9	1	2	Kitchen sink does not drain properly.	Problem confirmed. Plumber scheduled.	6	2	11/12/2019
9	12	6	2	New sofa requested.	Open	2	0	

FIGURE 1-8   Sample service request category

RESIDENTS

RESIDENT_ID	FIRST_NAME	SURNAME	PROPERTY_ID
1	Albie	O'Ryan	1
2	Tariq	Khan	1
3	Ismail	Salib	1
4	Callen	Beck	2
5	Milosz	Polansky	2
6	Ashanti	Lucas	2
7	Randy	Woodrue	2
8	Aislinn	Lawrence	3
9	Monique	French	3
10	Amara	Dejsuwan	4
12	Rosalie	Blackmore	4
13	Carina	Britton	4
14	Valentino	Ortega	5
15	Kaylem	Kent	5
16	Alessia	Wagner	6
17	Tyrone	Galvan	6
18	Constance	Fleming	6
19	Eamonn	Bain	6
20	Misbah	Yacob	7
21	Gianluca	Esposito	7
22	Elinor	Lake	7
23	Ray	Rosas	8
24	Damon	Caldwell	8
25	Dawood	Busby	8
26	Dora	Harris	8
27	Leroy	Stokes	8
28	Tamia	Hess	9
29	Amelia	Sanders	9
30	Zarah	Byers	10
31	Sara	Farrow	10
32	Delilah	Roy	10
33	Dougie	McDaniel	11
34	Tahir	Halabi	11
35	Mila	Zhikin	12
36	Glenn	Donovan	12
37	Zayn	Fowler	12

FIGURE 1-9   Sample data for StayWell residents

Module Summary

- KimTay Pet Supplies is an organization whose information requirements include sales reps, customers, items, invoices, and invoice lines.
- StayWell Student Accommodation is an organization whose information requirements include management offices, property details, owners, residents, and services requests.

Key Term

database

Case Exercises

KimTay Pet Supplies

Answer each of the following questions using the KimTay Pet Supplies data shown in Figure 1-2. No computer work is required.

1. List the first and last names of all customers that have a credit limit above, but not including, $500.
2. List the invoice numbers for invoices placed by customer ID 435 on November 18, 2021.
3. List the item ID, item description, and on-hand value for each item in category HOR. (*Hint*: On-hand value is the result of multiplying the number of units on hand by the price.)
4. List the item ID and item description of all items that are in category DOG.
5. How many customers have a balance that exceeds their credit limit?
6. What is the item ID, description, and price of the least expensive item in the database?
7. For each invoice, list the invoice number, invoice date, customer ID, and customer first and last names.
8. For each invoice placed on November 16, 2021, list the invoice number, customer ID, and customer first and last names.
9. List the sales rep ID, and first and last names, for every sales rep who represents at least one customer with a credit limit of $1,000.
10. For each invoice placed on November 15, 2021, list the invoice number, item ID, item description, and category for each item ordered.

Critical Thinking

1. KimTay Pet Supplies needs to be able to contact customers when problems arise concerning an invoice. What other types of data could KimTay include in the CUSTOMER table to assist in contacting customers?

StayWell Student Accommodation

Answer each of the following questions using the StayWell data shown in Figures 1-4 through 1–9. No computer work is required.

1. List the owner number, last name, and first name of every property owner.
2. List the last name and first name of every owner located in Seattle.
3. List the property ID for each condo that is smaller than 1,600 square feet.
4. List the last name, first name, and city of every owner who owns more than one property in the database.
5. List the last name, first name, and city of every owner with a property that has a monthly rent of less than $1,400 per month.
6. List all the residents staying at 782 Queen Ln.
7. How many properties have two floors?
8. How many owners live outside of Washington state (WA)?
9. List the owner's last and first names and property IDs for each property that has a scheduled or open service request.
10. List the property ID and square footage for each property that has a maintenance service request.
11. List the property ID and office number for all service requests for which the estimated number of hours is greater than 5.
12. What is the average rent for all three-bedroom properties?

Critical Thinking

1. The StayWell database does not include a column for service fees. In which table would you place the information for service fees? Why?

DATABASE DESIGN FUNDAMENTALS

OBJECTIVES

- Understand the terms *entity*, *attribute*, and *relationship*.
- Understand the terms *relation* and *relational database*.
- Understand functional dependence and identify when one column is functionally dependent on another.
- Understand the term *primary key* and identify primary keys in tables.
- Design a database to satisfy a set of requirements.
- Convert an unnormalized relation to first normal form.
- Convert tables from first normal form to second normal form.
- Convert tables from second normal form to third normal form.
- Create an entity-relationship diagram to represent the design of a database.

INTRODUCTION

In Module 1, you reviewed the tables and columns in the KimTay Pet Supplies and StayWell Student Accommodation databases that you use to complete the rest of this text. The process of determining the particular tables and columns that comprise a database is known as **database design**. In this module, you learn a method for designing a database to satisfy a set of requirements. In the process, you learn how to identify the tables and columns in the database. You also learn how to identify the relationships between the tables.

This module begins by examining some important concepts related to databases. It also presents the design method using the set of requirements that KimTay Pet Supplies identified to produce the appropriate database design. The module then examines the process of normalization, in which you identify and fix potential problems in database designs. Finally, you learn a way of visually representing the design of a database.

DATABASE CONCEPTS

Before learning how to design a database, you need to be familiar with some important database concepts related to relational databases, which are the types of databases you examined in Module 1 and that you use throughout the rest of this text. The terms entity, attribute, and relationship are important to understand when designing a database; the concepts of functional dependence and primary keys are critical when learning about the database design process.

Relational Databases

A **relational database** is a collection of tables like the ones you examined for KimTay Pet Supplies in Module 1 and that appear in Figure 2-1. Formally, these tables are called relations, and this is how this type of database gets its name.

SALES_REP

REP_ID	FIRST_NAME	LAST_NAME	ADDRESS	CITY	STATE	POSTAL	CELL_PHONE	COMMISSION	RATE
05	Susan	Garcia	42 Mountain Ln	Cody	WY	82414	307-824-1245	$12,743.16	0.04
10	Richard	Miller	87 Pikes Dr	Ralston	WY	82440	307-406-4321	$20,872.11	0.06
15	Donna	Smith	312 Oak Rd	Powell	WY	82440	307-982-8401	$14,912.92	0.04
20	Daniel	Jackson	19 Lookout Dr	Elk Butte	WY	82433	307-883-9481	$0.00	0.04

CUSTOMER

CUST_ID	FIRST_NAME	LAST_NAME	ADDRESS	CITY	STATE	POSTAL	EMAIL	BALANCE	CREDIT_LIMIT	REP_ID
125	Joey	Smith	17 Fourth St	Cody	WY	82414	jsmith17@example.com	$80.68	$500.00	05
182	Billy	Rufton	21 Simple Cir	Garland	WY	82435	billyruff@example.com	$43.13	$750.00	10
227	Sandra	Pincher	53 Verde Ln	Powell	WY	82440	spinch2@example.com	$156.38	$500.00	15
294	Samantha	Smith	14 Rock Ln	Ralston	WY	82440	ssmith5@example.com	$58.60	$500.00	10
314	Tom	Rascal	1 Rascal Farm Rd	Cody	WY	82414	trascal3@example.com	$17.25	$250.00	15
375	Melanie	Jackson	42 Blackwater Way	Elk Butte	WY	82433	mjackson5@example.com	$252.25	$250.00	05
435	James	Gonzalez	16 Rockway Rd	Wapiti	WY	82450	jgonzo@example.com	$230.40	$1,000.00	15
492	Elmer	Jackson	22 Jackson Farm Rd	Garland	WY	82435	ejackson4@example.com	$45.20	$500.00	10
543	Angie	Hendricks	27 Locklear Ln	Powell	WY	82440	ahendricks7@example.com	$315.00	$750.00	05
616	Sally	Cruz	199 18th Ave	Ralston	WY	82440	scruz5@example.com	$8.33	$500.00	15
721	Leslie	Smith	123 Sheepland Rd	Elk Butte	WY	82433	lsmith12@example.com	$166.65	$1,000.00	10
795	Randy	Blacksmith	75 Stream Rd	Cody	WY	82414	rblacksmith6@example.com	$61.50	$500.00	05

FIGURE 2-1   Sample data for KimTay Pet Supplies

INVOICES

INVOICE_NUM	INVOICE_DATE	CUST_ID
14216	11/15/2021	125
14219	11/15/2021	227
14222	11/16/2021	294
14224	11/16/2021	182
14228	11/18/2021	435
14231	11/18/2021	125
14233	11/18/2021	435
14237	11/19/2021	616

INVOICE_LINE

INVOICE_NUM	ITEM_ID	QUANTITY	QUOTED_PRICE
14216	CA75	3	$37.99
14219	AD72	2	$79.99
14219	DT12	4	$39.99
14222	LD14	1	$47.99
14224	KH81	4	$18.99
14228	FS42	1	$124.99
14228	PF19	1	$74.99
14231	UF39	2	$189.99
14233	KH81	1	$19.99
14233	QB92	4	$109.95
14233	WB49	4	$74.95
14237	LP73	3	$54.95

ITEM

ITEM_ID	DESCRIPTION	ON_HAND	CATEGORY	LOCATION	PRICE
AD72	Dog Feeding Station	12	DOG	B	$79.99
BC33	Feathers Bird Cage (12×24×18)	10	BRD	B	$79.99
CA75	Enclosed Cat Litter Station	15	CAT	C	$39.99
DT12	Dog Toy Gift Set	27	DOG	B	$39.99
FM23	Fly Mask with Ears	41	HOR	C	$24.95
FS39	Folding Saddle Stand	12	HOR	C	$39.99
FS42	Aquarium (55 Gallon)	5	FSH	A	$124.99
KH81	Wild Bird Food (25 lb)	24	BRD	C	$19.99
LD14	Locking Small Dog Door	14	DOG	A	$49.99
LP73	Large Pet Carrier	23	DOG	B	$59.99
PF19	Pump & Filter Kit	5	FSH	A	$74.99
QB92	Quilted Stable Blanket	32	HOR	C	$119.99
SP91	Small Pet Carrier	18	CAT	B	$39.99
UF39	Underground Fence System	7	DOG	A	$199.99
WB49	Insulated Water Bucket	34	HOR	C	$79.99

FIGURE 2-1 Sample data for KimTay Pet Supplies (Continued)

HELPFUL HINT

The names of columns and tables in this text follow a common naming convention in which column names use uppercase letters and replace spaces between words with an underscore (_). For example, KimTay Pet Supplies uses the column named FIRST_NAME to store first names and the column named INVOICE_NUM to store invoice numbers.

Entities, Attributes, and Relationships

There are some terms and concepts that are very important for you to know when working in the database environment. The terms *entity*, *attribute*, and *relationship* are fundamental when discussing databases. An **entity** is like a noun; it is a person, place, thing, or event. For example, the entities of interest to KimTay Pet Supplies are customers, invoices, and sales reps. The entities that are of interest to a school include students, faculty, and classes; a real estate agency is interested in clients, houses, and agents; and a used car dealer is interested in vehicles, customers, and manufacturers.

An **attribute** is a property of an entity. The term is used here exactly as it is used in everyday English. For example, for the entity *person*, the list of attributes might include such things as eye color and height. For KimTay Pet Supplies, the attributes of interest for the entity *customer* are first name, last name, address, city, and so on. For the entity *faculty* at a school, the attributes are faculty ID, name, office number, phone, and so on. For the entity *vehicle* at a car dealership, the attributes are the vehicle identification number, model, color, year, and so on.

A **relationship** is the association between entities. For example, at KimTay Pet Supplies there is an association between customers and sales reps. A sales rep is associated with all of his or her customers, and a customer is associated with his or her sales rep. Technically, you say that a sales rep is *related* to all of his or her customers, and a customer is *related* to his or her sales rep.

The relationship between sales reps and customers is an example of a **one-to-many relationship** because one sales rep is associated with many customers, but each customer is associated with only one sales rep. In this type of relationship, the word *many* is used in a way that is different from everyday English; it might not always mean a large number. In this context, for example, the term *many* means that a sales rep might be associated with *any* number of customers. That is, one sales rep can be associated with zero, one, or more customers.

How does a relational database handle entities, attributes of entities, and relationships between entities? Entities and attributes are fairly simple. Each entity has its own table. In the KimTay Pet Supplies database, there is one table for sales reps, one table for customers, and so on. The attributes of an entity become the columns in the table. In the table for sales reps, for example, there is a column for the sales rep ID, a column for the sales rep's first name, and so on.

What about relationships? At KimTay Pet Supplies, there is a one-to-many relationship between sales reps and customers, meaning each sales rep is related to the *many* customers that he or she represents, and each customer is related to the *one* sales rep who represents the customer. How is this relationship implemented in a relational database?

Consider Figure 2-1 again. If you want to determine the name of the sales rep who represents Billy Rufton (customer ID 182), you would locate the row for Billy Rufton in the CUSTOMER table and determine that the value for REP_ID is 10. Then you would look for the row in the SALES_REP table in which the REP_ID is 10. The *one* rep with REP_ID 10 is Richard Miller, who represents Billy Rufton.

On the other hand, if you want to determine the names of all the customers of the rep named Susan Garcia, you locate the row for Susan Garcia in the SALES_REP table and determine that the value in the REP_ID column is 05. Then you look for all the rows in the CUSTOMER table on which the REP_ID is 05. After identifying Susan Garcia's rep number, you find that the *many* customers she represents are numbered 125 (Joey Smith), 375 (Melanie Jackson), 543 (Angie Hendricks), and 795 (Randy Blacksmith).

You implement these relationships by having common columns in two or more tables. The REP_ID column in the SALES_REP table and the REP_ID column in the CUSTOMER table are used to implement the relationship between sales reps and customers. Given a sales rep, you can use these columns to determine all the customers that he or she represents; given a customer, you can use these columns to find the sales rep who represents the customer.

In this context, a relation is essentially a two-dimensional table. If you consider the tables shown in Figure 2-1, however, you can see that certain restrictions are placed on relations. Each column has a unique name, and entries within each column should *match* this column name. For example, if the column name is CREDIT_LIMIT, all entries in that column must be credit limits. In addition, each row should be unique—when two rows are identical, the second row does not provide any new information. For maximum flexibility, the order of the columns and rows should be immaterial. Finally, the table's design should be as simple as possible by restricting each position to a single entry and by preventing multiple entries (also called **repeating groups**) in an individual location in the table. Figure 2-2 shows a table design that includes repeating groups.

INVOICES

INVOICE_NUM	INVOICE_DATE	CUST_ID	ITEM_ID	QUANTITY	QUOTED_PRICE
14216	11/15/2021	125	CA75	3	$37.99
14219	11/15/2021	227	AD72	2	$79.99
			DT12	4	$39.99
14222	11/16/2021	294	LD14	1	$47.99
14224	11/16/2021	182	KH81	4	$18.99
14228	11/18/2021	435	FS42	1	$124.99
			PF19	1	$74.99
14231	11/18/2021	125	UF39	2	$189.99
14233	11/18/2021	435	KH81	1	$19.99
			QB92	4	$109.95
			WB49	4	$74.95
14237	11/19/2021	616	LP73	3	$54.95

FIGURE 2-2   Table with repeating groups

Figure 2-3 shows a better way to represent the same information shown in Figure 2-2. In Figure 2-3, every position in the table contains a single value.

INVOICES

INVOICE_NUM	INVOICE_DATE	CUST_ID	ITEM_ID	QUANTITY	QUOTED_PRICE
14216	11/15/2021	125	CA75	3	$37.99
14219	11/15/2021	227	AD72	2	$79.99
14219	11/15/2021	227	DT12	4	$39.99
14222	11/16/2021	294	LD14	1	$47.99
14224	11/16/2021	182	KH81	4	$18.99
14228	11/18/2021	435	FS42	1	$124.99
14228	11/18/2021	435	PF19	1	$74.99
14231	11/18/2021	125	UF39	2	$189.99
14233	11/18/2021	435	KH81	1	$19.99
14233	11/18/2021	435	QB92	4	$109.95
14233	11/18/2021	435	WB49	4	$74.95
14237	11/19/2021	616	LP73	3	$54.95

FIGURE 2-3   INVOICES table without repeating groups

When you remove the repeating groups from Figure 2-2, all of the rows in Figure 2-3 are single-valued. This structure is formally called a relation. A **relation** is a two-dimensional table in which the entries in the table are single-valued (each location in the table contains a single entry), each column has a distinct name, all values in the column match this name, the order of the rows and columns is immaterial, and each row contains unique values. A relational database is a collection of relations.

HELPFUL HINT

Rows in a table (relation) are also called **records** or **tuples**. Columns in a table (relation) are also called **fields** or attributes. This text uses the terms tables, columns, and rows unless the more formal terms of relation, attributes, and tuples are necessary for clarity.

There is a commonly accepted shorthand representation to show the tables and columns in a relational database: for each table, you write the name of the table and then within parentheses list all of the columns in the table. In this representation, each table appears on its own line. Using this method, you represent the KimTay Pet Supplies database as follows:

```
SALES_REP (REP_ID, FIRST_NAME, LAST_NAME, ADDRESS, CITY, STATE, POSTAL,
     CELL_PHONE, COMMISSION, RATE)
CUSTOMER (CUST_ID, FIRST_NAME, LAST_NAME, ADDRESS, CITY, STATE, POSTAL,
     EMAIL, BALANCE, CREDIT_LIMIT, REP_ID)
INVOICES (INVOICE_NUM, INVOICE_DATE, CUST_ID)
INVOICE_LINE (INVOICE_NUM, ITEM_ID, QUANTITY, QUOTED_PRICE)
ITEM (ITEM_ID, DESCRIPTION, ON_HAND, CATEGORY, LOCATION, PRICE)
```

Notice that some tables contain columns with duplicate names. For example, the REP_ID column appears in both the SALES_REP table *and* the CUSTOMER table. Suppose a situation existed wherein someone, or the **database management system (DBMS)** might confuse the two columns. Note the DBMS is a set of programs that allows users to store, manipulate, and retrieve data efficiently. For example, if you write REP_ID, it is not clear which REP_ID column you want to use. You need a mechanism for indicating the REP_ID column to which you are referring. One common approach to solving this problem is to write both the table name and the column name, separated by a period. Thus, you reference the REP_ID column in the CUSTOMER table as CUSTOMER.REP_ID, and you reference the REP_ID column in the SALES_REP table as SALES_REP.REP_ID. Technically, when you reference columns in this format, you say that you **qualify** the names. It is *always* acceptable to qualify column names, even when there is no potential for confusion. If confusion might arise, however, it is *essential* to qualify column names.

FUNCTIONAL DEPENDENCE

The concept of functional dependence is crucial to understanding the rest of the material in this module. Functional dependence is a formal name for what is basically a simple idea. To illustrate functional dependence, suppose that the SALES_REP table for KimTay

Pet Supplies is structured as shown in Figure 2-4. The only difference between the SALES_REP table shown in Figure 2-4 and the one shown in Figure 2-1 is the addition of an extra column named PAY_CLASS.

SALES_REP

REP_ID	FIRST NAME	LAST NAME	ADDRESS	CITY	STATE	POSTAL	CELL PHONE	COMMISSION	PAY_CLASS	RATE
05	Susan	Garcia	42 Mountain Ln	Cody	WY	82414	307-824-1245	$12,743.16	1	0.04
10	Richard	Miller	87 Pikes Dr	Ralston	WY	82440	307-406-4321	$20,872.11	2	0.06
15	Donna	Smith	312 Oak Rd	Powell	WY	82440	307-982-8401	$14,912.92	1	0.04
20	Daniel	Jackson	19 Lookout Dr	Elk Butte	WY	82433	307-883-9481	$0.00	1	0.04

FIGURE 2-4   SALES_REP table with a PAY_CLASS column

Suppose that one of the policies at KimTay Pet Supplies is that all sales reps in any given pay class earn their commissions at the same rate. To describe this situation, you could say that a sales rep's pay class *determines* his or her commission rate. Alternatively, you could say that a sales rep's commission rate *depends on* his or her pay class. This phrasing uses the words *determines* and *depends on* in the same way that you describe functional dependency. If you wanted to be formal, you would precede either expression with the word *functionally*. For example, you might say, "A sales rep's pay class *functionally determines* his or her commission rate," and "A sales rep's commission rate *functionally depends on* his or her pay class." You can also define functional dependency by saying that when you know a sales rep's pay class, you can determine his or her commission rate.

In a relational database, column B is **functionally dependent** on another column (or a collection of columns), A, if at any point in time a value for A determines a single value for B. You can think of this as follows: When you are given a value for A, do you know that you can find a single value for B? If so, B is functionally dependent on A (often written as A → B). You also can say that A **functionally determines** B.

At KimTay Pet Supplies, is the LAST_NAME column in the SALES_REP table functionally dependent on the REP_ID column? Yes, it is. If you are given a value for REP_ID, such as 10, there is a *single* LAST_NAME, Miller, associated with it. This is represented as: REP_ID → LAST_NAME

Q & A

Question: In the CUSTOMER table, is LAST_NAME functionally dependent on REP_ID?
Answer: No. Given the REP_ID 10, for example, you do not find a single customer last name because the sales rep with REP_ID 10 appears on more than one row in the table because he has four customers.

Q & A

Question: In the INVOICE_LINE table, is QUANTITY functionally dependent on INVOICE_NUM?
Answer: No. An INVOICE_NUM might be associated with several items in an invoice, so having just an INVOICE_NUM does not provide enough information.

Q & A

Question: Is QUANTITY functionally dependent on ITEM_ID?

Answer: No. Again, just as with INVOICE_NUM, an item ID might be associated with more than one invoice, so ITEM_ID does not provide enough information.

Q & A

Question: On which columns in the INVOICE_LINE table is QUANTITY functionally dependent?

Answer: To determine a value for QUANTITY, you need both an invoice number and an item ID. In other words, QUANTITY is functionally dependent on the combination (formally called the **concatenation**) of INVOICE_NUM and ITEM_ID. That is, given an invoice number *and* an item ID, you can find a single value for QUANTITY.

At this point, a question naturally arises: How do you determine functional dependencies? Can you determine them by looking at sample data, for example? The answer is no.

Consider the SALES_REP table in Figure 2-5, in which last names are unique. It is very tempting to say that LAST_NAME functionally determines ADDRESS, CITY, STATE, and POSTAL (or equivalently that ADDRESS, CITY, STATE, and POSTAL are all functionally dependent on LAST_NAME). After all, given the last name of a rep, you can find the single complete address; however, this is not always the case. What would happen if multiple sales reps had the same last name?

SALES_REP

REP_ID	FIRST_NAME	LAST_NAME	ADDRESS	CITY	STATE	POSTAL	CELL_PHONE	COMMISSION	RATE
05	Susan	Garcia	42 Mountain Ln	Cody	WY	82414	307-824-1245	$12,743.16	0.04
10	Richard	Miller	87 Pikes Dr	Ralston	WY	82440	307-406-4321	$20,872.11	0.06
15	Donna	Smith	312 Oak Rd	Powell	WY	82440	307-982-8401	$14,912.92	0.04
20	Daniel	Jackson	19 Lookout Dr	Elk Butte	WY	82433	307-883-9481	$0.00	0.04

FIGURE 2-5 SALES_REP table

What would happen if the last name of rep 20 was also Garcia? You would have the situation illustrated in Figure 2-6. Because there are now two reps with the last name of Garcia, you can no longer find a single address using a rep's last name—you were misled by the original data. The only way to determine functional dependencies is to examine the user's policies. This process can involve discussions with users, an examination of user documentation, and so on. For example, if managers at KimTay Pet Supplies have a policy not to hire two reps with the same last name, then LAST_NAME would indeed determine the other columns. Without such a policy, however, LAST_NAME would not determine the other columns.

SALES_REP

REP_ID	FIRST_NAME	LAST_NAME	ADDRESS	CITY	STATE	POSTAL	CELL_PHONE	COMMISSION	RATE
05	Susan	Garcia	42 Mountain Ln	Cody	WY	82414	307-824-1245	$12,743.16	0.04
10	Richard	Miller	87 Pikes Dr	Ralston	WY	82440	307-406-4321	$20,872.11	0.06
15	Donna	Smith	312 Oak Rd	Powell	WY	82440	307-982-8401	$14,912.92	0.04
20	Daniel	Garcia	19 Lookout Dr	Elk Butte	WY	82433	307-883-9481	$0.00	0.04

FIGURE 2-6   SALES_REP table with two reps named Garcia

PRIMARY KEYS

Another important database design concept is the primary key. In the simplest terms, the **primary key** is the unique identifier for a table. For example, the REP_ID column is the unique identifier for the SALES_REP table. Given a rep ID in the table, such as 10, there is only one row on which that rep ID occurs. Thus, the rep ID 10 uniquely identifies a row (in this case, the second row).

In this text, the definition of primary key needs to be more precise than just a unique identifier for a table. Specifically, column A (or a collection of columns) is the primary key for a table if the following is true:

Property 1. *All* columns in the table are functionally dependent on A.

Property 2. No subcollection of the columns in A (assuming A is a collection of columns and not just a single column) also has Property 1.

Q & A

Question: Is the CATEGORY column the primary key for the ITEM table?
Answer: No, because the other columns are not functionally dependent on CATEGORY. Given the category DOG, for example, you cannot determine an item ID, description, or anything else, because there are several rows on which the category is DOG.

Q & A

Question: Is the CUST_ID column the primary key for the CUSTOMER table?
Answer: Yes, because KimTay Pet Supplies assigns unique customer ID values. A specific customer ID cannot appear on more than one row. Thus, all columns in the CUSTOMER table are functionally dependent on CUST_ID.

Q & A

Question: Is the INVOICE_NUM column the primary key for the INVOICE_LINE table?
Answer: No, because it does not functionally determine either QUANTITY or QUOTED_PRICE.

Q & A

Question: Is the combination of the INVOICE_NUM and ITEM_ID columns the primary key for the INVOICE_LINE table?

Answer: Yes, because you can determine all columns by this combination of columns, and, further, neither the INVOICE_NUM nor the ITEM_ID alone has this property.

Q & A

Question: Is the combination of the ITEM_ID and DESCRIPTION columns the primary key for the ITEM table?

Answer: No. Although it is true that you can determine all columns in the ITEM table by this combination, ITEM_ID alone also has this property.

You can indicate a table's primary key with a shorthand representation of a database by underlining the column or collection of columns that comprise the primary key. The complete shorthand representation for the KimTay Pet Supplies database is as follows:

```
SALES_REP (REP_ID, FIRST_NAME, LAST_NAME, ADDRESS, CITY, STATE, POSTAL,
    CELL_PHONE, COMMISSION, RATE)
CUSTOMER (CUST_ID, FIRST_NAME, LAST_NAME, ADDRESS, CITY, STATE, POSTAL,
    EMAIL, BALANCE, CREDIT_LIMIT, REP_ID)
INVOICES (INVOICE_NUM, INVOICE_DATE, CUST_ID)
INVOICE_LINE (INVOICE_NUM, ITEM_ID, QUANTITY, QUOTED_PRICE)
ITEM (ITEM_ID, DESCRIPTION, ON_HAND, CATEGORY, LOCATION, PRICE)
```

HELPFUL HINT

Sometimes you might identify one or more columns that you can use as a table's primary key. For example, if the KimTay Pet Supplies database also included an EMPLOYEE table that contains employee numbers and Social Security numbers, either the employee number or the Social Security number could serve as the table's primary key. In this case, both columns are referred to as candidate keys. Like a primary key, a **candidate key** is a column or collection of columns on which all columns in the table are functionally dependent—the definition for primary key really defines candidate key as well. From all the candidate keys, you would choose one to be the primary key.

HELPFUL HINT

According to the definition of a candidate key, a Social Security number is a legitimate primary key. Many databases, such as those that store data about students at a college or university or those that store data about employees at a company, store a person's Social Security number as a primary key. However, many institutions and organizations are moving away from using Social Security numbers as primary keys because of privacy issues. Instead of using Social Security numbers, many institutions and organizations use unique student ID values or employee numbers as primary keys.

DATABASE DESIGN

This section presents a specific method you can follow to design a database when given a set of requirements that the database must support. The determination of the requirements is part of the process known as systems analysis. A systems analyst interviews users, examines existing and proposed documents, and examines organizational policies to determine exactly the type of data needs the database must support. This text does not cover this analysis. Rather, it focuses on how to take the set of requirements that this process produces and determine the appropriate database design.

After presenting the database design method, this section presents a sample set of requirements and illustrates the design method by designing a database to satisfy these requirements.

Design Method

To design a database for a set of requirements, complete the following steps:

1. Read the requirements, identify the entities (objects) involved, and name the entities. For example, when the design involves departments and employees, you might use the entity names DEPARTMENT and EMPLOYEE. When the design involves customers and sales reps, you might use the entity names CUSTOMER and SALES_REP.

2. Identify the unique identifiers for the entities you identified in Step 1. For example, when one of the entities is ITEM, determine what information is required to uniquely identify each individual item. In other words, what information does the organization use to distinguish one item from another? For the ITEM entity, the unique identifier for each item might be ITEM_ID; for a CUSTOMER entity, the unique identifier might be CUST_ID. When no unique identifier is available from the data you know about the entity, you need to create one. For example, you might use a unique number to identify items when no item numbers exist.

3. Identify the attributes for all the entities. These attributes become the columns in the tables. It is possible for two or more entities to contain the same attributes.

4. Identify the functional dependencies that exist among the attributes. Ask yourself the following question: If you know a unique value for an attribute, do you also know the unique values for other attributes? For example, when

you have the three attributes REP_ID, FIRST_NAME, and LAST_NAME and you know a unique value for REP_ID, do you also know a unique value for FIRST_NAME and LAST_NAME? If so, then FIRST_NAME and LAST_NAME are functionally dependent on REP_ID (REP_ID → FIRST_NAME, LAST_NAME).

5. Use the functional dependencies to identify the tables by placing each attribute with the attribute or minimum combination of attributes on which it is functionally dependent. The attribute(s) for an entity on which all other attributes are dependent is the primary key of the table. The remaining attributes are the other columns in the table. Once you have determined all the columns in the table, you can give the table an appropriate name. Usually the name will be the same as the name you identified for the entity in Step 1.

6. Identify any relationships between tables. In some cases, you might be able to determine the relationships directly from the requirements. It might be clear, for example, that one sales rep is related to many customers and that each customer is related to exactly one sales rep. When it is not, look for matching columns in the tables you created. For example, if both the SALES_REP table and the CUSTOMER table contain a REP_ID column and the values in these columns must match, you know that reps and customers are related. The fact that the REP_ID column is the primary key in the SALES_REP table tells you that the SALES_REP table is the *one* part of the relationship and the CUSTOMER table is the *many* part of the relationship.

In the next section, you will apply this process to produce the design for the KimTay Pet Supplies database using the collection of requirements that this database must support.

Database Design Requirements

The analyst has interviewed users and examined documents at KimTay Pet Supplies. In the process, the analyst has determined that the database must support the following requirements:

1. For a sales rep, store the sales rep's ID, first name, last name, street address, city, state, postal code, cell phone number, total commission, and commission rate.

2. For a customer, store the customer's ID, first name, last name, street address, city, state, postal code, e-mail address, balance, and credit limit. In addition, store the ID, first name, and last name of the sales rep who represents this customer. The analyst has also determined that a sales rep can represent many customers, but a customer must have exactly one sales rep (in other words, a sales rep must represent a customer; a customer cannot be represented by zero or more than one sales reps).

3. For an item, store the item's ID, description, units on hand, category, the value of the location in which the item is located, and the price. All units of a particular item are stored in the same location.

4. For an invoice, store the invoice number, invoice date, along with the ID, first name, and last name of the customer that placed the invoice, as well as the ID of the sales rep who represents that customer.

5. For each invoice item within an invoice, store the item ID and description, the quantity ordered, and the quoted price. The analyst also obtained the following information concerning invoices:
   a. There is only one customer per invoice.
   b. On a given invoice, there is at most one line item for a given item. For example, item AD72 cannot appear on several lines *within* the *same* invoice.
   c. The quoted price might differ from the actual price when the sales rep discounts a certain item on a specific invoice.

Database Design Process Example

The following steps apply the design process to the requirements for KimTay Pet Supplies to produce the appropriate database design:

Step 1: There appear to be four entities: sales reps, customers, items, and invoices. The names assigned to these entities are SALES_REP, CUSTOMER, ITEM, and INVOICES, respectively.

Step 2: From the collection of entities, review the data and determine the unique identifier for each entity. For the SALES_REP, CUSTOMER, ITEM, and INVOICES entities, the unique identifiers are the rep ID, customer ID, item ID, and invoice number, respectively. These unique identifiers are named REP_ID, CUST_ID, ITEM_ID, and INVOICE_NUM, respectively.

Step 3: The attributes mentioned in the first requirement all refer to sales reps. The specific attributes mentioned in the requirement are the sales rep's ID, first name, last name, street address, city, state, postal code, cell phone number, total commission, and commission rate. Assigning appropriate names to these attributes produces the following list:

```
REP_ID
FIRST_NAME
LAST_NAME
ADDRESS
CITY
STATE
POSTAL
CELL_PHONE
COMMISSION
RATE
```

The attributes mentioned in the second requirement refer to customers. The specific attributes are the customer's ID, first name, last name, street address, city, state, postal code, e-mail address, balance, and credit limit. The requirement also mentions the rep ID, first name, and last name of the sales rep who represents this customer. Assigning appropriate names to these attributes produces the following list:

```
CUST_ID
FIRST_NAME
LAST_NAME
ADDRESS
CITY
STATE
POSTAL
EMAIL
BALANCE
CREDIT_LIMIT
REP_ID
REP_FIRST_NAME
REP_LAST_NAME
```

HELPFUL HINT

Note above that the names given to the first and last name for each customer is FIRST_NAME and LAST_NAME, similar to the names given to represent the first and last names of each sales rep when determining the list of attributes for the entity SALES_REP. However, in this case we are wanting to include both the first and last names for the customer and the first and last names for the sales rep, in the same list pertaining to the entity CUSTOMER. When naming attributes associated with a single entity, in this case CUSTOMER, no two attributes can have the same name. Therefore, we cannot use FIRST_NAME and LAST_NAME for the first and last name for the sales rep (as attributes associated with the entity CUSTOMER) and use FIRST_NAME and LAST_NAME as the first and last name of a customer. Instead, we can use REP_FIRST_NAME and REP_LAST_NAME to represent the first and last name of the sales rep as attributes related to CUSTOMER. You will see as we continue to progress through the design process that this will be remedied and not be an issue. However, it is important to note at this juncture. In summary, two attributes can have the same name if they refer to different entities (such as using FIRST_NAME and LAST_NAME as attributes for the entities SALES_REP and CUSTOMER independently; however, when associated with a single entity, no two attributes can have the same name.

There are attributes named FIRST_NAME, LAST_NAME, ADDRESS, CITY, STATE, and POSTAL for sales reps as well as attributes named FIRST_NAME, LAST_NAME, ADDRESS, CITY, STATE, and POSTAL for customers. To distinguish these attributes in the final collection, follow the name of the attribute by the name of the corresponding entity in parentheses. For example, the address for a sales rep is ADDRESS (SALES_REP) and the address for a customer is ADDRESS (CUSTOMER).

The attributes mentioned in the third requirement refer to items. The specific attributes are the item's ID, description, units on hand, category, value of the location in which the item is located, and price. Assigning appropriate names to these attributes produces the following list:

```
ITEM_ID
DESCRIPTION
ON_HAND
CATEGORY
LOCATION
PRICE
```

The attributes mentioned in the fourth requirement refer to invoices. The specific attributes include the invoice number, invoice date, customer's ID, first and last names of who placed the invoice, and ID of the sales rep who represents the customer. Assigning appropriate names to these attributes produces the following list:

```
INVOICE_NUM
INVOICE_DATE
CUST_ID
FIRST_NAME
LAST_NAME
REP_ID
```

The specific attributes associated with the statement in the requirements concerning invoice line items are the invoice number (to determine the invoice to which the line item corresponds), item ID, description, quantity ordered, and quoted price. If the quoted price must be the same as the price, you could simply call it PRICE. According to requirement 5c, however, the quoted price might differ from the price, so you must add the quoted price to the list. Assigning appropriate names to these attributes produces the following list:

```
INVOICE_NUM
ITEM_ID
DESCRIPTION
QUANTITY
QUOTED_PRICE
```

The complete list grouped by entity is as follows:

```
SALES_REP
REP_ID
FIRST_NAME (SALES_REP)
LAST_NAME (SALES_REP)
ADDRESS (SALES_REP)
CITY (SALES_REP)
STATE (SALES_REP)
POSTAL (SALES_REP)
CELL_PHONE
COMMISSION
RATE
```

CUSTOMER
CUST_ID
FIRST_NAME (CUSTOMER)
LAST_NAME (CUSTOMER)
ADDRESS (CUSTOMER)
CITY (CUSTOMER)
STATE (CUSTOMER)
POSTAL (CUSTOMER)
EMAIL
BALANCE
CREDIT_LIMIT
REP_ID
REP_FIRST_NAME
REP_LAST_NAME

ITEM
ITEM_ID
DESCRIPTION
ON_HAND
CATEGORY
LOCATION
PRICE

INVOICES
INVOICE_NUM
INVOICE_DATE
CUST_ID
FIRST_NAME
LAST_NAME
REP_ID

For invoice line items within an invoice:

INVOICE_NUM
ITEM_ID
DESCRIPTION
QUANTITY
QUOTED_PRICE

Step 4: The fact that the unique identifier for sales reps is the rep ID gives the following functional dependencies:

REP_ID → FIRST_NAME (SALES_REP), LAST_NAME (SALES_REP), ADDRESS (SALES_REP),
    CITY (SALES_REP), STATE (SALES_REP), POSTAL (SALES_REP), CELL_PHONE,
    COMMISSION, RATE

This notation indicates that the FIRST_NAME (SALES_REP), LAST_NAME (SALES_REP), ADDRESS (SALES_REP), CITY (SALES_REP), STATE (SALES_REP), POSTAL (SALES_REP), CELL_PHONE, COMMISSION, and RATE are all functionally dependent on REP_ID.

The fact that the unique identifier for customers is the customer ID gives the following functional dependencies:

```
CUST_ID → FIRST_NAME (CUSTOMER), LAST_NAME (CUSTOMER), ADDRESS
        (CUSTOMER), CITY (CUSTOMER), STATE (CUSTOMER), POSTAL (CUSTOMER),
        EMAIL, BALANCE, CREDIT_LIMIT, REP_ID, REP_FIRST_NAME, REP_LAST_NAME
```

Q & A

Question: Do you really need to include the first name and last name of a sales rep in the list of attributes determined by the customer ID?

Answer: There is no need to include them in this list because they both can be determined from the sales rep ID and are already included in the list of attributes determined by REP_ID.

Thus, the functional dependencies for the CUSTOMER entity are as follows:

```
CUST_ID → FIRST_NAME (CUSTOMER), LAST_NAME (CUSTOMER), ADDRESS
        (CUSTOMER), CITY (CUSTOMER), STATE (CUSTOMER), POSTAL (CUSTOMER),
        EMAIL, BALANCE, CREDIT_LIMIT, REP_ID
```

The fact that the unique identifier for items is the item number gives the following functional dependencies:

```
ITEM_ID → DESCRIPTION, ON_HAND, CATEGORY, LOCATION, PRICE
```

The fact that the unique identifier for invoices is the invoice number gives the following functional dependencies:

```
INVOICE_NUM → INVOICE_DATE, CUST_ID, FIRST_NAME (CUSTOMER), LAST_NAME
        (CUSTOMER), REP_ID
```

Q & A

Question: Do you really need to include the first name and last name of a customer and the ID of the customer's rep in the list of attributes determined by the invoice number?

Answer: There is no need to include the customer's first and last names and the rep ID in this list because you can determine them from the customer ID and they are already included in the list of attributes determined by CUST_ID.

The functional dependencies for the INVOICES entity are as follows:

```
INVOICE_NUM → INVOICE_DATE, CUST_ID
```

The final attributes to be examined are those associated with the invoice line items within the invoice: ITEM_ID, DESCRIPTION, QUANTITY, and QUOTED_PRICE.

Question: Why are QUANTITY and QUOTED_PRICE not included in the list of attributes determined by the invoice number?

Answer: To uniquely identify a particular value for QUANTITY or QUOTED_PRICE, INVOICE_NUM alone is not sufficient, because there can be multiple items purchased on a single invoice. Therefore, it requires the combination of INVOICE_NUM and ITEM_ID.

The following shorthand representation indicates that the combination of INVOICE_NUM and ITEM_ID functionally determines QUANTITY and QUOTED_PRICE:

```
INVOICE_NUM, ITEM_ID → QUANTITY, QUOTED_PRICE
```

Question: Does DESCRIPTION need to be included in this list?

Answer: No, because DESCRIPTION can be determined by the ITEM_ID alone, and it already appears in the list of attributes dependent on the ITEM_ID.

The complete list of functional dependencies is as follows:

```
REP_ID → FIRST_NAME (SALES_REP), LAST_NAME (SALES_REP), ADDRESS (SALES_REP),
     CITY (SALES_REP), STATE (SALES_REP), POSTAL (SALES_REP), CELL_PHONE,
     COMMISSION, RATE
CUST_ID → FIRST_NAME (CUSTOMER), LAST_NAME (CUSTOMER), ADDRESS
     (CUSTOMER), CITY (CUSTOMER), STATE (CUSTOMER), POSTAL (CUSTOMER),
     EMAIL, BALANCE, CREDIT_LIMIT, REP_ID
ITEM_ID → DESCRIPTION, ON_HAND, CATEGORY, LOCATION, PRICE
INVOICE_NUM → INVOICE_DATE, CUST_ID
INVOICE_NUM, ITEM_ID → QUANTITY, QUOTED_PRICE
```

Step 5: Using the functional dependencies, you can create tables with the attribute(s) to the left of the arrow being the primary key and the attribute(s) to the right of the arrow being the other columns. For relations corresponding to those entities identified in Step 1, you can use the name you already determined. Because you did not identify any entity that had a unique identifier that was the combination of INVOICE_NUM and ITEM_ID, you need to assign a name to the table whose primary key consists of these two columns. Because this table represents the individual lines within an invoice, the name INVOICE_LINE is a good choice. The final collection of tables is as follows:

```
SALES_REP (REP_ID, FIRST_NAME, LAST_NAME, ADDRESS, CITY, STATE, POSTAL,
     CELL_PHONE, COMMISSION, RATE)
CUSTOMER (CUST_ID, FIRST_NAME, LAST_NAME, ADDRESS, CITY, STATE, POSTAL,
     EMAIL, BALANCE, CREDIT_LIMIT, REP_ID)
ITEM (ITEM_ID, DESCRIPTION, ON_HAND, CATEGORY, LOCATION, PRICE)
INVOICES (INVOICE_NUM, INVOICE_DATE, CUST_ID)
INVOICE_LINE (INVOICE_NUM, ITEM_ID, QUANTITY, QUOTED_PRICE)
```

Step 6: Examining the tables and identifying common columns gives the following list of relationships between the tables:

- The CUSTOMER and SALES_REP tables are related using the REP_ID columns. Because the REP_ID column is the primary key for the SALES_REP table, this indicates a one-to-many relationship between SALES_REP and CUSTOMER (one rep to many customers).
- The INVOICES and CUSTOMER tables are related using the CUST_ID columns. Because the CUST_ID column is the primary key for the CUSTOMER table, this indicates a one-to-many relationship between CUSTOMER and INVOICES (one customer to many invoices).
- The INVOICE_LINE and INVOICES tables are related using the INVOICE_NUM columns. Because the INVOICE_NUM column is the primary key for the INVOICES table, this indicates a one-to-many relationship between INVOICES and INVOICE_LINE (one invoice to many invoice lines).
- The INVOICE_LINE and ITEM tables are related using the ITEM_ID columns. Because the ITEM_ID column is the primary key for the ITEM table, this indicates a one-to-many relationship between ITEM and INVOICE_LINE (one item to many invoice lines).

NORMALIZATION

After creating the database design, you must analyze it to make sure it is free of potential problems. To do so, you follow a process called **normalization**, in which you identify the existence of potential problems, such as data duplication and redundancy, and implement ways to correct these problems.

The goal of normalization is to convert **unnormalized relations** (tables that satisfy the definition of a relation except that they might contain repeating groups) into various types of **normal forms**. A table in a particular normal form possesses a certain desirable collection of properties. Although there are several normal forms, the most common are first normal form, second normal form, and third normal form. Normalization is a process in which a table that is in first normal form is better than a table that is not in first normal form, a table that is in second normal form is better than one that is in first normal form, and so on. The goal of this process is to allow you to take a table or collection of tables and produce a new collection of tables that represents the same information but is free of problems.

First Normal Form

According to the definition of a relation, a relation (table) cannot contain a repeating group in which multiple entries exist on a single row. However, in the database design process, you might create a table that has all the other properties of a relation but contains a repeating group. Removing repeating groups is the starting point when converting an unnormalized collection of data into a table that is in first normal form. A table (relation) is in **first normal form (1NF)** when it does not contain a repeating group.

For example, in the design process you might create the following INVOICES table, in which there is a repeating group consisting of ITEM_ID and QUANTITY. The notation for this table is as follows:

```
INVOICES (INVOICE_NUM, INVOICE_DATE, (ITEM_ID, QUANTITY))
```

This notation describes a table named INVOICES that consists of a primary key, INVOICE_NUM, and a column named INVOICE_DATE. The inner parentheses indicate a repeating group that contains two columns, ITEM_ID and QUANTITY. This table contains one row per invoice with values in the ITEM_ID and QUANTITY columns for each invoice with the number INVOICE_NUM and placed on INVOICE_DATE. Figure 2-7 shows a single invoice with multiple combinations of an item ID and a corresponding quantity of units ordered.

INVOICES

INVOICE_NUM	INVOICE_DATE	ITEM_ID	QUANTITY
14216	11/15/2021	CA75	3
14219	11/15/2021	AD72	2
		DT12	4
14222	11/16/2021	LD14	1
14224	11/16/2021	KH81	4
14228	11/18/2021	FS42	1
		PF19	1
14231	11/18/2021	UF39	2
14233	11/18/2021	KH81	1
		QB92	4
		WB49	4
14237	11/19/2021	LP73	3

FIGURE 2-7   Unnormalized invoice data

To convert the table to first normal form, you remove the repeating group as follows:
INVOICES (<u>INVOICE NUM</u>, INVOICE_DATE, <u>ITEM ID</u>, QUANTITY)

Figure 2-8 shows the table in first normal form.

INVOICES

INVOICE_NUM	INVOICE_DATE	ITEM_ID	QUANTITY
14216	11/15/2021	CA75	3
14219	11/15/2021	AD72	2
14219	11/15/2021	DT12	4
14222	11/16/2021	LD14	1
14224	11/16/2021	KH81	4
14228	11/18/2021	FS42	1
14228	11/18/2021	PF19	1
14231	11/18/2021	UF39	2
14233	11/18/2021	KH81	1
14233	11/18/2021	QB92	4
14233	11/18/2021	WB49	4
14237	11/19/2021	LP73	3

FIGURE 2-8   Invoice data converted to first normal form

In Figure 2-7, the second row indicates that item AD72 and item DT12 are both included in invoice 14219. In Figure 2-8, this information is represented by *two* rows, the second and third. The primary key for the unnormalized INVOICES table was the INVOICE_NUM column alone. The primary key for the normalized table is now the combination of the INVOICE_NUM and ITEM_ID columns.

When you convert an unnormalized table to a table in first normal form, the primary key of the table in first normal form is usually the primary key of the unnormalized table concatenated with the key for the repeating group. The key for the repeating group is the column in the repeating group that distinguishes one occurrence of the repeating group from another. In the INVOICES table, ITEM_ID was the key to the repeating group and INVOICE_NUM was the primary key for the table. When converting the unnormalized data to first normal form, the primary key becomes the concatenation of the INVOICE_NUM and ITEM_ID columns.

Second Normal Form

The following INVOICES table is in first normal form, because it does not contain a repeating group:

    INVOICES (INVOICE NUM, INVOICE_DATE, ITEM ID, DESCRIPTION, QUANTITY,
        QUOTED_PRICE)

The table contains the following functional dependencies:

    INVOICE_NUM → INVOICE_DATE
    ITEM_ID → DESCRIPTION
    INVOICE_NUM, ITEM_ID → QUANTITY, QUOTED_PRICE

This notation indicates that INVOICE_NUM alone determines INVOICE_DATE, and ITEM_ID alone determines DESCRIPTION, but it requires *both* INVOICE_NUM *and* ITEM_ID to determine either QUANTITY or QUOTED_PRICE. Consider the sample of this table shown in Figure 2-9.

INVOICES

INVOICE_NUM	INVOICE_DATE	ITEM_ID	DESCRIPTION	QUANTITY	QUOTED_PRICE
14216	11/15/2021	CA75	Enclosed Cat Litter Station	3	$37.99
14219	11/15/2021	AD72	Dog Feeding Station	2	$79.99
14219	11/15/2021	DT12	Dog Toy Gift Set	4	$39.99
14222	11/16/2021	LD14	Locking Small Dog Door	1	$47.99
14224	11/16/2021	KH81	Wild Bird Food (25 lb)	4	$18.99
14228	11/18/2021	FS42	Aquarium (55 Gallon)	1	$124.99
14228	11/18/2021	PF19	Pump & Filter Kit	1	$74.99
14231	11/18/2021	UF39	Underground Fence System	2	$189.99
14233	11/18/2021	KH81	Wild Bird Food (25 lb)	1	$19.99
14233	11/18/2021	QB92	Quilted Stable Blanket	4	$109.95
14233	11/18/2021	WB49	Insulated Water Bucket	4	$74.95
14237	11/19/2021	LP73	Large Pet Carrier	3	$54.95

FIGURE 2-9   Sample Invoices table

Although the INVOICES table is in first normal form (because it contains no repeating groups), problems exist within the table that require you to restructure it.

The description of a specific item, KH81 for example, occurs twice in the table. This duplication (formally called **redundancy**) causes several problems. It is certainly wasteful of space, but that is not nearly as serious as some of the other problems. These other problems are called **update anomalies** and they fall into four categories:

1. **Updates:** If you need to change to the description of item KH81, you must change it twice—once in each row on which item KH81 appears. Updating the item description more than once makes the update process much more cumbersome and time consuming.

2. **Inconsistent data:** There is nothing about the design that prohibits item KH81 from having two *different* descriptions in the database. In fact, if item KH81 occurs on 20 rows in the table, it is possible for this item to have 20 different descriptions in the database.

3. **Additions:** When you try to add a new item and its description to the database, you will face a real problem. Because the primary key for the INVOICES table consists of both INVOICE_NUM and ITEM_ID, you need values for both of these columns to add a new row to the table. If you add an item to the table that does not yet have any invoices, what do you use for INVOICE_NUM? The only solution is to create a dummy INVOICE_NUM and then replace it with a real INVOICE_NUM once an order for this item is actually received. Certainly, this is not an acceptable solution.

4. **Deletions:** If you delete invoice 14216 from the database and it is the only invoice that contains item CA75, deleting the invoice also deletes all information about item CA75. For example, you would no longer know that item CA75 is an Enclosed Cat Litter Station.

These problems occur because the DESCRIPTION column is dependent on only a portion of the primary key (ITEM_ID) and *not* on the complete primary key. This situation leads to the definition of second normal form. Second normal form represents an improvement over first normal form because it eliminates update anomalies in these situations. A table (relation) is in **second normal form (2NF)** when it is in first normal form and no **nonkey column** (that is, a column that is not part of the primary key) is dependent on only a portion of the primary key.

HELPFUL HINT

When the primary key of a table contains only a single column, the table is automatically in second normal form.

You can identify the fundamental problem with the INVOICES table: It is not in second normal form. Although it is important to identify the problem, what you really need is a method to *correct* it; you want to be able to convert tables to second normal form. First, take each subset of the set of columns that make up the primary key and begin a new table with this subset as its primary key. For the INVOICES table, the new design is as follows:

```
(INVOICE_NUM,
(ITEM_ID,
(INVOICE_NUM, ITEM_ID,
```

Next, place each of the other columns with the appropriate primary key; that is, place each one with the minimal collection of columns on which it depends. For the INVOICES table, add the new columns as follows:

```
(INVOICE_NUM, INVOICE_DATE)
(ITEM_ID, DESCRIPTION)
(INVOICE_NUM, ITEM_ID, QUANTITY, QUOTED_PRICE)
```

Each of these new tables is given a descriptive name based on the meaning and contents of the table, such as INVOICES, ITEM, and INVOICE_LINE. Figure 2-10 shows samples of these tables.

INVOICES

INVOICE_NUM	INVOICE_DATE	ITEM_ID	DESCRIPTION	QUANTITY	QUOTED_PRICE
14216	11/15/2021	CA75	Enclosed Cat Litter Station	3	$37.99
14219	11/15/2021	AD72	Dog Feeding Station	2	$79.99
14219	11/15/2021	DT12	Dog Toy Gift Set	4	$39.99
14222	11/16/2021	LD14	Locking Small Dog Door	1	$47.99
14224	11/16/2021	KH81	Wild Bird Food (25 lb)	4	$18.99
14228	11/18/2021	FS42	Aquarium (55 Gallon)	1	$124.99
14228	11/18/2021	PF19	Pump & Filter Kit	1	$74.99
14231	11/18/2021	UF39	Underground Fence System	2	$189.99
14233	11/18/2021	KH81	Wild Bird Food (25 lb)	1	$19.99
14233	11/18/2021	QB92	Quilted Stable Blanket	4	$109.95
14233	11/18/2021	WB49	Insulated Water Bucket	4	$74.95
14237	11/19/2021	LP73	Large Pet Carrier	3	$54.95

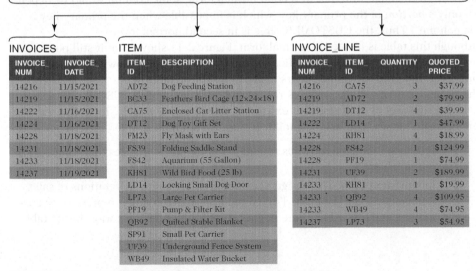

INVOICES

INVOICE_NUM	INVOICE_DATE
14216	11/15/2021
14219	11/15/2021
14222	11/16/2021
14224	11/16/2021
14228	11/18/2021
14231	11/18/2021
14233	11/18/2021
14237	11/19/2021

ITEM

ITEM_ID	DESCRIPTION
AD72	Dog Feeding Station
BC33	Feathers Bird Cage (12×24×18)
CA75	Enclosed Cat Litter Station
DT12	Dog Toy Gift Set
FM23	Fly Mask with Ears
FS39	Folding Saddle Stand
FS42	Aquarium (55 Gallon)
KH81	Wild Bird Food (25 lb)
LD14	Locking Small Dog Door
LP73	Large Pet Carrier
PF19	Pump & Filter Kit
QB92	Quilted Stable Blanket
SP91	Small Pet Carrier
UF39	Underground Fence System
WB49	Insulated Water Bucket

INVOICE_LINE

INVOICE_NUM	ITEM_ID	QUANTITY	QUOTED_PRICE
14216	CA75	3	$37.99
14219	AD72	2	$79.99
14219	DT12	4	$39.99
14222	LD14	1	$47.99
14224	KH81	4	$18.99
14228	FS42	1	$124.99
14228	PF19	1	$74.99
14231	UF39	2	$189.99
14233	KH81	1	$19.99
14233	QB92	4	$109.95
14233	WB49	4	$74.95
14237	LP73	3	$54.95

FIGURE 2-10   INVOICES table converted to second normal form

In Figure 2-10, converting the original INVOICES table to a new INVOICES table, an ITEM table, and an INVOICE_LINE table eliminates the update anomalies. A description appears only once for each item, so you do not have the redundancy that existed in the original table design. Changing the description of item KH81 from Wild Bird Food (25 lb) to KimTay Premium Wild Bird Food (25 lb), for example, is now a simple process involving a single change. Because the description for an item occurs in a single place, it is not possible to have multiple descriptions for a single item in the database at the same time.

To add a new item and its description, you create a new row in the ITEM table, regardless of whether that item has pending or actual invoices. In addition, deleting invoice 14216 does not delete item number CA75 from the database because it still exists in the ITEM table. Finally, you have not lost any information by converting the INVOICES table to second normal form. You can reconstruct the data in the original table from the data in the new tables.

Third Normal Form

Problems can still exist with tables that are in second normal form. For example, suppose that you create the following CUSTOMER table:

```
CUSTOMER (CUST_ID, FIRST_NAME, LAST_NAME, BALANCE, CREDIT_LIMIT, REP_ID,
    REP_FIRST_NAME, REP_LAST_NAME)
```

This table has the following functional dependencies:

```
CUST_ID → FIRST_NAME, LAST_NAME, BALANCE, CREDIT_LIMIT, REP_ID,
    REP_FIRST_NAME, REP_LAST_NAME
REP_ID → REP_FIRST_NAME, REP_LAST_NAME
```

CUST_ID determines all the other columns. In addition, REP_ID determines REP_FIRST_NAME and REP_LAST_NAME.

When a table's primary key is a single column, the table is automatically in second normal form. (If the table were not in second normal form, some column would be dependent on only a *portion* of the primary key, which is impossible when the primary key is just one column.) Thus, the CUSTOMER table is in second normal form.

Although this table is in second normal form, Figure 2-11 shows that it still possesses update problems similar to those identified for the INVOICES table shown in Figure 2-9. In Figure 2-11, the sales rep name occurs many times in the table.

The redundancy of including a sales rep ID and full name in the CUSTOMER table results in the same set of problems that existed for the INVOICES table. In addition to the problem of wasted space, you have the following update anomalies:

1. **Updates:** Changing the sales rep full name requires changes to multiple rows in the table.

2. **Inconsistent data:** The design does not prohibit multiple iterations of sales rep names in the database. For example, a sales rep might represent 20 customers, and his or her name might be entered 20 different ways in the table.

CUSTOMER

CUST_ID	FIRST_ NAME	LAST_ NAME	BALANCE	CREDIT_ LIMIT	REP_ID	REP_ FIRST_NAME	REP_ LAST_NAME
125	Joey	Smith	$80.68	$500.00	05	Susan	Garcia
375	Melanie	Jackson	$252.25	$250.00	05	Susan	Garcia
543	Angie	Hendricks	$315.00	$750.00	05	Susan	Garcia
795	Randy	Blacksmith	$61.50	$500.00	05	Susan	Garcia
182	Billy	Rufton	$43.13	$750.00	10	Richard	Miller
294	Samantha	Smith	$58.60	$500.00	10	Richard	Miller
492	Elmer	Jackson	$45.20	$500.00	10	Richard	Miller
721	Leslie	Smith	$166.65	$1,000.00	10	Richard	Miller
227	Sandra	Pincher	$156.38	$500.00	15	Donna	Smith
314	Tom	Rascal	$17.25	$250.00	15	Donna	Smith
435	James	Gonzalez	$230.40	$1,000.00	15	Donna	Smith
616	Sally	Cruz	$8.33	$500.00	15	Donna	Smith

FIGURE 2-11   Sample CUSTOMER table

3. **Additions:** To add sales rep 25 (Juanita Sanchez) to the database, she must represent at least one customer. If Juanita does not yet represent any customers, you either cannot record the fact that her name is Juanita Sanchez, or you must create a fictitious customer for her to represent until she represents an actual customer. Neither of these solutions is desirable.

4. **Deletions:** If you delete all the customers of sales rep 05 from the database, you will also lose all information about sales rep 05.

These update anomalies are because the REP_ID determines REP_FIRST_NAME and REP_LAST_NAME, but REP_ID is not the primary key. As a result, the same REP_ID and consequently the same REP_FIRST_NAME and REP_LAST_NAME can appear on many different rows.

You have seen that tables in second normal form represent an improvement over tables in first normal form, but to eliminate problems with tables in second normal form, you need an even better strategy for creating tables. Third normal form provides that strategy. Before looking at third normal form, however, you need to become familiar with the special name that is given to any column that determines another column (like REP_ID in the CUSTOMER table). Any column (or collection of columns) that determines another column is called a **determinant**. A table's primary key is a determinant. In fact, by definition, any candidate key is a determinant. (Remember that a candidate key is a column or collection of columns that could function as the primary key.) In Figure 2-11, REP_ID is a determinant, but it is not a candidate key, and that is the problem.

A table is in **third normal form (3NF)** when it is in second normal form and the only determinants it contains are candidate keys.

Now you have identified the problem with the CUSTOMER table: It is not in third normal form. There are several steps for converting tables to third normal form.

First, for each determinant that is not a candidate key, remove from the table the columns that depend on this determinant (but do not remove the determinant). Next, create a new table containing all the columns from the original table that depend on this determinant. Finally, make the determinant the primary key of this new table.

In the CUSTOMER table, for example, remove REP_FIRST_NAME and REP_LAST_NAME because they depend on the determinant REP_ID, which is not a candidate key. A new table, SALES_REP, is formed, consisting of REP_ID as the primary key and the columns REP_FIRST_NAME and REP_LAST__NAME, as follows:

```
CUSTOMER (CUST ID, FIRST_NAME, LAST_NAME, BALANCE, CREDIT_LIMIT,
    REP_ID)
```

and

```
SALES_REP (REP ID, REP_FIRST_NAME, REP_LAST_NAME)
```

Previously the first and last names for the sales rep were named REP_FIRST_NAME and REP_LAST_NAME, respectively. It was not possible to use the identifiers FIRST_NAME and LAST_NAME because in the CUSTOMER table FIRST_NAME and LAST_NAME were being used to identify the first and last names of the customer. Because the fields REP_FIRST_NAME and REP_LAST_NAME are now being removed from the CUSTOMER table and placed into the SALES_REP table, it is now possible to use the identifiers of FIRST_NAME and LAST_NAME to correspond to the first and last names for a sales rep. The SALES_REP table will now be noted as follows, incorporating the desired identifiers for the first and last names for the sales rep:

```
SALES_REP (REP ID, FIRST_NAME, LAST_NAME)
```

Figure 2-12 shows the original CUSTOMER table and the tables created when converting the original table to third normal form.

Has this new design for the CUSTOMER table corrected all of the previously identified problems? A sales rep's name appears only once, thus avoiding redundancy and simplifying the process of storing a sales rep's first and last name. This design prohibits a sales rep from having different names in the database. To add a new sales rep to the

CUSTOMER

CUST_ID	FIRST_NAME	LAST_NAME	BALANCE	CREDIT_LIMIT	REP_ID	REP_FIRST_NAME	REP_LAST_NAME
125	Joey	Smith	$80.68	$500.00	05	Susan	Garcia
375	Melanie	Jackson	$252.25	$250.00	05	Susan	Garcia
543	Angie	Hendricks	$315.00	$750.00	05	Susan	Garcia
795	Randy	Blacksmith	$61.50	$500.00	05	Susan	Garcia
182	Billy	Rufton	$43.13	$750.00	10	Richard	Miller
294	Samantha	Smith	$58.60	$500.00	10	Richard	Miller
492	Elmer	Jackson	$45.20	$500.00	10	Richard	Miller
721	Leslie	Smith	$166.65	$1,000.00	10	Richard	Miller
227	Sandra	Pincher	$156.38	$500.00	15	Donna	Smith
314	Tom	Rascal	$17.25	$250.00	15	Donna	Smith
435	James	Gonzalez	$230.40	$1,000.00	15	Donna	Smith
616	Sally	Cruz	$8.33	$500.00	15	Donna	Smith

Note updated identifier names

CUSTOMER

CUST_ID	FIRST_NAME	LAST_NAME	BALANCE	CREDIT_LIMIT	REP_ID
125	Joey	Smith	$80.68	$500.00	05
375	Melanie	Jackson	$252.25	$250.00	05
543	Angie	Hendricks	$315.00	$750.00	05
795	Randy	Blacksmith	$61.50	$500.00	05
182	Billy	Rufton	$43.13	$750.00	10
294	Samantha	Smith	$58.60	$500.00	10
492	Elmer	Jackson	$45.20	$500.00	10
721	Leslie	Smith	$166.65	$1,000.00	10
227	Sandra	Pincher	$156.38	$500.00	15
314	Tom	Rascal	$17.25	$250.00	15
435	James	Gonzalez	$230.40	$1,000.00	15
616	Sally	Cruz	$8.33	$500.00	15

SALES_REP

REP_ID	FIRST_NAME	LAST_NAME
05	Susan	Garcia
10	Richard	Miller
15	Donna	Smith
20	Daniel	Jackson

FIGURE 2-12   CUSTOMER table converted to third normal form

database, you add a row to the SALES_REP table; it is not necessary for a new rep to represent a customer. Finally, deleting all customers of a given sales rep will not remove the sales rep's record from the SALES_REP table, retaining the sales rep's first and last name in the database. You can reconstruct all the data in the original table from the data in the new collection of tables. All previously mentioned problems have indeed been solved.

Q & A

Question: Convert the following table to third normal form. In this table, STUDENT_NUM determines STUDENT_NAME, NUM_CREDITS, ADVISOR_NUM, and ADVISOR_NAME. ADVISOR_NUM determines ADVISOR_NAME. COURSE_NUM determines DESCRIPTION. The combination of a STUDENT_NUM and a COURSE_NUM determines GRADE.

```
STUDENT (STUDENT NUM, STUDENT_NAME, NUM_CREDITS, ADVISOR_NUM,
    ADVISOR_NAME, (COURSE_NUM, DESCRIPTION, GRADE))
```

Answer: Complete the following steps:

Step 1: Remove the repeating group to convert the table to first normal form, as follows:

```
STUDENT (STUDENT NUM, STUDENT_NAME, NUM_CREDITS, ADVISOR_NUM,
    ADVISOR_NAME, COURSE NUM, DESCRIPTION, GRADE)
```

The STUDENT table is now in first normal form because it has no repeating groups. It is not, however, in second normal form because STUDENT_NAME is dependent only on STUDENT_NUM, which is only a portion of the primary key.

Step 2: Convert the STUDENT table to second normal form. First, for each subset of the primary key, start a table with that subset as its key yielding the following:

```
(STUDENT_NUM,
(COURSE_NUM,
(STUDENT_NUM, COURSE_NUM,
```

Next, place the rest of the columns with the smallest collection of columns on which they depend, as follows:

```
(STUDENT NUM, STUDENT_NAME, NUM_CREDITS, ADVISOR_NUM, ADVISOR_NAME)
(COURSE NUM, DESCRIPTION)
(STUDENT NUM, COURSE NUM, GRADE)
```

Finally, assign names to each of the new tables:

```
STUDENT (STUDENT NUM, STUDENT_NAME, NUM_CREDITS, ADVISOR_NUM,
    ADVISOR_NAME)
COURSE (COURSE NUM, DESCRIPTION)
STUDENT_COURSE (STUDENT NUM, COURSE NUM, GRADE)
```

Although these tables are all in second normal form, the COURSE and STUDENT_COURSE tables are also in third normal form. The STUDENT table is not in third normal form, however, because it contains a determinant (ADVISOR_NUM) that is not a candidate key.

Step 3: Convert the STUDENT table to third normal form by removing the column that depends on the determinant ADVISOR_NUM and placing it in a separate table, as follows:

```
(STUDENT NUM, STUDENT_NAME, NUM_CREDITS, ADVISOR_NUM)
(ADVISOR NUM, ADVISOR_NAME)
```

Step 4: Name the tables and put the entire collection together, as follows:

```
STUDENT (STUDENT NUM, STUDENT_NAME, NUM_CREDITS, ADVISOR_NUM)
ADVISOR (ADVISOR NUM, ADVISOR_NAME)
COURSE (COURSE NUM, DESCRIPTION)
STUDENT_COURSE (STUDENT NUM, COURSE NUM, GRADE)
```

DIAGRAMS FOR DATABASE DESIGN

For many people, an illustration of a database's structure is quite useful. A popular type of illustration used to represent the structure of a database is the **entity-relationship (E-R)** diagram. In an E-R diagram, a rectangle represents an entity (table). One-to-many relationships between entities are drawn as lines between the corresponding rectangles.

Several different styles of E-R diagrams are used to diagram a database design. In the version shown in Figure 2-13, an arrowhead indicates the *many* side of the relationship between tables. In the relationship between the SALES_REP and CUSTOMER tables, for example, the arrow points from the SALES_REP table to the CUSTOMER table, indicating that one sales rep is related to many customers. The INVOICE_LINE table has two one-to-many relationships, as indicated by the line from the INVOICES table to the INVOICE_LINE table and the line from the ITEM table to the INVOICE_LINE table.

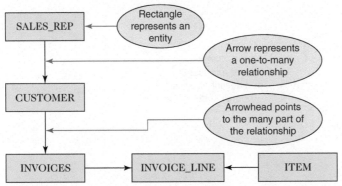

FIGURE 2-13   E-R diagram for the KimTay Pet Supplies database with rectangles and arrows

HELPFUL HINT

In this style of E-R diagram, you can put the rectangles in any position to represent the entities and relationships. The important thing is that the arrows connect the appropriate rectangles.

Another style of E-R diagram is to represent the *many* side of a relationship between tables with a crow's foot, as shown in Figure 2-14.

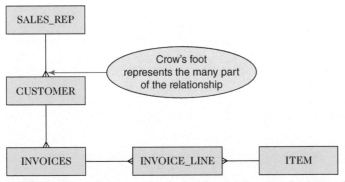

FIGURE 2-14   E-R diagram for the KimTay Pet Supplies database with crow's foot

The E-R diagram shown in Figure 2-15 represents the original style of E-R diagrams. In this style, relationships are indicated in diamonds that describe the relationship. The relationship between the SALES_REP and CUSTOMER tables, for example, is named REPRESENTS, reflecting the fact that a sales rep represents a customer. The relationship between the CUSTOMER and INVOICES table is named PLACED, reflecting the fact that customers place invoices. The relationship between the INVOICES and INVOICE_LINE tables is named CONTAINS, reflecting the fact that an invoice contains invoice lines. The relationship between the ITEM and INVOICE_LINE tables is named IS_ON, reflecting the fact that a given item is on many invoices. In this style of E-R diagram, the number 1 indicates the *one* side of the relationship and the letter *n* represents the *many* side of the relationship.

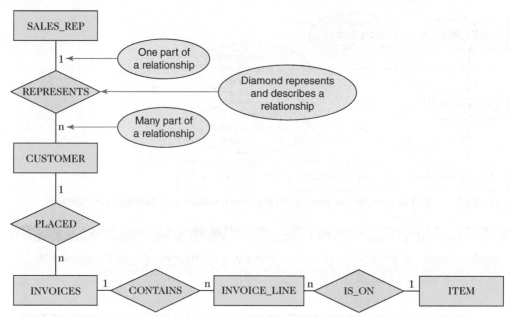

FIGURE 2-15   E-R diagram for the KimTay Pet Supplies database with named relationships

Module Summary

- An entity is a person, place, thing, or event. An attribute is a property of an entity. A relationship is an association between entities.

- A relation is a two-dimensional table in which the entries in the table contain only single values, each column has a distinct name, all values in a column match this name, the order of the rows and columns is immaterial, and each row contains unique values. A relational database is a collection of relations.

- Column B is functionally dependent on another column, A (or possibly a collection of columns), when a value for A determines a single value for B at any one time.

- Column A (or a collection of columns) is the primary key for a relation (table), R, if *all* columns in R are functionally dependent on A and no subcollection of the columns in A (assuming A is a collection of columns and not just a single column) also has Property 1.

- To design a database to satisfy a particular set of requirements, first read the requirements and identify the entities (objects) involved. Give names to the entities and identify the unique identifiers for these entities. Next, identify the attributes for all the entities and the functional dependencies that exist among the attributes and then use the functional dependencies to identify the tables and columns. Finally, identify any relationships between tables by looking at matching columns.

- A table (relation) is in first normal form (1NF) when it does not contain a repeating group. To convert an unnormalized table to first normal form, remove the repeating group and expand the primary key to include the original primary key along with the key to the repeating group.

- A table (relation) is in second normal form (2NF) when it is in first normal form and no nonkey column (that is, a column that is not part of the primary key) is dependent on only a portion of the primary key. To convert a table in first normal form to a collection of tables in second normal form, take each subset of the set of columns that make up the primary key and begin a new table with this subset as its primary key. Next, place each of the other columns with the appropriate primary key; that is, place each one with the minimal collection of columns on which it depends. Finally, give each of these new tables a name that is descriptive of the meaning and contents of the table.

- A table is in third normal form (3NF) when it is in second normal form and the only determinants (columns on which at least one other column depends) it contains are candidate keys (columns that could function as the primary key). To convert a table in second normal form to a collection of tables in third normal form, first, for each determinant that is not a candidate key, remove from the table the columns that depend on this determinant (but do not remove the determinant). Next, create a new table containing all the columns from the original table that depend on this determinant. Finally, make the determinant the primary key of this new table.

- An entity-relationship (E-R) diagram is an illustration that represents the design of a database. There are several common styles of illustrating database design that use shapes to represent entities and connectors to illustrate the relationships between those entities.

Key Terms

attribute

Boyce-Codd normal form (BCNF)

candidate key

~~concatenation~~

database design

database management system (DBMS)

determinant

entity

entity-relationship (E-R) diagram

field

first normal form (1NF)

functionally dependent

functionally determine

nonkey column

normal form

normalization

one-to-many relationship

primary key

~~qualify~~

record

redundancy

relation

relational database

relationship

repeating group

second normal form (2NF)

third normal form (3NF)

tuple

unnormalized relation

update anomaly

Review Questions

Module Quiz

1. What is an entity?
2. What is an attribute?
3. What is a relationship? What is a one-to-many relationship?
4. What is a repeating group?
5. What is a relation?
6. What is a relational database?
7. Describe the shorthand representation of the structure of a relational database. Why is it important to be able to represent the structure of a database in a shorthand fashion?
8. How do you qualify the name of a field, and when do you need to do this?
9. What does it mean for a column to be functionally dependent on another column?
10. What is a primary key? Why is a primary key required for proper database design?
11. A database at a college must support the following requirements:

    a. For a department, store its number and name.

    b. For an advisor, store his or her number, last name, first name, and the department number to which the advisor is assigned.

    c. For a course, store its code and description (for example, DBA210, SQL Programming).

d. For a student, store his or her number, first name, and last name. For each course the student takes, store the course code, course description, and grade earned. Also, store the number and name of the student's advisor. Assume that an advisor might advise any number of students but that each student has just one advisor.

   Design the database for the preceding set of requirements. Use your own experience as a student to determine any functional dependencies. List the tables, columns, and relationships. In addition, represent your design with an E-R diagram.

12. Define first normal form. What types of problems might you encounter using tables that are not in first normal form?

13. Define second normal form. What types of problems might you encounter using tables that are not in second normal form?

14. Define third normal form. What types of problems might you encounter using tables that are not in third normal form?

15. Using the functional dependencies that you determined in Question 11, convert the following table to an equivalent collection of tables that are in third normal form.

> STUDENT (STUDENT_NUM, STUDENT_LAST_NAME, STUDENT_FIRST_NAME, ADVISOR_NUM, ADVISOR_LAST_NAME, ADVISOR_FIRST_NAME, (COURSE_CODE, DESCRIPTION, GRADE))

Critical Thinking

1. List the changes to your answer for Question 11 needed to make the requirements change so a student can have more than one advisor.

2. List the changes to your answer for Question 11 needed to make the requirements change so that you must store the year and the semester in which a student took a course and received a grade.

Case Exercises

KimTay Pet Supplies

Answer each of the following questions using the KimTay Pet Supplies data shown in Figure 2-1. No computer work is required.

1. Indicate the changes (using the shorthand representation) that you would need to make to the original KimTay Pet Supplies database design (see Figure 2-1) to support the following requirements. A customer is not necessarily represented by a single sales rep, but they can be represented by several sales reps. When a customer places an order, the sales rep who gets the commission on the invoice must be in the collection of sales reps who represent the customer.

2. Indicate the changes (using the shorthand representation) that you would need to make to the original KimTay Pet Supplies database design to support the following requirements. There is no relationship between customers and sales reps. When a customer places an order, any sales rep can process the order and create the invoice. On the invoice, you need to identify both the customer placing the order and the sales rep responsible for the invoice. Draw an E-R diagram for the new design.

3. Indicate the changes (using the shorthand representation) that you would need to make to the original KimTay Pet Supplies database design in the event that the original Requirement 3 is changed as follows. For an item, store the item's ID, description, category, and price. In addition, for each location in which the item is located, store the value of the location, the description of the location, and the number of units of the item stored in the location. Draw an E-R diagram for the new design.

4. Using your knowledge of KimTay Pet Supplies, determine the functional dependencies that exist in the following table. After determining the functional dependencies, convert this table to an equivalent collection of tables that are in third normal form.

```
ITEM (ITEM _ ID, DESCRIPTION, ON _ HAND, CATEGORY, LOCATION, PRICE,
     (INVOICE _ NUM, INVOICE _ DATE, CUST _ ID, FIRST _ NAME,
     LAST _ NAME, QUANTITY, QUOTED _ PRICE))
```

Critical Thinking

1. Indicate the changes you need to make to the KimTay Pet Supplies database to support the following additional requirement. Each location has a manager who is identified by a manager ID, a manager first name, and a manager last name.

StayWell Student Accommodation

Answer each of the following questions using the StayWell Student Accommodation data shown in Figures 1-4 through 1-9 in Module 1. No computer work is required.

1. Determine the functional dependencies that exist in the following table and then convert this table to an equivalent collection of tables that are in third normal form.

```
OFFICE (OFFICE _ NUM, OFFICE _ NAME, (ADDRESS, SQR _ FT, BDRMS,
     FLOORS, MONTHLY _ RENT, OWNER _ NUM))
```

2. Determine the functional dependencies that exist in the following table and then convert this table to an equivalent collection of tables that are in third normal form.

```
PROPERTY (PROPERTY _ ID, OFFICE _ NUM, ADDRESS, SQR _ FT,
     BDRMS, FLOORS, MONTHLY _ RENT, OWNER _ NUM, LAST _ NAME,
     FIRST _ NAME)
```

3. StayWell also rents out properties on a weekly basis to students attending summer school in the Seattle area. Design a database to meet the following requirements, using the short-hand representation and a diagram of your choice.

    a. For each student renter, list his or her number, first name, middle initial, last name, address, city, state, postal code, telephone number, and e-mail address.

    b. For each property, list the office number, property address, city, state, postal code, square footage, number of bedrooms, number of floors, maximum number of persons that can sleep in the unit, and the base weekly rate.

    c. For each rental agreement, list the renter number, first name, middle initial, last name, address, city, state, postal code, telephone number, start date of the rental, end date of the rental, and the weekly rental amount. The rental period is one or more weeks.

MODULE **3**

CREATING TABLES

OBJECTIVES

- Create and run SQL commands.
- Create and activate a database.
- Create tables.
- Identify and use data types to define columns in tables.
- Understand and use nulls.
- Add rows to tables.
- View table data.
- Correct errors in a table.
- Save SQL commands to a file.
- Describe a table's layout using SQL.

INTRODUCTION

You already might be an experienced user of a database management system (DBMS). You might find a DBMS at your school's library, at a site on the Internet, or in any other place where you retrieve data using a computer. In this module, you begin your study of **Structured Query Language (SQL)**, which is one of the most popular and widely used languages for retrieving and manipulating database data.

In the mid-1970s, SQL was developed as the data manipulation language for IBM's prototype relational model DBMS, System R, under the name SEQUEL at IBM's San Jose research facilities. In 1980, the language was renamed SQL (but still pronounced *sequel* although the equally popular pronunciation of *S-Q-L* [*ess-cue-ell*] is preferable) to avoid confusion with an unrelated hardware product named SEQUEL. Most DBMSs use a version of SQL as their data manipulation language.

In this module, you learn the basics of working in SQL. You learn how to create tables and assign data types to columns. You also learn about a special type of value, called a null value, and learn how to manage these values in tables. You learn how to insert data into your tables after you create them. Finally, you learn how to describe a table's layout using SQL.

CREATING AND RUNNING SQL COMMANDS

You accomplish tasks in SQL by creating and running commands using a DBMS that supports SQL. This text uses MySQL to create and run SQL commands. The text also indicates differences you find if you are using Oracle or Microsoft SQL Server.

The version of MySQL used in this text is MySQL 8.0 (specifically MySQL Community Server 8.0.18). You can download and install the latest version, and previous versions, of MySQL 8.0 edition for free from the MySQL Web site (https://dev.mysql.com). Although you may choose any of the setup types during installation dependent upon your needs, to be able to perform operations presented in this text, it is suggested you choose the Developer Default setup type or the Full option. Either of these options include the installation of the MySQL Workbench. MySQL Workbench contains many powerful tools that allows developers and database administrators to visually design, develop, and administer MySQL databases. The MySQL Workbench also contains an SQL editor that is used throughout the text to enter commands and view the results of the commands entered. Be sure to remember the password selected during installation.

Using MySQL Workbench

After installing MySQL 8.0, run the MySQL Workbench 8.0 CE app using whatever method you prefer for running an app. On the MySQL Workbench opening window, you notice links where you may browse MySQL documentation, access a MySQL blog, and participate in forums related to MySQL. On this main window, you also see a list of the MySQL connections currently available to you. The one connection listed is to the server created during the installation of MySQL. See Figure 3-1.

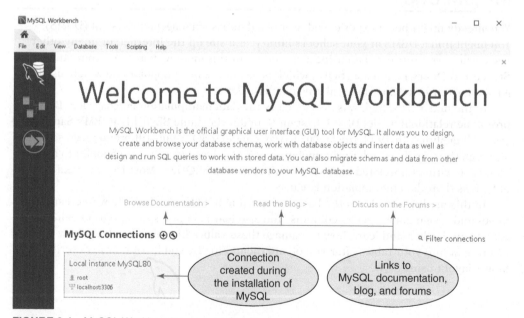

FIGURE 3-1   MySQL Workbench opening window

Click on the connection box *Local instance MySQL80*. MySQL80 was the default name given during installation if you accepted the defaults. The name may be different if you changed the name during installation. Next provide the password to access the server you created during installation. See Figure 3-2.

FIGURE 3-2   Entering password for server

Once you have successfully submitted the password for the connection, you are given access to the main MySQL Workbench environment for that connection. See Figure 3-3.

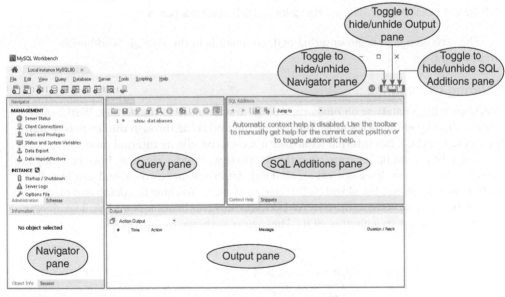

FIGURE 3-3   Main MySQL Workbench environment

Remember that MySQL Workbench is a very powerful tool that contains many features. We only use the SQL editor within the MySQL Workbench for our purposes. Therefore, we can simplify, or unclutter, the window by hiding some of the panes. The two panes we would like to hide are the Navigation pane and the MySQL Additions pane. To hide these two panes, click on their corresponding toggle button as show in Figure 3-3.

The result of hiding the Navigator pane and the SQL Additions pane gives more room for the Query pane and the Output pane. Each pane expands to fill the original window as shown in Figure 3-4.

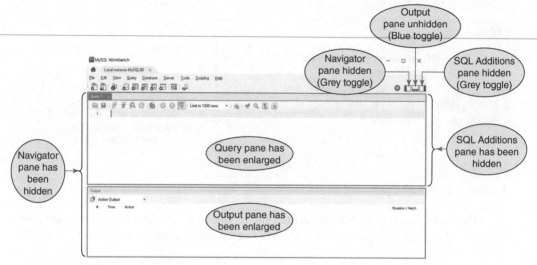

FIGURE 3-4   Outcome of hiding the Navigator and SQL Additions panes

The next step is to begin entering SQL commands in the MySQL Workbench environment.

Entering Commands

Before creating a database on our own, we can first get used to the MySQL Workbench environment by entering a simple SQL command and going through the process to have it executed. MySQL has internal databases it uses to handle its internal processing. These databases will be separate from the database we will be creating; however, they are viewable. Because we have not yet created any databases on our own, and just installed MySQL, any databases listed will be internal to MySQL. To show the databases on a MySQL server host you use the **SHOW DATABASES** command followed by a semicolon. A semicolon ends a statement in SQL. The syntax is shown in Figure 3-5.

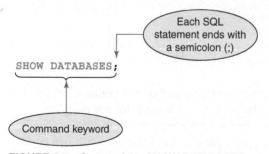

FIGURE 3-5   Syntax of the SHOW DATABASES command

The next step is to enter the SHOW DATABASES command into the MySQL Workbench SQL editor. Enter the command on the first line as show in Figure 3-6. Be sure to enter the semicolon after the command.

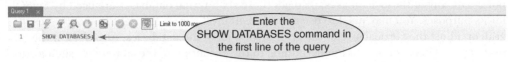

FIGURE 3-6   Enter SHOW DATABASES command

Notice as you entered the command, the keywords of SHOW DATABASES turn blue. This color of blue is used to represent keywords in the SQL editor within the MySQL Workbench. This color scheme is the Microsoft Windows default scheme and can be modified if preferred; however, for the remainder of the text we continue using this color of blue for keywords.

The next step is to execute the command entered. On the main menu, select the Query menu and select Execute Current Statement as shown in Figure 3-7. This executes the statement you just entered. Note that you could have also selected Execute (All or Selected) because there was only one SQL statement entered.

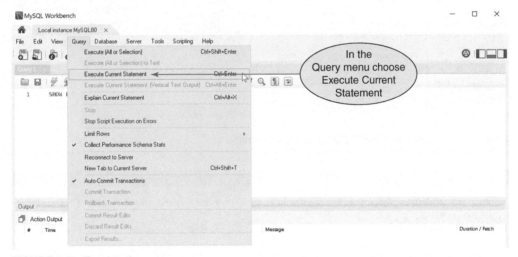

FIGURE 3-7   Execute the query

HELPFUL HINT

Although some environments may not require a semicolon to end an SQL statement, it is always good practice to do so. For in the event you are using an environment in which it is required and do not include the semicolon, an error will occur. Always follow proper coding practice for any language you are using, regardless of whether the environment is forgiving or not.

Once the command is executed, a result grid is displayed between the query pane and output pane. Note on the right-hand side of the result grid there are other options available; however, we will not be using them at present. The result of the command SHOW DATABASES lists the databases available in the MySQL server connection. Note we did not create any of these databases; instead, these six internal databases are used by MySQL for its purposes. You may need to use the vertical scroll bar on the right side of the result grid, or adjust the vertical size of the grid, to view all of the databases. Also note in the output pane there is information pertaining to the execution of the statement, such as the time of day it was executed, general description of the processing, outcome, and the time it took for the processing to occur. Note under the message column in the output pane that six rows were returned, which corresponds to the six databases listed. The green circle with a checkmark indicates the command executed successfully. See Figure 3-8.

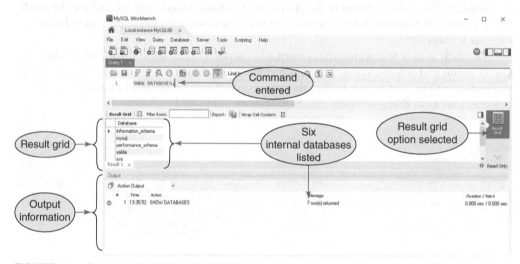

FIGURE 3-8 Outcome of SHOW DATABASES command

HELPFUL HINT

Note that your specific version of MySQL may have a different number of internal databases listed. This presents no issues.

To clear the result grid, click on the "x" located on the bottom left of the result grid after "Result #." The grid is removed, and the query and output panes remain. To remove the details from output pane, you may right-click anywhere while the cursor is on the row or pane pertaining to the action. When the menu appears, select the Clear option from the menu, and the information is removed. If you wish to review any history of processing commands, you can click the drop-down arrow beside Action Output in the output pane and select History Output. See Figure 3-9.

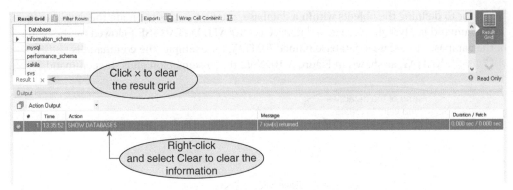

FIGURE 3-9   To clear results of the SHOW DATABASES command

Now that you have entered and executed an SQL command in MySQL Workbench, the next step is to create your own database. Prior to creating your own database, you can clear the query pane by simply highlighting the command and deleting it, or any other method you prefer. You should now have a MySQL Workbench window similar to Figure 3-4, prior to entering any commands and only the query and output panes showing.

HELPFUL HINT

Although it is not necessary to clear the query and output panes as you progress to creating a database of your own, it is cleared during the presentation in the textbook to make the examples more readable and easier to understand. This way you can focus on one command, or group of commands, at a time and not constantly viewing previous commands or results.

CREATING A DATABASE

There are many objects within a database, including tables and fields. All of these objects have identifiers, or names, associated with them. DBMS rules for naming identifiers vary dependent upon the DBMS. For example, in the version of MySQL used in this text, identifier names for a database, table, or a field can be up to 64 characters; however, that does not mean that you should give your identifiers names of that length. It is simply permitted if the need arises to properly describe the object. If you want to name identifiers very uniquely in any DBMS, you should consult the documentation for that specific DMBS. The documentation for naming identifiers in the version of MySQL used in this text can be found at https://dev.mysql.com/doc/refman/8.0/en/identifiers.html. General guidelines that are acceptable to most DBMS are given below. If you adhere to these guidelines for naming identifiers when using a DBMS, it is rare that you will have an issue.

1.   The identifier name cannot exceed 30 characters.
2.   The identifier name must start with a letter.
3.   The identifier name can contain letters, numbers, and underscores (_).
4.   The identifier name cannot contain spaces.

Prior to defining the objects within a database, the first step is to create the database itself. The command in MySQL to create a database is **CREATE DATABASE** followed by the name of the database. To create a database named KIMTAY, for example, the command is CREATE DATABASE KIMTAY; as shown in Figure 3-10. Note that a semicolon ends the command.

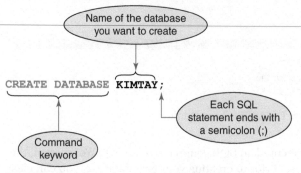

CREATE DATABASE KIMTAY;

Name of the database you want to create

Each SQL statement ends with a semicolon (;)

Command keyword

FIGURE 3-10   Syntax of the CREATE DATABASE command

Enter the command to create the KimTay database into the MySQL Workbench SQL editor. Execute the command similar to how you executed the SHOW DATABASES command and view the results. See Figure 3-11.

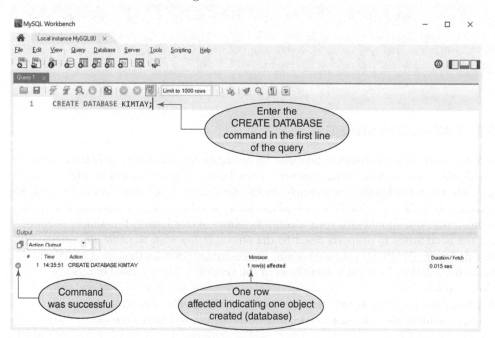

FIGURE 3-11   Enter SHOW DATABASES command

Execute the SHOW DATABASES; command as you did previously and view the results in Figure 3-12. The results are now different because the KimTay database has been added, with seven databases now listed. Six of the databases will be internal to MySQL; however, the one additional database is the one you just created.

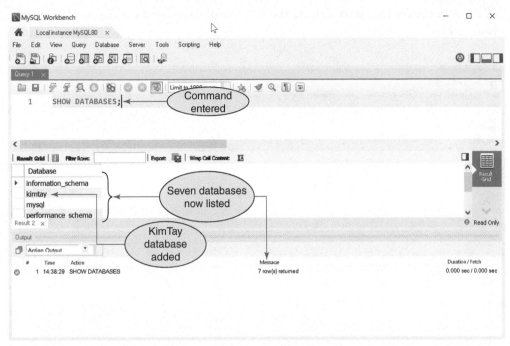

FIGURE 3-12   Outcome of SHOW DATABASES command after creating the KimTay database

Now the KimTay database has been created, you need to create the tables that will reside within the database. In addition, you need to populate the tables with the data from the previous modules. First, we begin by creating the table that holds the sales reps.

Changing the Default Database

To work with a database, you must change the default database to the one you need to use. The **default database** is the database to which all subsequent commands pertain. To activate the default database, execute the **USE** command followed by the name of the database. For example, to change the default database to the one you just created for KimTay Pet Supplies, the command would be USE KIMTAY;, as shown in Figure 3-13. Changing the default database is also known as activating or using the database.

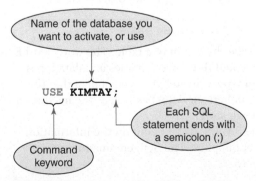

FIGURE 3-13   Syntax of the USE command

Execute the command to activate the KIMTAY database and see the results in Figure 3-14.

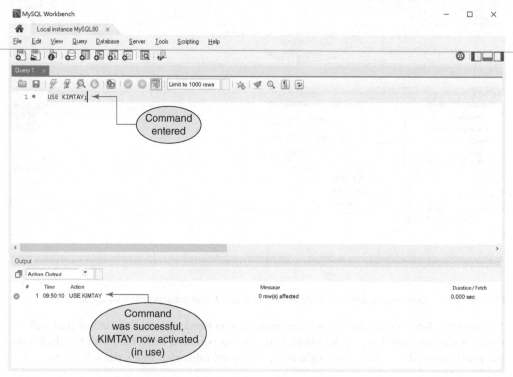

FIGURE 3-14   Enter USE command to activate the KIMTAY database

Now that the default database has been set to the KIMTAY database, you can now begin to add the tables to the database.

CREATING A TABLE

The first step in creating a table is to describe the layout of the table to the DBMS.

EXAMPLE 1: Describe the layout of the SALES_REP table to the DBMS.

You use the **CREATE TABLE** command to describe the layout of a table. The word TABLE is followed by the name of the table to be created and then by the names and data types of the columns that the table contains. The **data type** indicates the type of data that the column can contain (for example, characters, numbers, or dates) as well as the maximum number of characters or digits that the column can store.

In the previous modules we chose the name SALES_REP to contain the information pertaining to sales reps employed by KimTay Pet Supplies. The SQL command that creates the SALES_REP table is shown in Figure 3-15.

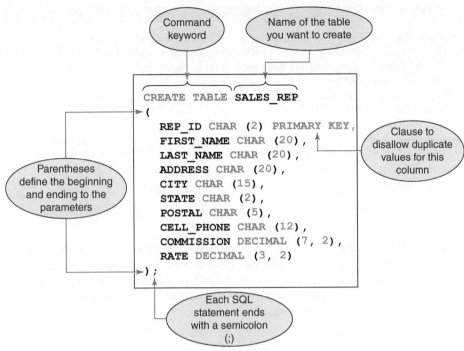

FIGURE 3-15   CREATE TABLE command to create the SALES_REP table

This CREATE TABLE command, which uses the data definition features of SQL, describes a table named SALES_REP. The table contains ten columns: REP_ID, FIRST_NAME, LAST_NAME, ADDRESS, CITY, STATE, POSTAL, CELL_PHONE, COMMISSION, and RATE. The REP_ID column can store two characters and is the table's primary key. The FIRST_NAME and LAST_NAME columns can store 20 characters each, and the STATE column can store two characters. The COMMISSION column can store only numbers, and those numbers are limited to seven digits, including two decimal places. Similarly, the RATE column can store three-digit numbers, including two decimal places. You can think of the SQL command shown in Figure 3-15 as creating an empty table with column headings for each column name.

In SQL, commands are free format; that is, no rule says that a particular word must begin in a particular position on the line. For example, you could have written the CREATE TABLE command shown in Figure 3-15 as follows:

```
CREATE TABLE SALES_REP (REP_ID CHAR(2) PRIMARY KEY, FIRST_NAME
CHAR(20), LAST_NAME CHAR(20), ADDRESS CHAR(20), CITY
CHAR(15), STATE CHAR(2), POSTAL CHAR(5), CELL_PHONE
CHAR(12), COMMISSION DECIMAL(7,2), RATE DECIMAL(3,2));
```

It should be noted that the PRIMARY KEY clause in the previous statement specifies that REP_ID will be the unique identifier to the row meaning "No Duplicate" are allowed for the column.

The manner in which the CREATE TABLE command shown in Figure 3-15 was written makes the command more readable. This text strives for such readability when writing SQL commands.

To create the SALES_REP table in MySQL Workbench, enter and execute the command shown in Figure 3-15 as you did with the previous commands. Once again, there is a
different color scheme for various parts of the command as you enter it. Figure 3-16 shows
the executed command and results. The figures in this text may show the panes resized so
that more of the command or results is visible to the user.

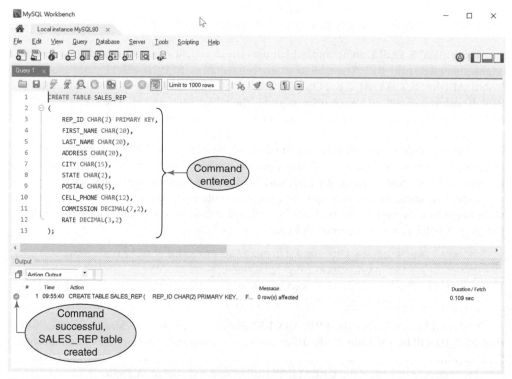

FIGURE 3-16   Enter CREATE TABLE command to create the SALES_REP table

ORACLE USER NOTE

Oracle 19c Enterprise/Standard Edition database is adopted in this book; however, you may use Oracle 19c Express Edition. Oracle provides several tools to connect to the database to issue SQL commands. These tools vary from the traditional SQL*Plus command line interface to the graphical user interface SQL Developer which is user friendly and offers many capabilities that assist developers in their SQL development tasks. Oracle SQL Developer is used in this book. Using Oracle SQL Developer enter the query shown in Oracle Figure 3-1 to create SALES_REP table and click on the green arrow button located in worksheet navigation toolbar to run the command.

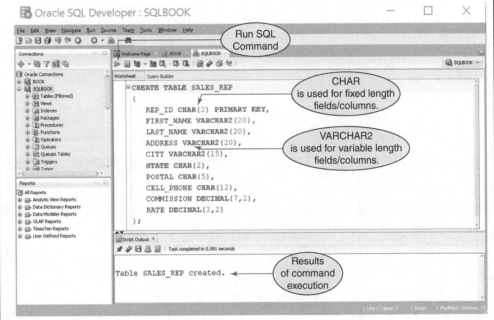

Source: Oracle Corporation

ORACLE FIGURE 3-1   CREATE TABLE statement to create SALES_REP table using Oracle

▶ SQL SERVER USER NOTE

Microsoft offers a competitive enterprise DBMS comparable to Oracle designed for use in client-server applications. There are three versions of SQL Server Enterprise Edition that require a paid license, whereas Developer and Express editions are free. You may connect to Microsoft SQL Server database from your own computer through a set of client database tools called SQL Server Management Studio. Management Studio includes a Query Editor window that you can use to run SQL commands. If you are using Management Studio and connecting to a database on your local computer, accept the default values for Server Type, Server Name, and Authentication, and then click the Connect button in the Connect to Server dialog box. When Management Studio is displayed, open the database in which you want to run SQL commands and click the New Query button on the toolbar. Type the SQL command in the Query Editor window that opens and then click the Execute button on the toolbar to execute the command. The command shown in SQL Server Figure 3-1 creates the SALES_REP table and displays a message in the Messages pane to indicate that the command completed successfully.

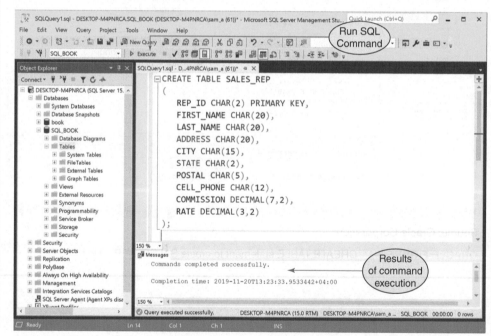

SQL SERVER FIGURE 3-1   CREATE TABLE statement to create SALES_REP table using SQL Server

Although there was verification from MySQL that the table was created, you may view the list of tables within an activated database by using the SHOW TABLES; command. This command is similar to the SHOW DATABASES command you used previously, but instead it gives you a list of tables residing in the current database in use. In our case, this results in a list of the tables residing in the KIMTAY database. See Figure 3-17 for the results of the command.

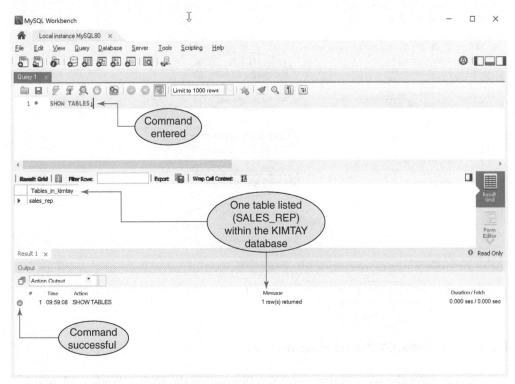

FIGURE 3-17   Outcome of SHOW TABLES command listing the tables in the KIMTAY database

Correcting Errors in SQL Commands

Suppose that you attempted to create the SALES_REP table using the CREATE TABLE command shown in Figure 3-18, which contains several mistakes. Instead of displaying a message that the table was created successfully, MySQL displays an error message about a problem that it encountered. In reviewing the command, you see that CHAR is misspelled on line 5, the CITY column was omitted, and line 8 should be deleted. If you run a command and MySQL Workbench displays an error, you can use the mouse and the arrow keys on the keyboard to position the insertion point in the correct position so you can correct these errors using the same techniques that you might use in a word processor. For example, you can use the pointer to select the word CHR on line 5 and type CHAR, and then you can use the pointer to move the insertion point to the end of line 5 so you can press Enter to insert the missing information to create the CITY column. You can use the pointer to select the contents of line 8 and then press Delete to remove it. After making these changes, you can click the Run button to execute the command again. If the command contains additional errors, you see an error message again. If the command is correct, you see the message that the table was created.

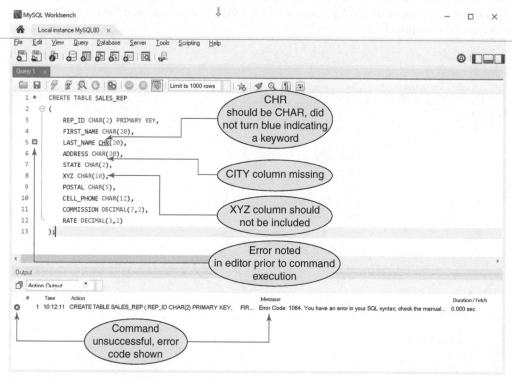

FIGURE 3-18   CREATE TABLE command with errors

You may have also noticed that the SQL editor within the MySQL Workbench indicated there was a syntax error in the command on line 5 prior to executed, as indicated by the small red box with an X in it beside the line. The SQL editor is quite advanced and understands the correct syntax as you enter the commands. In addition, note that omitting the CITY column and inserting a XYZ column do not produce syntax errors. Instead, they are considered logic errors on your part.

Dropping a Table

After creating a table, you might notice that you added a column that you do not need or that you assigned the wrong data type or size to a column. One way to correct such errors in a table is simply to delete (drop) the table and start over. For example, suppose you wrote a CREATE TABLE command that contained a column named LST instead of LAST or defined a column as CHAR(5) instead of CHAR(15). Suppose you do not discover the error and you execute the command, creating a table with these problems. In this case, you can delete the entire table using the **DROP TABLE** command and then re-create the table using the correct CREATE TABLE command.

To drop a table, execute the DROP TABLE command, followed by the name of the table you want to delete and a semicolon. To delete the SALES_REP table, for example, you would enter and execute the following command:

```
DROP TABLE SALES_REP;
```

Dropping a table also deletes any data that you entered into the table. It is a good idea to check your CREATE TABLE commands carefully before executing them and to correct any problems before adding data. Later in this text, you learn how to change a table's structure without having to delete the entire table.

Q & A

Question: How can I correct a mistake that I made when I created a table?
Answer: Later in the text, you see how to alter a table to make any necessary corrections. For now, the easiest way is to drop the table using the DROP TABLE command and then to execute the correct CREATE TABLE command.

USING DATA TYPES

For each column in a table, you must specify the data type to use to store the type of data that the column contains. Figure 3-19 describes some common data types used in databases.

Data Type	Description
CHAR(*n*)	Stores a character string *n* characters long. You use the CHAR data type for columns that contain letters and special characters, and for columns containing numbers that will not be used in any calculations. Because neither sales rep ID numbers nor customer ID numbers will be used in any calculations, for example, the REP_ID and CUST_ID columns are both assigned the CHAR data type.
VARCHAR(*n*)	An alternative to CHAR that stores a character string up to *n* characters long. Unlike CHAR, only the actual character string is stored. If a character string 20 characters long is stored in a CHAR(30) column, for example, it will occupy 30 characters (20 characters plus 10 blank spaces). If it is stored in a VARCHAR(30) column, it will only occupy 20 spaces. In general, tables that use VARCHAR instead of CHAR occupy less space, but the DBMS does not process them as rapidly during queries and updates. However, both are legitimate choices. This text uses CHAR, but VARCHAR works equally well.
DATE	Stores date data. The specific format in which dates are stored varies from one SQL implementation to another. In MySQL and SQL Server, dates are enclosed in single quotation marks and have the format YYYY-MM-DD (for example, '2020-10-23' is October 23, 2020). In Oracle, dates are enclosed in single quotation marks and have the format DD-MON-YYYY (for example, '23-OCT-2020' is October 23, 2020).

FIGURE 3-19 Commonly used data types

Data Type	Description
DECIMAL(p,q)	Stores a decimal number p digits long with q of the digits being decimal places to the right of the decimal point. For example, the data type DECIMAL(5,2) represents a number with three places to the left and two places to the right of the decimal (for example, 123.45). You can use the contents of DECIMAL columns in calculations. You also can use the NUMERIC(p,q) data type in MySQL to store a decimal number. Oracle and SQL Server also use NUMBER(p,q) to store a decimal number.
INT	Stores integers, which are numbers without a decimal part. The valid range is –2147483648 to 2147483647. You can use the contents of INT columns in calculations. If you follow the word INT with AUTO_INCREMENT, you create a column for which SQL will automatically generate a new sequence number for each time you add a new row. This would be the appropriate choice, for example, when you want the DBMS to generate a value for a primary key.
SMALLINT	Stores integers but uses less space than the INT data type. The valid range is –32768 to 32767. SMALLINT is a better choice than INT when you are certain that the column will store numbers within the indicated range. You can use the contents of SMALLINT columns in calculations.

FIGURE 3-19 Commonly used data types (Continued)

USING NULLS

Occasionally, when you enter a new row into a table or modify an existing row, the values for one or more columns are unknown or unavailable. For example, you can add a customer's name and address to a table even though the customer does not have an assigned sales rep or an established credit limit. In other cases, some values might never be known—perhaps there is a customer that does not have a sales rep. In SQL, you handle this situation by using a special value to represent cases in which an actual value is unknown, unavailable, or not applicable. This special value is called a **null data value**, or simply a **null**. When creating a table, you can specify whether to allow nulls in the individual columns.

Q & A

Question: Should a user be allowed to enter null values for the primary key?
Answer: No. The primary key is supposed to uniquely identify a given row, and this would be impossible if nulls were allowed. For example, if you stored two customer records without values in the primary key column, you would have no way to tell them apart.

In SQL, you use the **NOT NULL** clause in a CREATE TABLE command to indicate columns that *cannot* contain null values. The default is to allow nulls; columns for which you do not specify NOT NULL can accept null values.

For example, suppose that the FIRST_NAME and LAST_NAME columns in the SALES_REP table cannot accept null values, but all other columns in the SALES_REP table can. The CREATE TABLE command in Figure 3-20 accomplishes this goal.

```
CREATE TABLE SALES_REP
(
    REP_ID CHAR (2) PRIMARY KEY,
    FIRST_NAME CHAR (20) NOT NULL,
    LAST_NAME CHAR (20) NOT NULL,
    ADDRESS CHAR (20),
    CITY CHAR (15),
    STATE CHAR (2),
    POSTAL CHAR (5),
    CELL_PHONE CHAR (12),
    COMMISSION DECIMAL (7, 2),
    RATE DECIMAL (3, 2)
);
```

NOT NULL clauses added to the FIRST_NAME and LAST_NAME fields

FIGURE 3-20   CREATE TABLE command with NOT NULL clauses

If you created the SALES_REP table with this CREATE TABLE command, the DBMS would reject any attempt to store a null value in either the FIRST_NAME or LAST_NAME column. The database allows storing NULL values in the ADDRESS column because it was created without specifying NOT NULL when the table was created. Because the primary key column cannot accept null values, you do not need to specify the REP_ID column as NOT NULL.

ADDING ROWS TO A TABLE

After you have created a table in a database, you can load data into the table by using the INSERT command.

The INSERT Command

The **INSERT** command adds rows to a table. You type INSERT INTO followed by the name of the table into which you are adding data. Then you type the word VALUES followed by the specific values to be inserted in parentheses. When adding rows to character columns, make sure you enclose the values in single quotation marks (for example, "Susan"). You also must enter the values in the appropriate case, because character data is stored exactly as you enter it.

HELPFUL HINT

You must enclose values in single quotation marks for any column whose type is character (CHAR), even when the data contains numbers. Because the POSTAL column in the SALES_REP table has a CHAR data type, for example, you must enclose postal codes in single quotation marks, even though they are numbers.

If you need to enter an apostrophe (single quotation mark) into a column, you type two single quotation marks. For example, to enter the name O'Toole in the LAST_NAME column, you would type "O'Toole" as the value in the INSERT command.

EXAMPLE 2: Add sales rep 05 to the SALES_REP table.

The command for this example is shown in Figure 3-21. Note that the character strings ("05," "Susan," "Garcia," and so on) are enclosed in single quotation marks. When you execute the command, the record is added to the SALES_REP table.

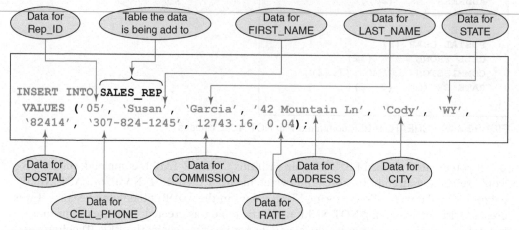

FIGURE 3-21   INSERT command to add sales rep 05 to the SALES_REP table

The result of the command being entered and executed is shown in Figure 3-22.

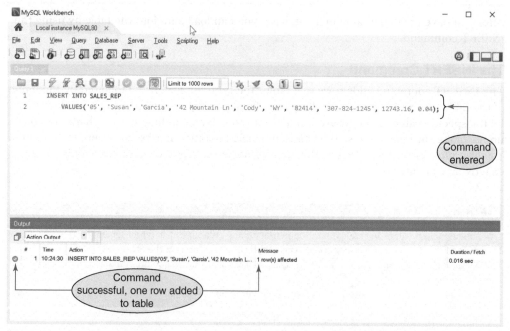

FIGURE 3-22   INSERT command executed for the first record in the SALES_REP table

Make sure that you type the values in the same case as those shown in the figures to avoid problems later when retrieving data from the database.

EXAMPLE 3: Add sales reps 10 and 15 to the SALES_REP table.

You could enter and execute new INSERT commands to add the new rows to the table. However, an easier and faster way to add these new rows to the table is to use the mouse and the keyboard to modify the previous INSERT command and execute it to add the record for the second sales rep. Figure 3-23 shows the new command to add the second record containing the data for sales rep 10. Simply use the mouse and keyboard to modify the command and execute it. Note that if it is easier for you to delete the previous command and enter the new command from the beginning, it is absolutely fine.

```
INSERT INTO SALES_REP
    VALUES ('10', 'Richard', 'Miller', '87 Pikes Dr', 'Ralston', 'WY',
    '82440', '307-406-4321', 20872.11, 0.06);
```

FIGURE 3-23   INSERT command to add sales rep 10 to the SALES_REP table

Figure 3-24 shows the results of the command being entered and executed to add the second record to the SALES_REP table, containing the data for sales rep 10.

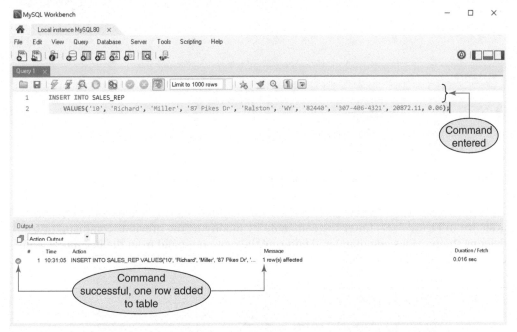

FIGURE 3-24   INSERT command executed for the second record in the SALES_REP table

The next command to add the third record, containing the data for sales rep 15, is shown in Figure 3-25. Enter the command by modifying the previous command, or deleting the previous command and entering the new command from the beginning. Once entered, execute the command.

```
INSERT INTO SALES_REP
    VALUES ('15', 'Donna', 'Smith', '312 Oak Rd', 'Powell', 'WY',
    '82440', '307-982-8401', 14912.92, 0.04);
```

FIGURE 3-25   INSERT command to add sales rep 15 to the SALES_REP table

Figure 3-26 shows the results of the command being entered and executed to add the third record to the SALES_REP table, containing the data for sales rep 15.

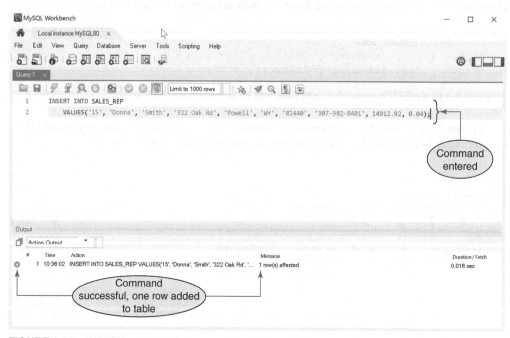

FIGURE 3-26   INSERT command executed for the third record in the SALES_REP table

The next command to add the fourth record, containing the data for sales rep 20, is shown in Figure 3-27. Enter the command by modifying the previous command or by deleting the previous command and entering the new command from the beginning. Once entered, execute the command.

```
INSERT INTO SALES_REP
    VALUES ('20', 'Daniel', 'Jackson', '19 Lookout Dr', 'Elk Butte',
    'WY', '82433', '307-833-9481', 0.00, 0.04);
```

FIGURE 3-27   INSERT command to add sales rep 20 to the SALES_REP table

Figure 3-28 shows the results of the command being entered and executed to add the fourth record to the SALES_REP table, containing the data for sales rep 20.

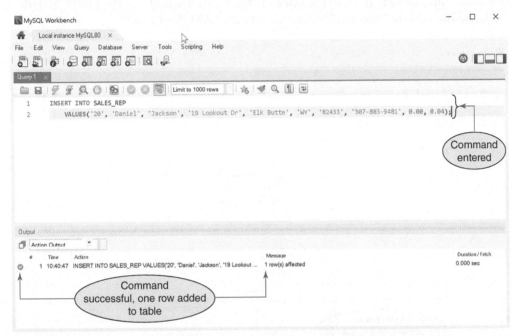

FIGURE 3-28   INSERT command executed for the fourth record in the SALES_REP table

Inserting a Row that Contains Nulls

To enter a null value into a table, you use a special form of the INSERT command in which you identify the names of the columns that accept non-null values and then list only these non-null values after the VALUES command, as shown in Example 4.

EXAMPLE 4: Add sales rep 25 to the SALES_REP table. Her name is Donna Sanchez. All columns, except REP_ID, FIRST_NAME, and LAST_NAME, are null.

In this case, you do not enter a value of *null*; you enter only the non-null values. To do so, you must indicate precisely which values you are entering by listing the corresponding columns as shown in Figure 3-29. The command shown in Figure 3-29 indicates that you are entering data in only the REP_ID, FIRST_NAME, and LAST_NAME columns and that you are *not* entering values in any other columns; the other columns contain null values.

```
INSERT INTO SALES_REP (REP_ID, FIRST_NAME, LAST_NAME)
    VALUES ('25', 'Donna', 'Sanchez');
```

FIGURE 3-29   INSERT command to add sales rep 25 to the SALES_REP table (containing null values)

Figure 3-30 shows the results of the command being entered and executed to add the fifth record to the SALES_REP table, containing the data for sales rep 25; however, only the REP_ID, FIRST_NAME, and LAST_NAME fields are added. The remaining fields contain null values. The order of the data aligns with the order of the fields. The value of "25" is inserted into the REP_ID field, the value of "Donna" is inserted into the FIRST_NAME field, and the value of "Sanchez" is inserted into the LAST_NAME field.

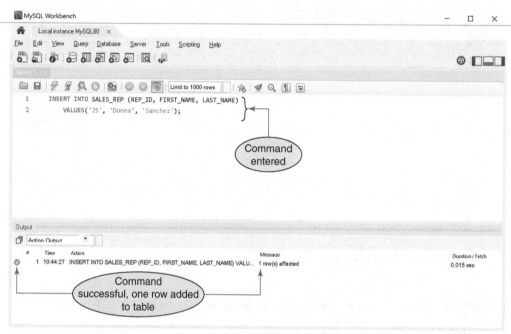

FIGURE 3-30   INSERT command executed for the fifth record in the SALES_REP table containing null values

VIEWING TABLE DATA

To view the data in a table, you use the **SELECT** command, which is described in more detail in Modules 4 and 5.

EXAMPLE 5: Display all the rows and columns in the SALES_REP table.

You can use a simple version of the SELECT command to display all the rows and columns in a table by typing the word SELECT, followed by an asterisk (*), followed by the keyword FROM and the name of the table containing the data you want to view. Just as with other SQL commands, the command ends with a semicolon. In MySQL, you type the command shown in Figure 3-31.

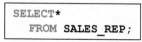

```
SELECT*
   FROM SALES_REP;
```

FIGURE 3-31   Select command to list all records in the SALES_REP table

Figure 3-32 shows the results of the command being entered and executed, along with the results shown in the results grid. As you can see, in the fifth record the data for the REP_ID, FIRST_NAME, and LAST_NAME fields have been inserted as you wanted. The remaining fields in the fifth record contain null values.

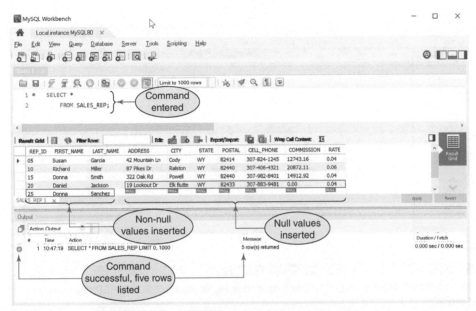

FIGURE 3-32   Using a SELECT command to view a table

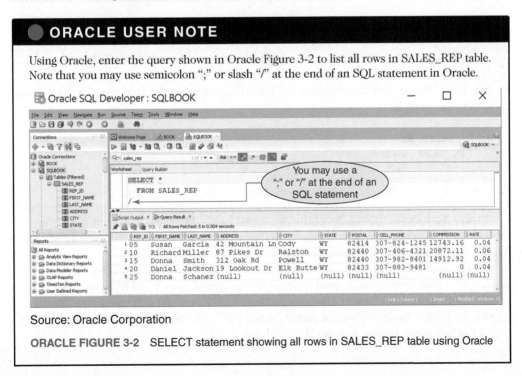

ORACLE USER NOTE

Using Oracle, enter the query shown in Oracle Figure 3-2 to list all rows in SALES_REP table. Note that you may use semicolon ";" or slash "/" at the end of an SQL statement in Oracle.

Source: Oracle Corporation

ORACLE FIGURE 3-2   SELECT statement showing all rows in SALES_REP table using Oracle

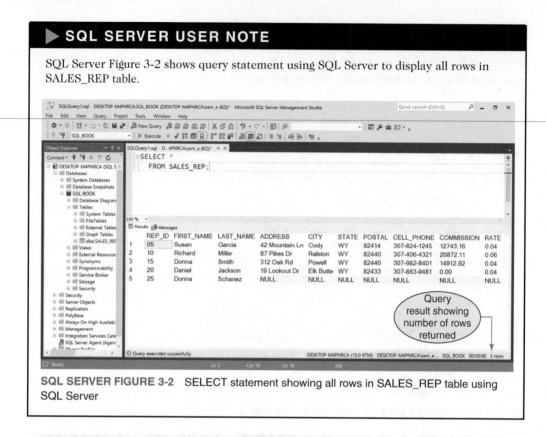

SQL SERVER USER NOTE

SQL Server Figure 3-2 shows query statement using SQL Server to display all rows in SALES_REP table.

SQL SERVER FIGURE 3-2   SELECT statement showing all rows in SALES_REP table using SQL Server

CORRECTING ERRORS IN A TABLE

After executing a SELECT command to view a table's data, you might find that you need to change the value in a column. You can use the **UPDATE** command to change a value in a table. The UPDATE command shown in Figure 3-33 changes the last name in the row on which the sales rep ID is 25 to Salinas.

```
UPDATE SALES_REP
    SET LAST_NAME = 'Salinas'
        WHERE REP_ID = '25';
```

FIGURE 3-33   UPDATE command to change the LAST_NAME for sales rep 25

Figure 3-34 shows the results of the command being enter and executed. Note the message in the output gives further detail that one row was affected, with one row matching the criteria and one row being changed.

The same SELECT command used in Figure 3-31 to list all of the records in the SALES_REP table can be used again to show the results of the UPDATE command just executed in Figure 3-34. Figure 3-35 shows the SELECT command being entered and executed, along with displaying the results of the UPDATE command from Figure 3-34, in which the last name for rep number 25 is Salinas.

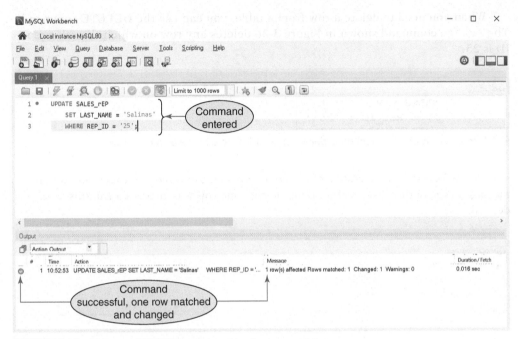

FIGURE 3-34   Using an UPDATE command to change a value

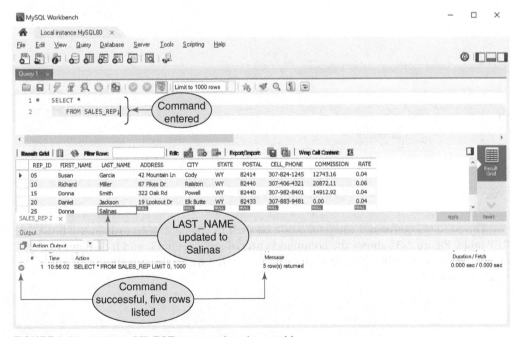

FIGURE 3-35   Using a SELECT command to view a table

When you need to delete a row from a table, you can use the **DELETE** command. The `DELETE` command shown in Figure 3-36 deletes any row on which the sales rep ID is 25.

```
DELETE
      FROM SALES_REP
           WHERE REP_ID = '25';
```

FIGURE 3-36   DELETE command to delete all records where the sales rep id is 25

Figure 3-37 shows the results of the command being entered and executed. Note the message in the output gives further detail in that one row was affected, or in this case deleted.

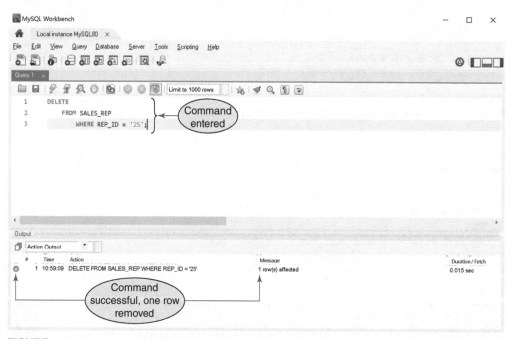

FIGURE 3-37   Using the DELETE command to delete a row

The SELECT command can once again be used to display the records in the SALES_REP table. Figure 3-38 shows the command entered and executed, and it displays the updated data in the table. Note that the data associated with sales rep ID 25 no longer resides in the table.

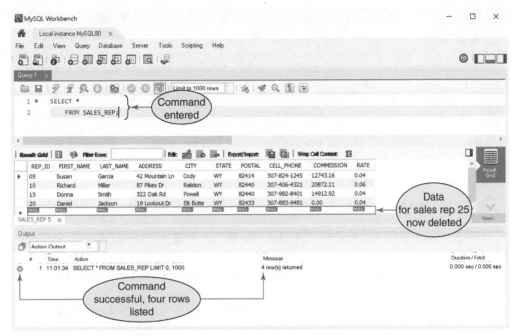

FIGURE 3-38 Using a SELECT command to view a table

Q & A

Question: How do I correct errors in my data?

Answer: The method you use to correct an error depends on the type of error you need to correct. If you added a row that should not be in the table, use a DELETE command to remove it. If you forgot to add a row, you can use an INSERT command to add it. If you added a row that contains incorrect data, you can use an UPDATE command to make the necessary corrections. Alternatively, you could use a DELETE command to remove the row containing the error and then use an INSERT command to insert the correct row.

SAVING SQL COMMANDS

MySQL lets you save SQL commands so you can use them again without retyping them. In MySQL, as well as in many other DBMSs, you save commands in a **script file**, or simply a **script**, which is a text file. In MySQL, script files have the .sql filename extension. Some DBMSs, such as Oracle, have a special location called the **script repository** to store the scripts. With MySQL, you can save your scripts in the location of your choice on your local file system (such as on a hard drive or USB flash drive), therefore, creating your own repository. The following steps describe how to create and use scripts in the MySQL Workbench. If you are using a different version of MySQL or another DBMS, use Help, consult the system documentation, or search the Internet to determine how to accomplish the same tasks.

Q & A

Question: What are advantages of creating scripts?
Answer: Creating a script offers some distinct advantages. You can create or edit a script using a text editor or word processor and save the script into your own script repository to be used in MySQL. A script can be created separately from the MySQL Workbench environment. Scripts allow you to create a group of SQL commands you would like to execute regularly and have them ready for use without rekeying them. Additionally, there are some advanced features you see later in this text that are only available when using scripts.

To create a script in MySQL:

1. Enter the command, or commands, you would like to comprise the script in the query pane.
2. On the MySQL Workbench main menu, click on the File menu and select the Save Script As option.
3. You may now navigate to a location in your file system you would like to save the script.
4. Enter a name for your script in the File name: text box. Note the file type is an SQL file with an extension of .sql.
5. When you are finished, click the Save button. You return to the query pane with the name of the tab being the name of your script.

To view or edit a script in MySQL:

1. On the MySQL Workbench main menu, click on the File menu and select Open SQL Script.
2. Navigate to the location in your file system where the script is saved.
3. Select the script and click Open.
4. Your script is now in a new tab in the query pane with the name being the same name as your script.
5. You may now edit the script.

To run an existing script in MySQL (Option #1):

1. On the MySQL Workbench main menu, click on the File menu and select Open SQL Script.
2. Navigate to the location in your file system where the script is saved.
3. Select the script and click Open.
4. Your script is now in a new tab in the query pane with the name being the same name as your script.
5. You may now execute the script by clicking Query on the MySQL Workbench main menu and selecting the appropriate execute option (for example, Execute (All or Selection)).

To run an existing script in MySQL (Option #2):

1. On the MySQL Workbench main menu, click on the File menu and select Run SQL Script.
2. Navigate to the location in your file system where the script is saved.
3. Select the script and click Open.
4. In the Run SQL Script dialog box, select the Default Schema Name from the drop-down menu and click Run.
5. After the results are displayed, you click on Close to close the Run SQL Script dialog box.

When you are finished using a script and no longer need to store it, you can delete it. To delete a script in MySQL:

1. Navigate to the location in your file system where the script is saved.
2. Delete the file containing the script by the normal methods for your file system.

● ORACLE USER NOTE

Oracle SQL Developer allows to save scripts any folder on your local system. All scripts created in Oracle SQL Developer are text files with the .sql filename extension. To create a script file in Oracle SQL Developer:

1. Load the Oracle SQL Developer tool, under Oracle Connections pane click on the desired database. (*Note:* Initially, you must create a connection entering account credentials as shown in Oracle Figure 3-3.)
2. Enter query statement you desire to store and execute the statement to validate it is syntactically correct and it returns the expected results.
3. Click the Save button and then enter a name for the script.

To view, edit, or run an existing script:

1. Load Oracle SQL Developer and double click on Database Connection created previously.
2. Click the Open File button on the toolbar.
3. Navigate to the folder containing the script file and then click the Open button in the Open File dialog box. The script appears in the Query Editor window. You can view the content of the script to make changes to it by editing the commands. If you want to save your edits to a script, click the Save button to save your changes.
4. To run a script, click the Execute button.

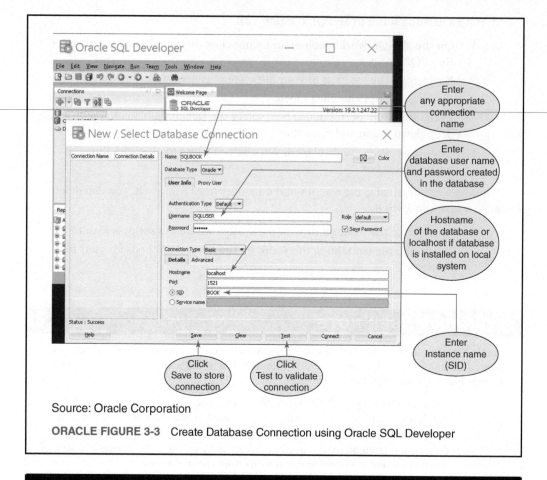

Source: Oracle Corporation

ORACLE FIGURE 3-3   Create Database Connection using Oracle SQL Developer

---

▶ **SQL SERVER USER NOTE**

SQL Server can store scripts in any folder on your local system. All scripts created in SQL Server are text files with the .sql filename extension. To create a script file in SQL Server:

1. Load SQL Server Management Studio and then click the Connect button in the Connect to Server dialog box.
2. Open the appropriate database and then click the New Query button.
3. Type the command or commands to save in the script. When necessary, click the Execute button to execute the commands saved in the script.
4. When you are finished, click the Save button and then enter a name for the script.

To view, edit, or run an existing script:

1. Load SQL Server Management Studio and then click the Connect button in the Connect to Server dialog box.
2. Open the appropriate database and then click the New Query button.
3. Click the Open File button on the toolbar.

4. Navigate to the folder containing the script file and then click the Open button in the Open File dialog box. The script appears in the Query Editor window. You can view the content of the script to make changes to it by editing the commands. If you want to save your edits to a script, click the Save button to save your changes.

5. To run a script, click the Execute button.

CREATING THE REMAINING DATABASE TABLES

To create the remaining tables in the KimTay Pet Supplies database (KIMTAY), you need to execute the appropriate CREATE TABLE and INSERT commands. You should save these commands as scripts so you can re-create your database, if necessary, by running the scripts.

HELPFUL HINT

Your instructor might give you the script files to use to create the tables for KimTay Pet Supplies and StayWell Student Accommodation databases and to insert data into them.

Figure 3-39 shows the CREATE TABLE command for the CUSTOMER table. Notice that the FIRST_NAME and LAST_NAME columns are specified as NOT NULL. Additionally, the CUST_ID column is the table's primary key, indicating that the CUST_ID column is the unique identifier of rows in the table. With this column designated as the primary key, the DBMS rejects any attempt to store a customer ID that already exists in the table.

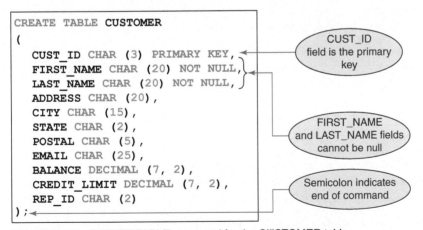

```
CREATE TABLE CUSTOMER
(
    CUST_ID CHAR (3) PRIMARY KEY,
    FIRST_NAME CHAR (20) NOT NULL,
    LAST_NAME CHAR (20) NOT NULL,
    ADDRESS CHAR (20),
    CITY CHAR (15),
    STATE CHAR (2),
    POSTAL CHAR (5),
    EMAIL CHAR (25),
    BALANCE DECIMAL (7, 2),
    CREDIT_LIMIT DECIMAL (7, 2),
    REP_ID CHAR (2)
);
```

- CUST_ID field is the primary key
- FIRST_NAME and LAST_NAME fields cannot be null
- Semicolon indicates end of command

FIGURE 3-39   CREATE TABLE command for the CUSTOMER table

After creating the CUSTOMER table, you can create another file containing the INSERT commands to add the customer rows to the table. When a script file contains more than one command, each command must end with a semicolon. Figure 3-40 shows the INSERT commands to add rows to the CUSTOMER table.

```
INSERT INTO CUSTOMER
    VALUES ('125', 'Joey', 'Smith', '17 Fourth St',
    'Cody', 'WY', '82414', 'jsmith17@example.com',
    80.68, 500.00, '05');
INSERT INTO CUSTOMER
    VALUES ('182', 'Billy', 'Rufton', '21 Simple Cir',
    'Garland', 'WY', '82435', 'billyruff@example.com',
    43.13, 750.00, '10');
INSERT INTO CUSTOMER
    VALUES ('227', 'Sandra', 'Pincher', '53 Verde Ln',
    'Powell', 'WY', '82440', 'spinch2@example.com',
    156.38, 500.00, '15');
INSERT INTO CUSTOMER
    VALUES ('294', 'Samantha', 'Smith', '14 Rock Ln',
    'Ralston', 'WY', '82440', 'ssmith5@example.com',
    58.60, 500.00, '10');
INSERT INTO CUSTOMER
    VALUES ('314','Tom', 'Rascal', '1 Rascal Farm Rd',
    'Cody', 'WY', '82414', 'trascal3@example.com',
    17.25, 250.00, '15');
INSERT INTO CUSTOMER
    VALUES ('375', 'Melanie', 'Jackson', '42 Blackwater
    Way', 'Elk Butte', 'WY', '82433',
    'mjackson5@example.com', 252.25, 250.00, '05');
```

Data for first row

Data for second row

```
INSERT INTO CUSTOMER
    VALUES ('435', 'James', 'Gonzalez', '16 Rockway Rd',
    'Wapiti', 'WY', '82450', 'jgonzo@example.com',
    230.40, 1000.00, '15');
INSERT INTO CUSTOMER
    VALUES ('492', 'Elmer', 'Jackson', '22 Jackson Farm
    Rd', 'Garland', 'WY', '82435',
    'ejackson4@example.com', 45.20, 500.00, '10');
INSERT INTO CUSTOMER
    VALUES ('543', 'Angie', 'Hendricks', '27 Locklear
    Ln', 'Powell', 'WY', '82440',
    'ahendricks7@example.com', 315.00, 750.00,'05');
INSERT INTO CUSTOMER
    VALUES ('616', 'Sally', 'Cruz', '199 18th Ave',
    'Ralston', 'WY', '82440', 'scruz5@example.com',
    8.33, 500.00, '15');
INSERT INTO CUSTOMER
    VALUES ('721', 'Leslie', 'Smith', '123 Sheepland
    Rd', 'Elk Butte', 'WY', '82433',
    'lsmith12@example.com', 166.65, 1000.00,'10');
INSERT INTO CUSTOMER
    VALUES ('795', 'Randy', 'Blacksmith', '75 Stream
    Rd', 'Cody', 'WY', '82414',
    'rblacksmith6@example.com', 61.50, 500.00, '05');
```

Each command ends with a semicolon

FIGURE 3-40   INSERT commands for the CUSTOMER table

Figures 3-41 through 3-46 show the scripts for the CREATE TABLE and INSERT commands for creating and inserting data into the INVOICES, ITEM, and INVOICE_LINE tables in the KimTay Pet Supplies database. Figure 3-41 contains the CREATE TABLE command for the INVOICES table.

```
CREATE TABLE INVOICES
(
    INVOICE_NUM CHAR(5) PRIMARY KEY,
    INVOICE_DATE DATE,
    CUST_ID CHAR(3)
);
```

INVOICE_NUM field is the primary key

FIGURE 3-41 CREATE TABLE command for the INVOICES table

Figure 3-42 contains the INSERT commands to load data into the INVOICES table. Notice the way that dates are entered.

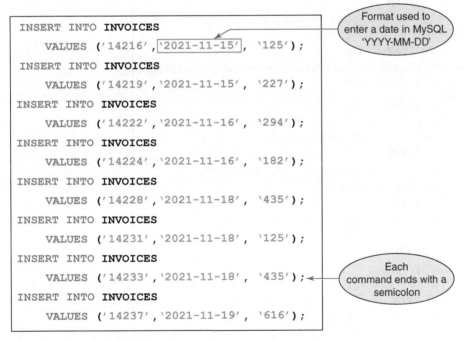

```
INSERT INTO INVOICES
    VALUES ('14216','2021-11-15', '125');
INSERT INTO INVOICES
    VALUES ('14219','2021-11-15', '227');
INSERT INTO INVOICES
    VALUES ('14222','2021-11-16', '294');
INSERT INTO INVOICES
    VALUES ('14224','2021-11-16', '182');
INSERT INTO INVOICES
    VALUES ('14228','2021-11-18', '435');
INSERT INTO INVOICES
    VALUES ('14231','2021-11-18', '125');
INSERT INTO INVOICES
    VALUES ('14233','2021-11-18', '435');
INSERT INTO INVOICES
    VALUES ('14237','2021-11-19', '616');
```

Format used to enter a date in MySQL 'YYYY-MM-DD'

Each command ends with a semicolon

FIGURE 3-42 INSERT commands for the INVOICES table

Figure 3-43 contains the CREATE TABLE command for the ITEM table.

```
CREATE TABLE ITEM
(
   ITEM_ID CHAR (4) PRIMARY KEY,
   DESCRIPTION CHAR (30),
   ON_HAND DECIMAL (4, 0),
   CATEGORY CHAR (3),
   LOCATION CHAR (1),
   PRICE DECIMAL (6, 2)
);
```

ITEM_ID field is the primary key

FIGURE 3-43   CREATE TABLE command for the ITEM table

Figure 3-44 contains the INSERT commands to load data into the ITEM table.

```
INSERT INTO ITEM
   VALUES ('AD72', 'Dog Feeding Station',
   12, 'DOG', 'B', 79.99);
INSERT INTO ITEM
   VALUES ('BC33', 'Feathers Bird Cage (12x24x18)',
   10, 'BRD', 'B', 79.99);
INSERT INTO ITEM
   VALUES ('CA75', 'Enclosed Cat Litter Station',
   15, 'CAT', 'C', 39.99);
INSERT INTO ITEM
   VALUES ('DT12', 'Dog Toy Gift Set', 27,
   'DOG', 'B', 39.99);
INSERT INTO ITEM
   VALUES ('FM23', 'Fly Mask with Ears', 41,
   'HOR', 'C', 24.95);
INSERT INTO ITEM
   VALUES ('FS39', 'Folding Saddle Stand', 12,
   'HOR', 'C', 39.99);
INSERT INTO ITEM
   VALUES ('FS42', 'Aquarium (55 Gallon)',
   5, 'FSH', 'A', 124.99);
INSERT INTO ITEM
   VALUES ('KH81', 'Wild Bird Food (25 lb)',
   24, 'BRD', 'C',19.99);
```

Each command ends with a semicolon

FIGURE 3-44   INSERT commands for the ITEM table

```
INSERT INTO ITEM
    VALUES ('LD14', 'Locking Small Dog Door', 14,
    'DOG', 'A', 49.99);
INSERT INTO ITEM
    VALUES ('LP73', 'Large Pet Carrier', 23,
    'DOG', 'B', 59.99);
INSERT INTO ITEM
    VALUES ('PF19', 'Pump & Filter Kit', 5,
    'FSH', 'A', 74.99);
INSERT INTO ITEM
    VALUES ('QB92', 'Quilted Stable Blanket',
    32, 'HOR', 'C', 119.99);
INSERT INTO ITEM
    VALUES ('SP91', 'Small Pet Carrier',
    18, 'CAT', 'B', 39.99);
INSERT INTO ITEM
    VALUES ('UF39', 'Underground Fence System',
    7, 'DOG', 'A', 199.99);
INSERT INTO ITEM
    VALUES ('WB49', 'Insulated Water Bucket',
    34, 'HOR', 'C', 79.99);
```

FIGURE 3-44   INSERT commands for the ITEM table (Continued)

Figure 3-45 contains the CREATE TABLE command for the INVOICE_LINE table. Notice the way that the primary key is defined when it consists of more than one column.

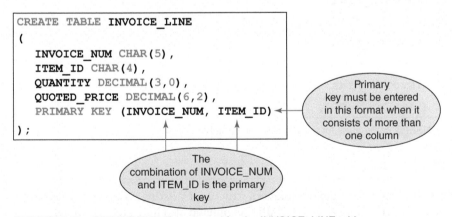

FIGURE 3-45   CREATE TABLE command for the INVOICE_LINE table

Figure 3-46 contains the INSERT commands to load data into the INVOICE_LINE table.

```
INSERT INTO INVOICE_LINE
     VALUES ('14216','CA75', 3, 37.99);
INSERT INTO INVOICE_LINE
     VALUES ('14219','AD72', 2, 79.99);
INSERT INTO INVOICE_LINE
     VALUES ('14219','DT12', 4, 39.99);
INSERT INTO INVOICE_LINE
     VALUES ('14222','LD14', 1, 47.99);
INSERT INTO INVOICE_LINE
     VALUES ('14224','KH81', 4, 18.99);
INSERT INTO INVOICE_LINE
     VALUES ('14228','FS42', 1, 124.99);
INSERT INTO INVOICE_LINE
     VALUES ('14228','PF19', 1, 74.99);
INSERT INTO INVOICE_LINE
     VALUES ('14231','UF39', 2, 189.99);
INSERT INTO INVOICE_LINE
     VALUES ('14233','KH81', 1, 19.99);
INSERT INTO INVOICE_LINE
     VALUES ('14233','QB92', 4, 109.95);
INSERT INTO INVOICE_LINE
     VALUES ('14233','WB49', 4, 74.95);
INSERT INTO INVOICE_LINE
     VALUES ('14237','LP73', 3, 54.95);
```

Each command ends with a semicolon

FIGURE 3-46   INSERT commands for the INVOICE_LINE table

DESCRIBING A TABLE

The CREATE TABLE command defines a table's structure by listing its columns, data types, and column lengths. The CREATE TABLE command also indicates which columns cannot accept nulls. When you work with a table, you might not have access to the

CREATE TABLE command that was used to create it. For example, another programmer might have created the table, or perhaps you created the table several months ago but did not save the command. You might want to examine the table's structure to see the details about the columns in the table. Each DBMS provides a method to examine a table's structure.

EXAMPLE 6: Describe the SALES_REP table.

In MySQL, you can use the **DESCRIBE** command to list all the columns in a table and their properties. Figure 3-47 shows the `DESCRIBE` command for the SALES_REP table, note that DESC, the abbreviated form of the DESCRIBE command, is accepted in MySQL and Oracle. The result indicates the name of each column in the table, along with its data type and length. The Null column indicates whether the field can accept a value of null. The Key column indicates which fields are part of the primary key.

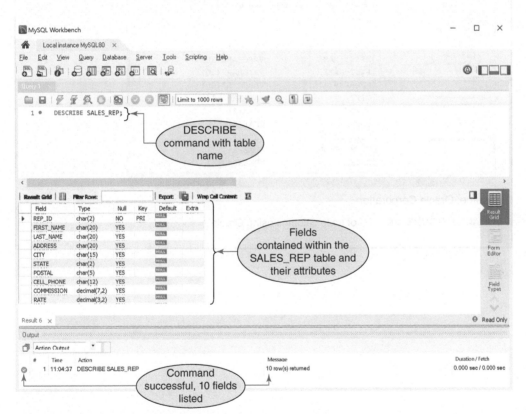

FIGURE 3-47 DESCRIBE command for the SALES_REP table

● ORACLE USER NOTE

Using Oracle, you may use DESCRIBE command or abbreviated DESC to display list of columns of any table as shown in Oracle Figure 3-4.

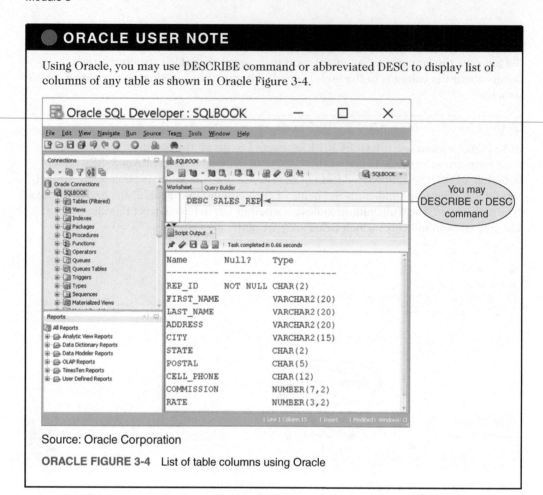

Source: Oracle Corporation

ORACLE FIGURE 3-4   List of table columns using Oracle

> ## ► SQL SERVER USER NOTE

In SQL Server, you may execute the system stored procedure, SP_COLUMNS (case insensitive), to list all the columns in a table as shown in SQL Server Figure 3-3.

The result indicates the name of each column in the SALES_REP table, along with its data type and length. A value of 1 in the Nullable column indicates a column that can accept null values. (The remaining columns that appear in the results are beyond the scope of this discussion.)

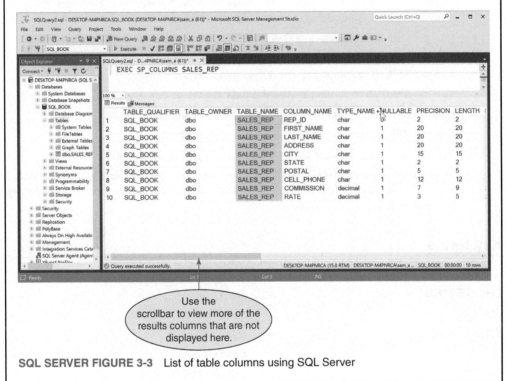

SQL SERVER FIGURE 3-3   List of table columns using SQL Server

Module Summary

- Use the CREATE TABLE command to create a table by typing the table name and then listing within a single set of parentheses the columns in the table.
- Use the DROP TABLE command to delete a table and all its data from the database.
- Some commonly used data types in are INT, SMALLINT, DECIMAL, CHAR, VARCHAR, and DATE.
- A null data value (or null) is a special value that is used when the actual value for a column is unknown, unavailable, or not applicable.
- Use the NOT NULL clause in a CREATE TABLE command to identify columns that cannot accept null values.
- Use the INSERT command to insert rows into a table.
- Use the SELECT command to view the data in a table.
- Use the UPDATE command to change the value in a column.
- Use the DELETE command to delete a row from a table.
- You can save SQL commands in a script file in MySQL, Oracle, and SQL Server.
- You can use the DESCRIBE command in MySQL and Oracle to display a table's structure and layout. In SQL Server, execute the SP_COLUMNS stored procedure to display the structure and layout of a table.

Key Terms

CREATE DATABASE	null data value
CREATE TABLE	script
data type	script file
default database	script repository
DELETE	SELECT
DESCRIBE	SHOW DATABASES
DROP TABLE	Structured Query Language (SQL)
INSERT	UPDATE
NOT NULL	USE
null	

Review Questions

Module Quiz

1. How do you create a table using SQL?
2. How do you delete a table using SQL?
3. What are common data types used to define columns using SQL?

4. Identify the best data type to use to store the following data in Oracle, in SQL Server, and in MySQL:

   a. The month, day, and year that an employee was hired

   b. An employee's Social Security number

   c. The department in which an employee works

   d. An employee's hourly pay rate

5. Identify the following column names as valid or invalid in MySQL:

   a. COMMISSIONRATE

   b. POSTAL_CODE_5CHAR

   c. SHIP TO ADDRESS

   d. INVOICE-NUMBER

6. What is a null value? How do you use SQL to identify columns that cannot accept null values?

7. Which SQL command do you use to add a row to a table?

8. Which SQL command do you use to view the data in a table?

9. Which SQL command do you use to change the value in a column in a table?

10. Which SQL command do you use to delete rows from a table?

11. How do you display the columns in a table and their characteristics in MySQL?

Critical Thinking

1. Explain the difference between the CHAR data type and the VARCHAR data type. Use the Internet to find examples of when to use VARCHAR and when to use CHAR. Be sure to cite the URL(s) that provided the examples as references at the end of your document.

2. Use the Internet to research BOOLEAN data types. What is a BOOLEAN data type and what is it called in Oracle, SQL Server, and MySQL? Be sure to cite the URL(s) that provided the information at the end of your document.

Case Exercises

To print a copy of your commands using MySQL, start Word or another word processor and create a new document. Select the SQL command(s) in SQL Server, copy it to the Clipboard, and then past it into the document. To export a command's results in MySQL, you can export a dataset to an external file by selecting the Export/Import option in the result grid. You can then choose the type of file you want to export the data to.

To print a copy of your commands and results using SQL Server, start Word or another word processor and create a new document. Select the SQL command(s) in MySQL or SQL Server, copy it to the Clipboard, and then paste it into the document. To copy and paste a command's results in SQL Server, right-click the datasheet selector (the box in the upper-left corner of the datasheet) to select the entire datasheet, copy it to the Clipboard, and then paste it into the document.

To print a copy of your commands and results using Oracle, use the browser's Print command on the File menu or click the Print button on the browser's toolbar.

You may also consult with your instructor for any specific instructions on how she/he would like your work submitted.

KimTay Pet Supplies

Use SQL to complete the following exercises.

1. Create a table named REP. The table has the same structure as the SALES_REP table shown in Figure 3-15 except the LAST_NAME column should use the VARCHAR data type and the COMMISSION and RATE columns should use the NUMERIC data type. Execute the command to describe the layout and characteristics of the REP table.

2. Add the following row to the REP table: rep ID: 35, first name: Fred; last name: Kiser; address: 427 Billings Dr.; city: Cody; state: WY; postal: 82414; cell phone: 307-555-6309; commission: 0.00; and rate: 0.05. Display the contents of the REP table.

3. Delete the REP table.

4. Run the script file for the KimTay Pet Supplies database to create the five tables and add records to the tables. Be sure to select the script file for the particular DBMS that you are using (MySQL, Oracle, or SQL Server). (*Note:* If you do not have the script files for this text, ask your instructor for assistance.)

5. Confirm that you have created the tables correctly by describing each table and comparing the results to Figures 3-15, 3-39, 3-41, 3-43, and 3-45.

6. Confirm that you have added all data correctly by viewing the data in each table and comparing the results to Figure 2-1 in Module 2.

Critical Thinking

1. Review the data for the ITEM table in Figure 2-1 in Module 2 and then review the data types used to create the ITEM table in Figure 3-34. Suggest alternate data types for the DESCRIPTION, ON_HAND, and STOREHOUSE fields and explain your recommendations.

StayWell Student Accommodation

Use SQL to complete the following exercises.

1. Create a table named SUMMER_SCHOOL_RENTALS. The table has the same structure as the PROPERTY table shown in Figure 3-48 except the PROPERTY_ID and OFFICE_NUMBER columns should use the NUMBER data type and the MONTHLY_RENT column should be changed to WEEKLY_RENT. Execute the command to describe the layout and characteristics of the SUMMER_SCHOOL_RENTALS table.

2. Add the following row to the SUMMER_SCHOOL_RENTALS table: property ID: 13; office ID: 1; address: 5867 Goodwin Ave; square feet: 1,650; bedrooms: 2; floors 1; weekly rent: 400; owner number: CO103.

3. Delete the SUMMER_SCHOOL_RENTALS table.

4. Run the script file for the StayWell database to create the six tables and add records to the tables. Be sure to select the script file for the particular DBMS that you are using (MySQL, Oracle, or SQL Server). (*Note:* If you do not have the script files for this text, ask your instructor for assistance.)

5. Confirm that you have created the tables correctly by describing each table and comparing the results to Figures 3-48.

6. Confirm that you have added all data correctly by viewing the data in each table and comparing the results to Figures 1-4 through 1-9 in Module 1.

OFFICE

COLUMN	TYPE	LENGTH	DECIMAL PLACES	NULLS ALLOWED	DESCRIPTION
OFFICE_NUM	DECIMAL	2	0	No	Office number (primary key)
OFFICE_NAME	CHAR	25			Office name
ADDRESS	CHAR	25			Office address
AREA	CHAR	25			Office area
CITY	CHAR	25			Office city
STATE	CHAR	2			Office state
ZIP_CODE	CHAR	5			Office zip code

OWNER

COLUMN	TYPE	LENGTH	DECIMAL PLACES	NULLS ALLOWED	DESCRIPTION
OWNER_NUM	CHAR	2		No	Office number (primary key)
LAST_NAME	CHAR	25			Owner last name
FIRST_NAME	CHAR	25			Owner first name
ADDRESS	CHAR	25			Owner street address
CITY	CHAR	25			Owner city
STATE	CHAR	2			Owner state
ZIP_CODE	CHAR	5			Owner zip code

PROPERTY

COLUMN	TYPE	LENGTH	DECIMAL PLACES	NULLS ALLOWED	DESCRIPTION
PROPERTY_ID	DECIMAL	2	0	No	Property ID (primary key)
OFFICE_NUM	DECIMAL	2	0		Number of office managing the property
ADDRESS	CHAR	25			Property address
SQR_FT	DECIMAL	5	0		Property size in square feet
BDRMS	DECIMAL	2	0		Number of bedrooms of the property
FLOORS	DECIMAL	2	0		Number of floors
MONTHLY_RENT	DECIMAL	6	2		Monthly property rent
OWNER_NUM	CHAR	5			Number of property owner

FIGURE 3-48   Table layouts for the StayWell Student Accommodation database

SERVICE_CATEGORY

COLUMN	TYPE	LENGTH	DECIMAL PLACES	NULLS ALLOWED	DESCRIPTION
CATEGORY_NUM	DECIMAL	2	0	No	Category number (primary key)
CATEGORY_DESCRIPTION	CHAR	35			Category description

SERVICE_REQUEST

COLUMN	TYPE	LENGTH	DECIMAL PLACES	NULLS ALLOWED	DESCRIPTION
SERVICE_ID	DECIMAL	2	0	No	Service ID (primary key)
PROPERTY_ID	DECIMAL	35			Property for which the service is requested
CATEGORY_NUMBER	DECIMAL	2			Category number of the service requested
OFFICE_ID	DECIMAL	2			Number of the office managing the property
DESCRIPTION	CHAR	255			Description of the specific service e required
STATUS	CHAR	255			Description of the status of the service request
EST_HOURS	DECIMAL	4			Estimated number of hours required to complete the service
SPENT_HOUSE	DECIMAL	4			Hours already spent on the service
NEXT_SERVICE_DATE	CHAR				Next scheduled date for work on this service (or null if no next service is required)

RESIDENTS

COLUMN	TYPE	LENGTH	DECIMAL PLACES	NULLS ALLOWED	DESCRIPTION
RESIDENT_ID	DECIMAL	2	0	No	ID of property resident (primary key)
FIRST_NAME	CHAR	25			First name of resident
SURNAME	CHAR	25			Last name of resident
PROPERTY_ID	DECIMAL	2			Property number

FIGURE 3-48   Table layouts for the StayWell Student Accommodation database (Continued)

Critical Thinking

1. The SERVICE_REQUEST table uses the CHAR data type for the DESCRIPTION and STATUS fields. Is there an alternate data type that could be used to store the values in these fields? Justify your reason for choosing an alternate data type or for leaving the data type as CHAR.

MODULE **4**

SINGLE-TABLE QUERIES

OBJECTIVES

- Retrieve data from a database using SQL commands.
- Use simple and compound conditions in queries.
- Use the BETWEEN, LIKE, and IN operators in queries.
- Use computed columns in queries.
- Sort data using the ORDER BY clause.
- Sort data using multiple keys and in ascending and descending order.
- Use aggregate functions in a query.
- Use subqueries.
- Group data using the GROUP BY clause.
- Select individual groups of data using the HAVING clause.
- Retrieve columns with null values.

INTRODUCTION

In this module, you learn about the SQL SELECT command that is used to retrieve data in a database. You examine ways to sort data and use SQL functions to count rows and calculate totals. You also learn about a special feature of SQL that lets you nest SELECT commands by placing one SELECT command inside another. Finally, you learn how to group rows that have matching values in a column.

CONSTRUCTING SIMPLE QUERIES

One of the most important features of a DBMS is its ability to answer a wide variety of questions concerning the data in a database. When you need to find data that answers a specific question, you use a query. A **query** is a question represented in a way that the DBMS can understand.

In SQL, you use the SELECT command to query a database. The basic form of the SELECT command is SELECT-FROM-WHERE. After you type the word SELECT, you list the columns that you want to include in the query results. This portion of the command is called the **SELECT clause**. Next, you type the word FROM followed by the name of the table that contains the data you need to query. This portion of the command is called the **FROM clause**. Finally, after the word WHERE, you list any conditions (restrictions) that apply to the data you want to retrieve. This optional portion of the command is called the **WHERE clause**. For example, when you need to retrieve the rows for only those customers with credit limits of $750, include a condition in the WHERE clause specifying that the value in the CREDIT_LIMIT column must be $750 (CREDIT_LIMIT = 750).

There are no special formatting rules in SQL. In this text, the FROM clause and the WHERE clause (when it is used) appear on separate lines only to make the commands more readable and understandable.

Retrieving Certain Columns and All Rows

You can write a command to retrieve specified columns and all rows from a table, as illustrated in Example 1.

EXAMPLE 1: List the number, first name, last name, and balance for all customers.

Because you need to list *all* customers, the WHERE clause is unnecessary; you do not need to put any restrictions on the data to retrieve. You list the columns to be included (CUST_ID, FIRST_NAME, LAST_NAME, and BALANCE) in the SELECT clause and the name of the table (CUSTOMER) in the FROM clause. Type a semicolon to indicate the end of the command. The query and its results appear in Figure 4-1.

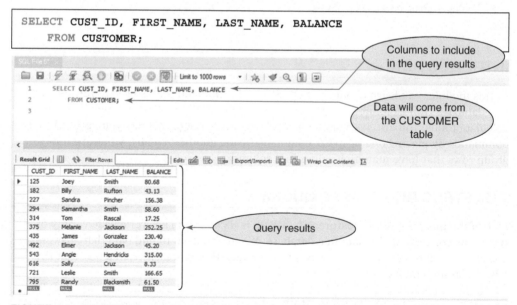

FIGURE 4-1 SELECT command to select certain columns from the CUSTOMER table

HELPFUL HINT

Notice in Figure 4-1 the dataset that was returned contained the rows you expected, but also returned a row of null values. Because MySQL Workbench is a very powerful tool, this row of null values is for you to enter an additional row of data. You could then create a new dataset to be used in the database. If you were using the MySQL Command Client and operating at a command prompt, this would not occur. MySQL Workbench was chosen to demonstrate the execution of the SQL commands due to its graphical interface.

HELPFUL HINT

During execution of a query in MySQL Workbench, the query is automatically limited to producing 1000 rows by default. This setting can be modified within the SQL editor preferences that can be found in the documentation if you prefer. The query results shown within this text include all results when possible due to their limited size, so there is no need to modify this preference.

HELPFUL HINT

You may change the size of output pane, and results grid, to accommodate your query results. To change the size of the area, use the vertical resize pointer that separates the two areas. For example, if you hover between the query pane and the output pane, the vertical resize pointer will appear, allowing you to move the border between the two areas vertically. It may be cumbersome for you to resize the panes each time to look exactly like the one in the text, so consider using the vertical scroll bar within the results grid.

Retrieving All Columns and All Rows

You can use the same type of command illustrated in Example 1 to retrieve all columns and all rows from a table. As Example 2 illustrates, however, you can use a shortcut to accomplish this task.

EXAMPLE 2: List the complete ITEM table.

Instead of including every column in the SELECT clause, you can use an asterisk (*) to indicate that you want to include all columns. The result lists all columns in the order in which you described them to the DBMS when you created the table. If you want the columns listed in a different order, type the column names in the order in which you want them to appear in the query results. In this case, assuming that the default order is appropriate, you can use the query shown in Figure 4-2 to display the complete ITEM table. This is similar to how you displayed the contents of the SALES_REP table in Figures 3-31 and 3-32 in Module 3.

```
SELECT *
    FROM ITEM;
```

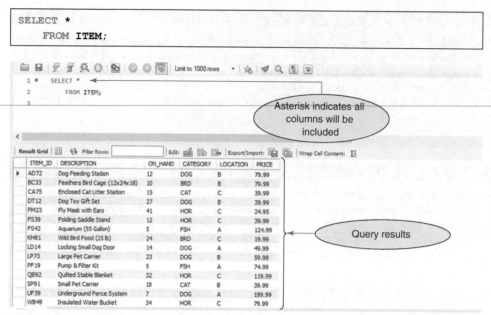

FIGURE 4-2   SELECT command to select all columns from the ITEM table

Using a WHERE Clause

When you need to retrieve rows that satisfy some condition, you include a WHERE clause in the SELECT command, as shown in Example 3.

EXAMPLE 3: What is the last name of the customer with the customer ID 125?

You can use a WHERE clause to restrict the query results to customer number 125, as shown in Figure 4-3. Because CUST_ID is a character column, the value 125 is enclosed in single quotation marks. In addition, because the CUST_ID column is the primary key of the CUSTOMER table, there can be only one customer whose number matches the number in the WHERE clause.

```
SELECT LAST_NAME
    FROM CUSTOMER
        WHERE CUST_ID = '125';
```

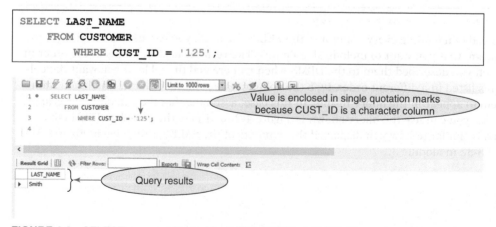

FIGURE 4-3   SELECT command to find the LAST_NAME of CUST_ID 125 in the CUSTOMER table

The condition in the preceding WHERE clause is called a simple condition. A **simple condition** has the form column name, comparison operator, and then either another column name or a value. Figure 4-4 lists the comparison operators that you can use in SQL.

Comparison Operator	Description
=	Equal to
>	Less than
<	Greater than
< =	Less than or equal to
> =	Greater than or equal to
< >	Not equal to

FIGURE 4-4 Comparison operators used in SQL commands

EXAMPLE 4: Find the last name of each customer located in the city Cody.

The only difference between this example and the previous one is that in Example 3, there could only be one row in the answer because the condition involved the table's primary key. In Example 4, the condition involves a column that is *not* the table's primary key. Because there is more than one customer located in the city of Cody, the results can and do contain more than one row, as shown in Figure 4-5.

```
SELECT LAST_NAME
    FROM CUSTOMER
        WHERE CITY = 'Cody';
```

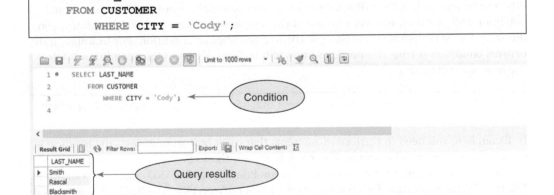

FIGURE 4-5 SELECT command to find the LAST_NAME of all customers living in the CITY of Cody

---

EXAMPLE 5: Find first name, last name, balance, and credit limit for all customers with balances that exceed their credit limits.

A simple condition can also compare the values stored in two columns. In Figure 4-6, the WHERE clause includes a comparison operator that selects only those rows in which the balance is greater than the credit limit.

```
SELECT FIRST_NAME, LAST_NAME, BALANCE, CREDIT_LIMIT
    FROM CUSTOMER
        WHERE BALANCE > CREDIT_LIMIT;
```

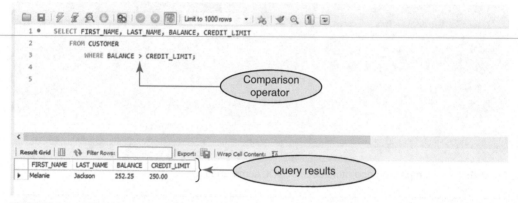

FIGURE 4-6   SELECT command to find specific information for customers with a BALANCE that exceeds their CREDIT_LIMIT

Using Compound Conditions

The conditions you have seen so far are called simple conditions. Examples 6, 7, and 8 require compound conditions. You form a **compound condition** by connecting two or more simple conditions with the AND, OR, and NOT operators. When the **AND** operator connects simple conditions, all the simple conditions must be true for the compound condition to be true. When the **OR** operator connects the simple conditions, the compound condition will be true whenever any one of the simple conditions is true. Preceding a condition by the **NOT** operator reverses the truth of the original condition. For example, if the original condition is true, the new condition will be false; if the original condition is false, the new one will be true.

EXAMPLE 6: List the descriptions of all items that are stored in location B and for which there are more than 15 units on hand.

In Example 6, you need to retrieve those items that meet *both* conditions—the location is equal to B *and* the number of units on hand is greater than 15.

To find the answer, you form a compound condition using the AND operator, as shown in Figure 4-7. The query examines the data in the ITEM table and lists the items that are stored in location B and for which there are more than 15 units on hand. When a WHERE clause uses the AND operator to connect simple conditions, it also is called an **AND condition**.

HELPFUL HINT

You may have noticed the word DESCRIPTION is not blue in the command in Figure 4-7; however, it is blue in the screen shot of the results. The word DESCRIPTION was added to the keyword list in version 8.0.4 of MySQL; however, it is a non-reserved keyword and can be used.

```
SELECT DESCRIPTION
    FROM ITEM
        WHERE LOCATION = 'B' AND
            ON_HAND > 15;
```

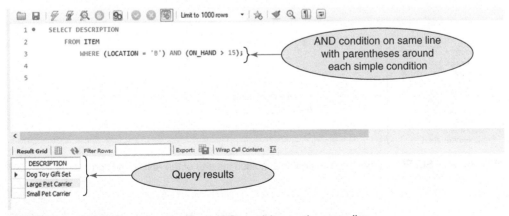

FIGURE 4-7   SELECT command with an AND condition on separate lines

For readability, each of the simple conditions in the query shown in Figure 4-7 appears on a separate line. Some people prefer to put the conditions on the same line with parentheses around each simple condition, as shown in Figure 4-8. These two methods accomplish the same thing. In this text, simple conditions within a compound condition appear on the same line with parentheses around each simple condition.

```
SELECT DESCRIPTION
    FROM ITEM
        WHERE (LOCATION = 'B') AND (ON_HAND > 15);
```

FIGURE 4-8   SELECT command with an AND condition on the same line

HELPFUL HINT

Notice that the simple conditions in the previous example are contained within parentheses. Although not necessary for the condition, it does make the condition more readable and easier to identify the simple conditions comprising the compound condition. As mentioned in a previous module, proper indenting also makes the command much more readable. Some coders like to also add a set of parentheses surrounding the entire compound condition, with the simple conditions also in parentheses. Just as in mathematical equations, the inner parentheses are evaluated first and helps to force proper interpretation of the condition. Additional parentheses can be helpful when you have very complicated compound conditions.

EXAMPLE 7: List the descriptions of all items that are stored in location B or for which there are more than 15 units on hand.

In Example 7, you need to retrieve descriptions for those items for which the location is equal to B, *or* the number of units on hand is greater than 15, *or* both. To do this, you form a compound condition using the OR operator, as shown in Figure 4-9. When a WHERE clause uses the OR operator to connect simple conditions, it also is called an **OR condition**.

```
SELECT DESCRIPTION
    FROM ITEM
        WHERE (LOCATION = 'B') OR (ON_HAND > 15);
```

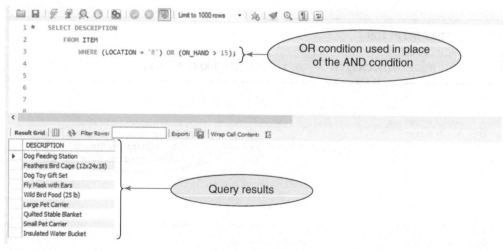

FIGURE 4-9   SELECT command with an OR condition instead of the AND condition

EXAMPLE 8: List the descriptions of all items that are not stored in location B.

For Example 8, you could use a simple condition and the *not equal to* operator (WHERE LOCATION < > 'B'). As an alternative, you could use the EQUAL operator (=) in the condition and precede the entire condition with the NOT operator, as shown in Figure 4-10. When a WHERE clause uses the NOT operator to connect simple conditions, it also is called a **NOT condition**. You do not need to enclose the condition LOCATION = 'B' in parentheses; however, doing so makes the command more readable.

```
SELECT DESCRIPTION
    FROM ITEM
        WHERE NOT (LOCATION = 'B');
```

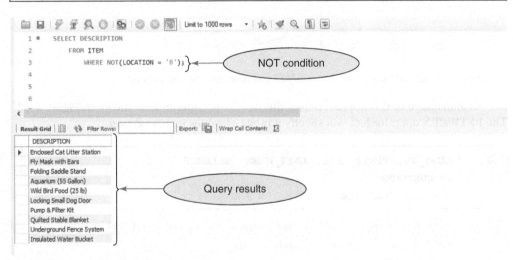

FIGURE 4-10   SELECT command with a NOT condition

Using the BETWEEN Operator

Example 9 requires a compound condition to determine the answer.

EXAMPLE 9: List the customer ID, first name, last name, and balance of all customers with balances greater than or equal to $125 and less than or equal to $250.

You can use a WHERE clause and the AND operator, as shown in Figure 4-11, to retrieve the data.

HELPFUL HINT

In SQL, numbers included in queries are entered without extra symbols, such as dollar signs and commas.

```
SELECT CUST_ID, FIRST_NAME, LAST_NAME, BALANCE
    FROM CUSTOMER
        WHERE (BALANCE >= 125) AND (BALANCE <= 250);
```

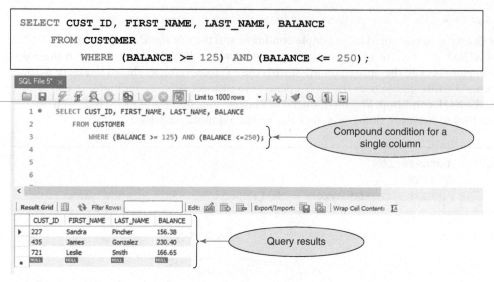

FIGURE 4-11   SELECT command with an AND condition for a single column

An alternative to this approach uses the BETWEEN operator, as shown in Figure 4-12. The **BETWEEN** operator lets you specify a range of values in a condition.

```
SELECT CUST_ID, FIRST_NAME, LAST_NAME, BALANCE
    FROM CUSTOMER
        WHERE (BALANCE BETWEEN 125 AND 250);
```

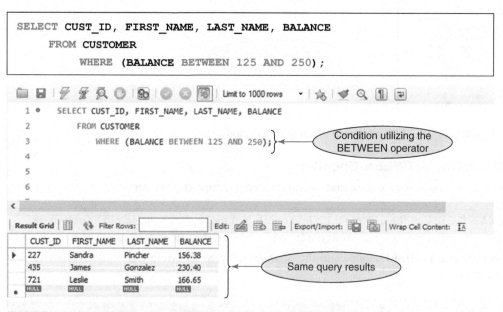

FIGURE 4-12   SELECT command using the BETWEEN operator

The BETWEEN operator is inclusive, meaning that the query selects a value equal to either value in the condition and in the range of the values. In the clause BETWEEN 125 AND 250, for example, values of 125 through 250 would make the condition true. You can use the BETWEEN operator in MySQL, Oracle, and SQL Server.

The BETWEEN operator is not an essential feature of SQL; you have just seen that you can obtain the same result without it. Using the BETWEEN operator, however, does make certain SELECT commands simpler to construct.

Using Computed Columns

You can perform computations using SQL queries. A **computed column** does not exist in the database but can be computed using data in the existing columns. Computations can involve any arithmetic operator shown in Figure 4-13.

Arithmetic Operator	Description
+	Addition
–	Subtraction
*	Multiplication
/	Division

FIGURE 4-13   Arithmetic operators

EXAMPLE 10: Find the number, first and last name, and available credit (the credit limit minus the balance) for each customer.

There is no column in the KimTay Pet Supplies database that stores a customer's available credit, but you can compute the available credit using the CREDIT_LIMIT and BALANCE columns. To compute the available credit, you use the expression CREDIT_LIMIT - BALANCE, as shown in Figure 4-14.

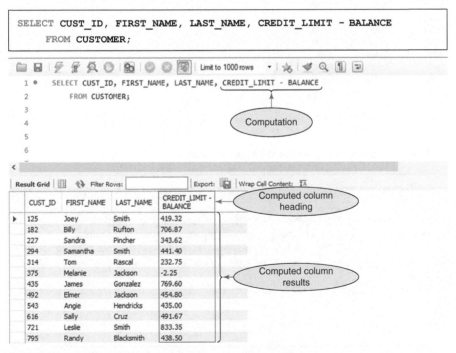

FIGURE 4-14   SELECT command with a computed column

You also can assign a name, or alias, to a computed column by following the computation with the word **AS** and the desired name. The command shown in Figure 4-15, for example, assigns the name AVAILABLE_CREDIT to the computed column using the AS keyword. Giving the column a descriptive name, such as AVAILABLE_CREDIT, is much more readable and easier to understand than using CREDIT_LIMIT – BALANCE. Because this calculation is very simple, using the calculation as the heading for the column is understandable; however, if the calculation were much more complicated and the column headings were not named accordingly, it could become quite difficult to understand.

```
SELECT CUST_ID, FIRST_NAME, LAST_NAME, CREDIT_LIMIT - BALANCE AS
AVAILABLE_CREDIT
        FROM CUSTOMER;
```

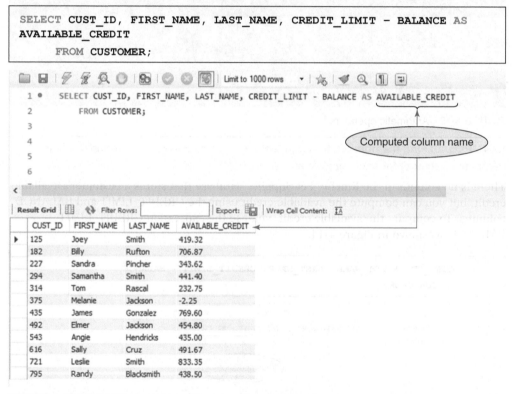

FIGURE 4-15   SELECT command with a named computed column

EXAMPLE 11: Find the customer ID, first name, last name, and available credit for each customer with at least $400 of available credit.

You also can use computed columns in comparisons, as shown in Figure 4-16. Notice it is not necessary to place parentheses around the computation (CREDIT_LIMIT – BALANCE); however, it does make the statement more readable.

```
SELECT CUST_ID, FIRST_NAME, LAST_NAME, CREDIT_LIMIT - BALANCE AS
AVAILABLE_CREDIT
     FROM CUSTOMER
          WHERE (CREDIT_LIMIT - BALANCE) >= 400;
```

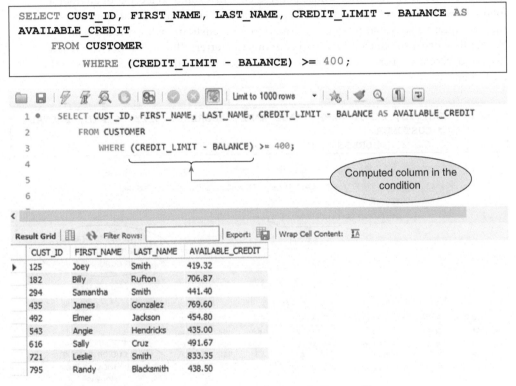

FIGURE 4-16   SELECT command with a computed column in the condition

Using the LIKE Operator

In most cases, the conditions in WHERE clauses involve exact matches, such as retrieving rows for each customer located in the city of Cody. In some cases, however, exact matches do not work. For example, you might know that the desired value contains only a certain collection of characters. In such cases, you use the LIKE operator with a wildcard symbol, as shown in Example 12. Rather than testing for equality, the **LIKE** operator uses one or more wildcard characters to test for a pattern match.

EXAMPLE 12: List the customer ID, first name, last name, and complete address of each customer located at an address that contains the letters "Rock."

All you know is that the addresses you want contain a certain collection of characters ("Rock") somewhere in the ADDRESS column, but you do not know where. In SQL, for MySQL, Oracle, SQL Server, the percent sign (%) is used as a wildcard to represent any collection of characters. As shown in Figure 4-17, the condition LIKE '%Rock%' retrieves information for each customer whose address contains some collection of characters, followed by the letters "Rock," followed potentially by some additional characters. Note that this query also would retrieve information for a customer whose address is "783 Rockabilly" because "Rockabilly" also contains the letters "Rock." Notice the results list two different occurrences where "Rock" is listed somewhere in the address of the customer.

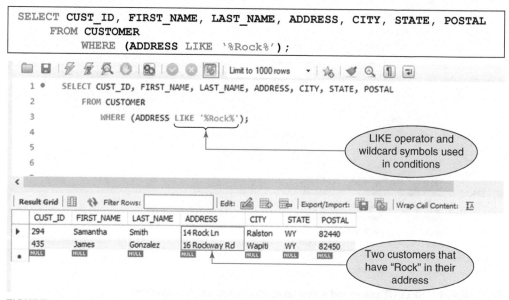

FIGURE 4-17   SELECT command with a LIKE operator and wildcard characters

Another wildcard symbol in SQL is the underscore (_), which represents any individual character. For example, "T_m" represents the letter "T" followed by any single character, followed by the letter "m," and would retrieve rows that include words such as Tim, Tom, or T3m.

HELPFUL HINT

In a large database, you should use wildcards only when absolutely necessary. Searches involving wildcards can be extremely slow to process.

Using the IN Operator

An **IN clause**, which consists of the IN operator followed by a collection of values, provides a concise way of phrasing certain conditions, as Example 13 illustrates. You will see another use for the IN clause in more complex examples later in this module.

EXAMPLE 13: List the customer ID, first name, last name, and credit limit for each customer with a credit limit of $500, $750, or $1,000.

In this query, you can use an IN clause to determine whether a credit limit is $500, $750, or $1,000. You could obtain the same answer by using the condition WHERE (CREDIT_LIMIT = 500) OR (CREDIT_LIMIT = 750) OR (CREDIT_LIMIT = 1000). The approach shown in Figure 4-18 is simpler because the IN clause contains a collection of values: 500, 750, and 1000. The condition is true for those rows in which the value in the CREDIT_LIMIT column is in this collection.

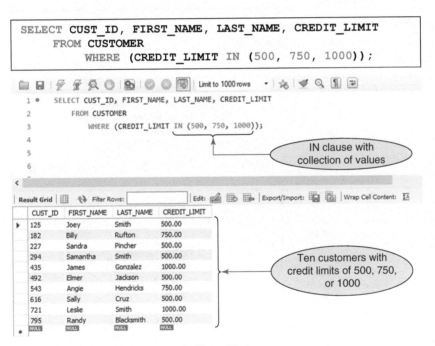

FIGURE 4-18   SELECT command with an IN clause

SORTING

Recall that the order of rows in a table is immaterial to the DBMS. From a practical standpoint, this means that when you query a relational database, there is no defined order in which to display the results. Rows might be displayed in the order in which the data was originally entered, but even this is not certain. If the order in which the data is displayed is important, you can specifically request that the results appear in a desired order. In SQL, you specify the results order by using the ORDER BY clause.

Using the ORDER BY Clause

You use the **ORDER BY clause** to list data in a specific order, as shown in Example 14.

EXAMPLE 14: List the customer ID, first name, last name, and balance of each customer. Order (sort) the output in ascending (increasing) order by balance.

The column on which to sort data is called a **sort key** or simply a **key**. In Example 14, you need to order the output by balance, so the sort key is the BALANCE column. To sort the output, use an ORDER BY clause followed by the sort key. If you do not specify a sort order, the default is ascending. The query appears in Figure 4-19.

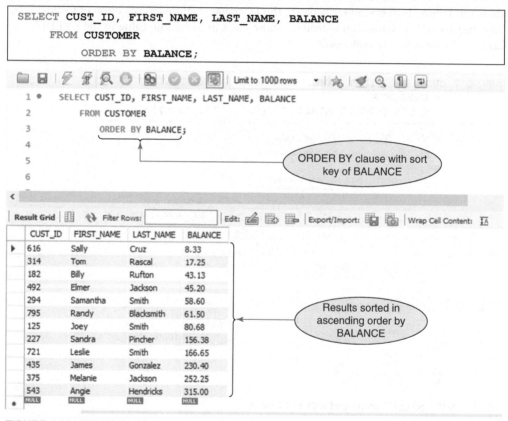

FIGURE 4-19   SELECT command to sort rows

Additional Sorting Options

Sometimes you might need to sort data using more than one key, as shown in Example 15.

EXAMPLE 15: List the customer ID, first name, last name, and credit limit of each customer. Order the customers by last name within descending credit limit. (In other words, first sort the customers by credit limit in descending order. Within each group of customers that have a common credit limit, sort the customers by last name in ascending order.)

Example 15 involves two new ideas: sorting on multiple keys—CREDIT_LIMIT and LAST_NAME—and sorting one of the keys in descending order. When you need to sort data on two columns, the more important column (in this case, CREDIT_LIMIT) is called the **major sort key** (or the **primary sort key**) and the less important column (in this case, LAST_NAME) is called the **minor sort key** (or the **secondary sort key**). To sort on multiple keys, you list the keys in order of importance in the ORDER BY clause. To sort in descending order, you follow the name of the sort key with the **DESC** operator, as shown in Figure 4-20.

```
SELECT CUST_ID, FIRST_NAME, LAST_NAME, CREDIT_LIMIT
     FROM CUSTOMER
          ORDER BY CREDIT_LIMIT DESC, LAST_NAME;
```

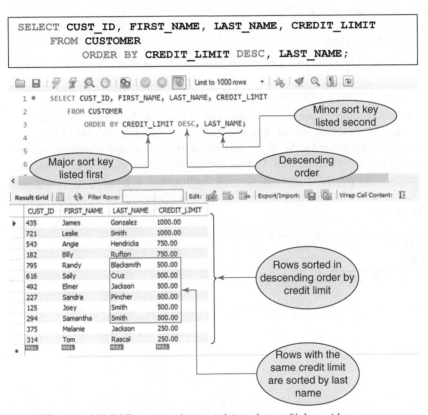

FIGURE 4-20   SELECT command to sort data using multiple sort keys

USING FUNCTIONS

SQL uses special functions, called **aggregate functions**, to calculate sums, averages, counts, maximum values, and minimum values. These functions apply to *groups* of rows. They could apply to all the rows in a table (for example, calculating the average balance of all customers). They also could apply to those rows satisfying some particular condition (for example, the average balance of all customers of sales rep 10). The descriptions of the aggregate functions appear in Figure 4-21.

FUNCTION	DESCRIPTION
AVG	Calculates the average value in a column
COUNT	Determines the number of rows in a table
MAX	Determines the maximum value in a column
MIN	Determines the minimum value in a column
SUM	Calculates the total of the values in a column

FIGURE 4-21   SQL aggregate functions

Using the COUNT Function

The **COUNT** function, as illustrated in Example 16, counts the number of rows in a table.

EXAMPLE 16: How many items are in the category DOG?

For this query, you need to determine the total number of rows in the ITEM table with the value DOG in the CATEGORY column. You use the COUNT function to assist you. You could count the item numbers in the query results, or the number of descriptions, or the number of entries in any other column. It does not matter which column you choose because all columns should provide the same answer. Rather than arbitrarily selecting one column, most SQL implementations let you use the asterisk (*) to represent any column, as shown in Figure 4-22.

```
SELECT COUNT(*)
     FROM ITEM
          WHERE (CATEGORY = 'DOG');
```

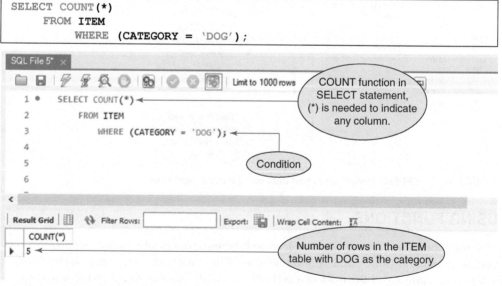

FIGURE 4-22   SELECT command to count rows

You also can count the number of rows in a query by selecting a specific column instead of using the asterisk, such as the ITEM_ID column, as show in Figure 4-23. This produces the same result as the command in Figure 4-22.

```
SELECT COUNT(ITEM_ID)
    FROM ITEM
        WHERE (CATEGORY = 'DOG');
```

FIGURE 4-23   SELECT command to count rows using a specific column

Using the SUM Function

If you need to calculate the total of all customers' balances, you can use the **SUM** function, as illustrated in Example 17.

EXAMPLE 17: Find the total number of KimTay Pet Supplies customers and the total of their balances.

When you use the SUM function, you must specify the column to total, and the column's data type must be numeric. (How could you calculate a sum of names or addresses?) Figure 4-24 shows the query and the results.

```
SELECT COUNT(*), SUM(BALANCE)
    FROM CUSTOMER;
```

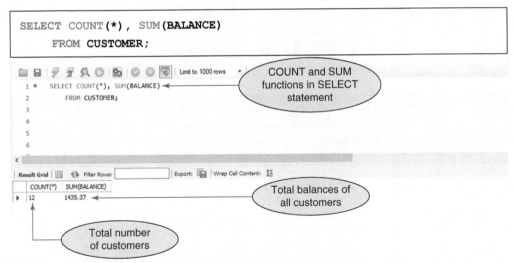

FIGURE 4-24   SELECT command to count rows and calculate a total

Using the AVG, MAX, and MIN Functions

Using the AVG, MAX, and MIN functions is similar to using SUM, except that different statistics are calculated. **AVG** calculates the average value in a numeric range, **MAX** calculates the maximum value in a numeric range, and **MIN** calculates the minimum value in a numeric range.

EXAMPLE 18: Find the sum of all balances, the average balance, the maximum balance, and the minimum balance of all KimTay Pet Supplies customers.

Figure 4-25 shows the query and the results.

```
SELECT SUM(BALANCE), AVG(BALANCE), MAX(BALANCE), MIN(BALANCE)
    FROM CUSTOMER;
```

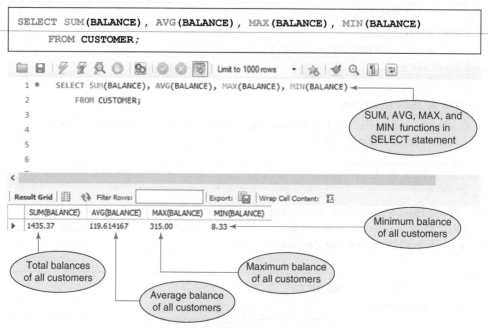

FIGURE 4-25   SELECT command with multiple functions

HELPFUL HINT

When you use the SUM, AVG, MAX, or MIN functions, SQL ignores any null value(s) in the column and eliminates them from the computations.

Null values in numeric columns can produce strange results when statistics are computed. For example, suppose the BALANCE column accepts null values, there are currently four customers in the CUSTOMER table, and their respective balances are $100, $200, $300, and null (unknown). When you calculate the average balance, SQL ignores the null value and obtains a result of $200 (($100 + $200 + $300) / 3). Similarly, when you calculate the total of the balances, SQL ignores the null value and calculates a total of $600. When you count the number of customers in the table, however, SQL includes the row containing the null value, and the result is 4. Thus, the total of the balances ($600) divided by the number of customers (4) results in an average balance of $150. Being aware of the details of how functions process their data prevents unexpected results.

HELPFUL HINT

You can use an AS clause with a function. For example, the following command computes a sum of the BALANCE column and displays the column heading as TOTAL_BALANCE in the query results:

```
SELECT SUM(BALANCE) AS TOTAL_BALANCE
    FROM CUSTOMER;
```

Using the DISTINCT Operator

In some situations, the **DISTINCT** operator is useful when used in conjunction with the COUNT function because it eliminates duplicate values in the query results. Examples 19 and 20 illustrate the most common uses of the DISTINCT operator.

EXAMPLE 19: Find the customer ID of each customer that currently has an invoice (that is, an invoice currently in the INVOICES table).

The command seems fairly simple. When a customer currently has an invoice, there must be at least one row in the INVOICES table on which that customer's ID appears. You could use the query shown in Figure 4-26 to find the customer IDs with invoices.

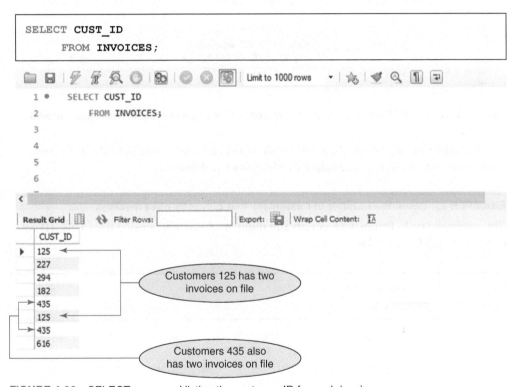

FIGURE 4-26   SELECT command listing the customer ID for each invoice

Notice that customer IDs 125 and 435 each appear more than once in the results; this means that both customers currently have more than one invoice in the INVOICES table. Suppose you want to list each customer ID only once, as illustrated in Example 20.

EXAMPLE 20: Find the number of each customer that currently has an open order. List each customer only once.

To ensure uniqueness, you can use the DISTINCT operator, as shown in Figure 4-27. Notice that customers 125 and 435 are only listed once in the results.

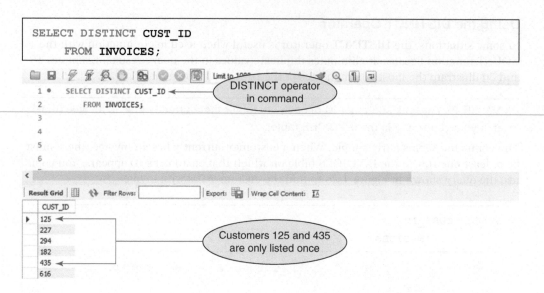

FIGURE 4-27   SELECT command listing the customer ID for all invoices with duplicates removed

You might wonder about the relationship between COUNT and DISTINCT, because both involve counting rows. Example 21 identifies the differences.

EXAMPLE 21: Count the number of customers that currently have invoices.

The query shown in Figure 4-28 counts the number of customers using the CUST_ID column in the INVOICES table.

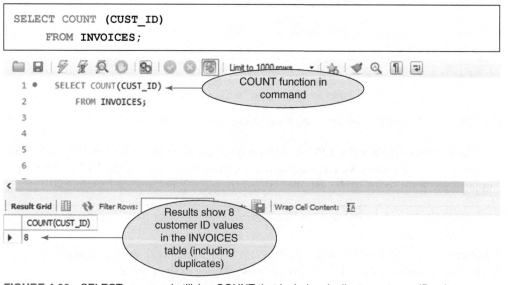

FIGURE 4-28   SELECT command utilizing COUNT that includes duplicate customer ID values

Q & A

Question: What is wrong with the query results shown in Figure 4-28?
Answer: The answer, 8, is the result of counting the customers that have invoices multiple times—once for each separate invoice currently on file. The result counts each customer ID and does not eliminate duplicate customer numbers to provide an accurate count of the number of customers.

Some SQL implementations, including MySQL, Oracle, and SQL Server, allow you to use the DISTINCT operator to calculate the correct count, as shown in Figure 4-29. Notice the results show 6 customer ID values that have invoices, excluding duplicates.

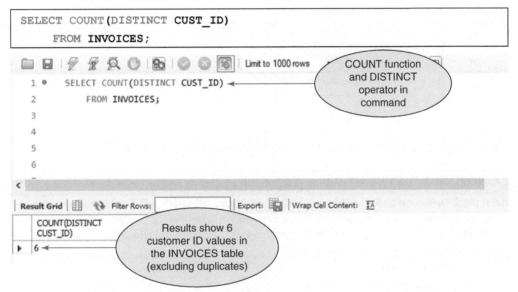

FIGURE 4-29   SELECT command utilizing COUNT and DISTINCT that eliminates duplicate customer ID values

NESTING QUERIES

Sometimes obtaining the results you need requires two or more steps, as shown in the next two examples.

EXAMPLE 22: List the item ID of each item in category HOR.

The command to obtain the results are shown in Figure 4-30. Notice the results show four item ID values with a category of HOR (FM23, FS39, QB92, and WB49).

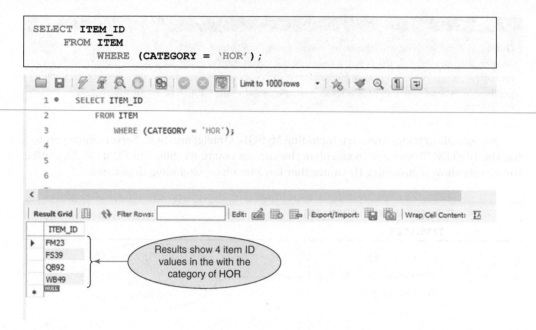

FIGURE 4-30   SELECT command to list all item ID values in the category HOR

EXAMPLE 23: List the invoice numbers that contain an invoice line for an item in category HOR.

Example 23 asks you to find the invoice numbers in the INVOICE_LINE table that correspond to the item ID values in the results of the query used in Example 22. After viewing those results (FM23, FS39, QB92, and WB49), you can use the command shown in Figure 4-31.

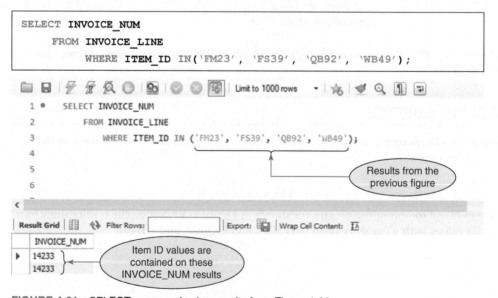

FIGURE 4-31   SELECT command using results from Figure 4-30

Subqueries

It is possible to place one query inside another. The inner query is called a **subquery**. The subquery is evaluated first. After the subquery has been evaluated, the outer query can use the results of the subquery to find its results, as shown in Example 24.

EXAMPLE 24: Find the answer to Examples 22 and 23 in one step.

You can find the same result as in the previous two examples in a single step by using a subquery. In Figure 4-32, the command shown in parentheses is the subquery. This sub-query is evaluated first, producing a temporary table. The temporary table is used only to evaluate the query—it is not available to the user or displayed—and it is deleted after the evaluation of the query is complete. In this example, the temporary table has only a single column (ITEM_ID) and four rows (FM23, FS39, QB92, and WB49). The outer query is evaluated next. In this case, the outer query retrieves the invoice number on every row in the INVOICE_LINE table for which the item ID is in the results of the sub-query. Because that table contains only the item numbers in category HOR, the results display the desired list of invoice numbers. The two items happen to be on the same invoice.

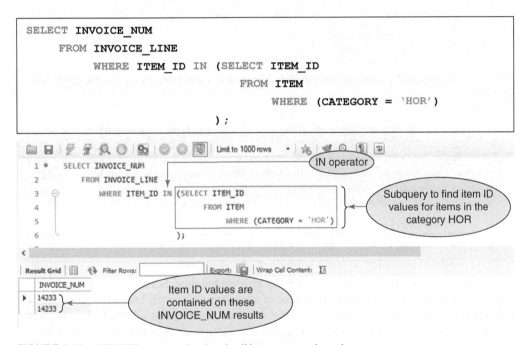

FIGURE 4-32   SELECT command using the IN operator and a subquery

Figure 4-32 shows duplicate invoice numbers in the results. To eliminate this duplication, you can use the DISTINCT operator as shown in Figure 4-33.

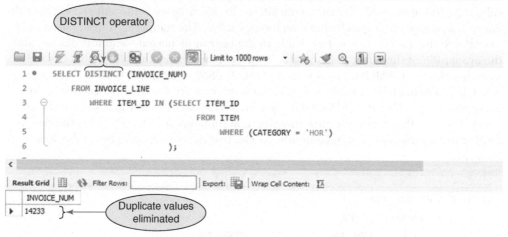

FIGURE 4-33   SELECT command using the IN operator and a subquery, along with the DISTINCT operator

---

HELPFUL HINT

Notice the indentions with the command for readability. As previously mentioned, there are many ways to indent code for better readability. This is the method this text uses, with the beginning and ending parentheses for the subquery aligning vertically.

EXAMPLE 25: List the customer ID, first name, last name, and balance for each customer whose balance exceeds the average balance of all customers.

In this case, you use a subquery to obtain the average balance. Because the subquery produces a single number (the average balance of all customers), each individual customer's balance is compared to this number, and the row for a customer is selected when the customer's balance is greater than the average balance. The query is shown in Figure 4-34. Notice the results show five customers whose balance exceeds the average balance for all customers.

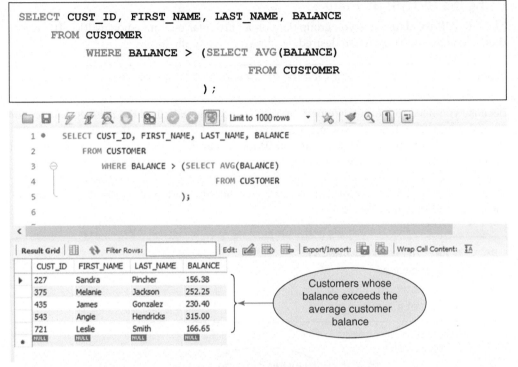

```
SELECT CUST_ID, FIRST_NAME, LAST_NAME, BALANCE
     FROM CUSTOMER
          WHERE BALANCE > (SELECT AVG(BALANCE)
                                FROM CUSTOMER
                      ) ;
```

FIGURE 4-34   SELECT command using an operator and a subquery

GROUPING

Grouping creates groups of rows that share some common characteristic. If you group customers by credit limit, for example, the first group contains customers with $250 credit limits, the second group contains customers with $500 credit limits, and so on. If, on the other hand, you group customers by sales rep ID, the first group contains those customers represented by sales rep 05, the second group contains those customers represented by sales rep 10, and the third group contains those customers represented by sales rep 15.

When you group rows, any calculations indicated in the SELECT command are performed for the entire group. For example, if you group customers by sales rep ID and the query requests the average balance, the results include the average balance for the group of customers represented by rep 05, the average balance for the group represented by rep 10, and the average balance for the group represented by rep 15. The following examples illustrate this process.

Using the GROUP BY Clause

The **GROUP BY clause** lets you group data on a particular column, such as REP_ID, and then calculate statistics, when desired, as shown in Example 26.

EXAMPLE 26: For each sales rep, list the rep ID and the average balance of the rep's customers.

Because you need to group customers by rep ID and then calculate the average balance for all customers in each group, you must use the GROUP BY clause. In this case, GROUP BY REP_ID puts customers with the same rep ID into separate groups. Any statistics indicated in the SELECT command are calculated for each group. It is important to note that the GROUP BY clause does not sort the data in a particular order; you must use the ORDER BY clause to sort data. Assuming that the results should be ordered by rep ID, you can use the command shown in Figure 4-35.

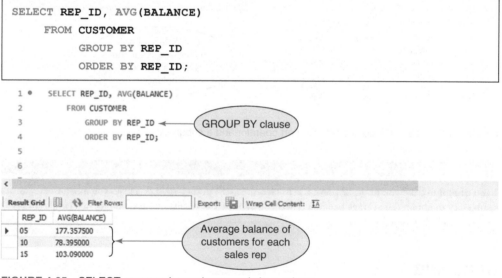

```
SELECT REP_ID, AVG(BALANCE)
      FROM CUSTOMER
            GROUP BY REP_ID
            ORDER BY REP_ID;
```

FIGURE 4-35   SELECT command grouping records in a column

When rows are grouped, one line of output is produced for each group. The only things that can be displayed are statistics calculated for the group or columns whose values are the same for all rows in a group.

Q & A

Question: Is it appropriate to display the rep ID in the query for Example 26?
Answer: Yes, because the rep ID in one row in a group must be the same as the rep ID in any other row in the group.

Q & A

Question: Would it be appropriate to display a customer ID in the query for Example 26?
Answer: No, because the customer ID varies on the rows in a group. (The same rep is associated with many customers.) The DBMS would not be able to determine which customer ID to display for the group, and would display an error message if you attempt to display a customer ID.

Using a HAVING Clause

The HAVING clause is used to restrict the groups that are included, as shown in Example 27.

EXAMPLE 27: Repeat the previous example, but list only those reps whose customers have an average balance greater than $100.

The only difference between Examples 26 and 27 is the restriction to display only those reps whose customers have an average balance greater than $100. This restriction does not apply to individual rows but rather to *groups*. Because the WHERE clause applies only to rows, you cannot use it to accomplish the kind of selection that is required. Fortunately, the HAVING clause does for groups what the WHERE clause does for rows. The **HAVING clause** limits the groups that are included in the results. In Figure 4-36, the row created for a group is displayed only when the average balance for the rows in the group is greater than $100.

```
SELECT REP_ID, AVG(BALANCE)
    FROM CUSTOMER
        GROUP BY REP_ID
        HAVING AVG (BALANCE) > 100
        ORDER BY REP_ID;
```

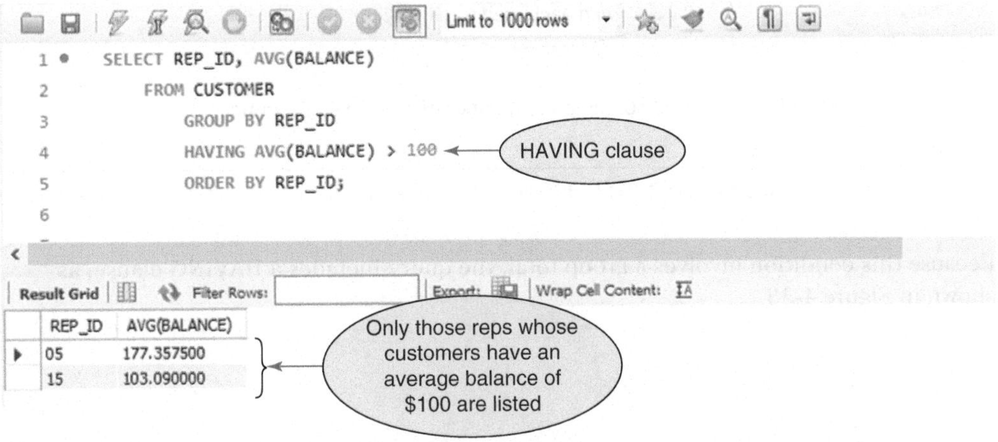

```
1 •   SELECT REP_ID, AVG(BALANCE)
2         FROM CUSTOMER
3            GROUP BY REP_ID
4            HAVING AVG(BALANCE) > 100  ◄──── ( HAVING clause )
5            ORDER BY REP_ID;
6
```

REP_ID	AVG(BALANCE)
▶ 05	177.357500
15	103.090000

Only those reps whose customers have an average balance of $100 are listed

FIGURE 4-36   SELECT command restricting the groups to include in the results

HAVING vs. WHERE

Just as you can use the WHERE clause to limit the *rows* that are included in a query's result, you can use the HAVING clause to limit the *groups* that are included. Examples 28, 29, and 30 illustrate the difference between these two clauses.

EXAMPLE 28: List each credit limit and the number of customers having each credit limit.

To count the number of customers that have a given credit limit, you must group the data by credit limit, as shown in Figure 4-37.

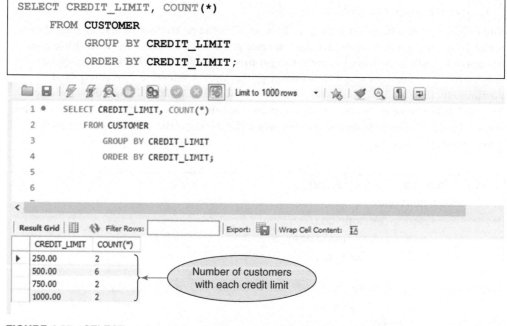

FIGURE 4-37　SELECT command counting the number of rows in each group

---

EXAMPLE 29: Repeat Example 28, but list only those credit limits held by more than two customers.

Because this condition involves a group total, the query includes a HAVING clause, as shown in Figure 4-38.

```
SELECT CREDIT_LIMIT, COUNT(*)
    FROM CUSTOMER
        GROUP BY CREDIT_LIMIT
        HAVING COUNT(*) > 2
        ORDER BY CREDIT_LIMIT;
```

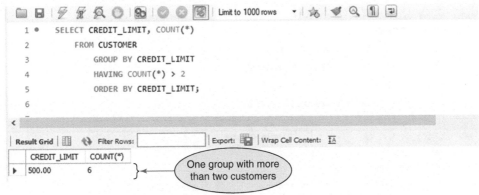

FIGURE 4-38 SELECT command displaying groups with more than two rows

EXAMPLE 30: List each credit limit and the number of customers of sales rep 05 that have this limit.

The condition involves only rows, so using the WHERE clause is appropriate, as shown in Figure 4-39.

```
SELECT CREDIT_LIMIT, COUNT(*)
    FROM CUSTOMER
        WHERE (REP_ID = '05')
            GROUP BY CREDIT_LIMIT
            ORDER BY CREDIT_LIMIT;
```

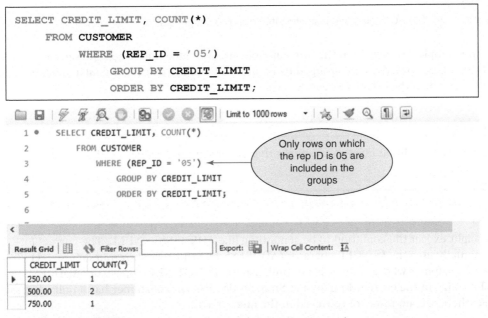

FIGURE 4-39 SELECT command restricting the rows to be grouped

EXAMPLE 31: Repeat Example 30, but list only those credit limits held by fewer than two customers.

Because the conditions involve rows and groups, you must use both a WHERE clause and a HAVING clause, as shown in Figure 4-40.

```
SELECT CREDIT_LIMIT, COUNT(*)
    FROM CUSTOMER
        WHERE (REP_ID = '05')
            GROUP BY CREDIT_LIMIT
            HAVING COUNT(*) < 2
            ORDER BY CREDIT_LIMIT;
```

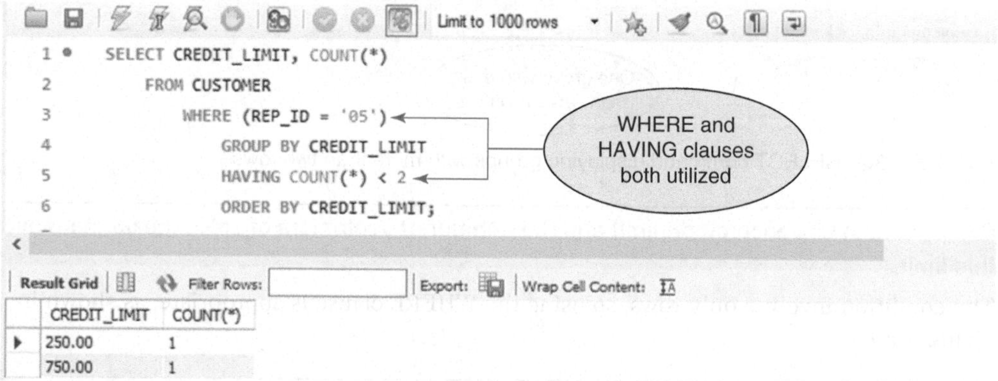

FIGURE 4-40   SELECT command restricting the rows and the groups

In Example 31, rows from the original table are evaluated only when the sales rep ID is 05. These rows then are grouped by credit limit and the count is calculated. Only groups for which the calculated count is less than two are displayed.

NULLS

Sometimes a condition involves a column that can accept null values, as illustrated in Example 32.

EXAMPLE 32: List the number and name of each customer with a null (unknown) address value.

You might expect the condition to be something like ADDRESS = NULL. The correct format actually uses the **IS NULL** operator (ADDRESS IS NULL), as shown in Figure 4-41. To select a customer whose address is not null, use the **IS NOT NULL** operator (ADDRESS IS NOT NULL). In the current KimTay Pet Supplies database, no customer has a null address value; therefore, no rows are retrieved in the query results.

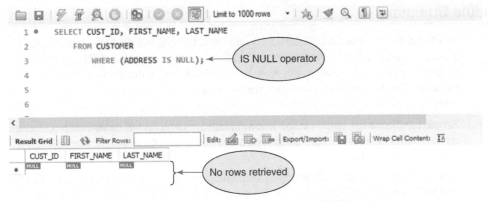

FIGURE 4-41   Selecting rows containing null values in the ADDRESS column

SUMMARY OF SQL CLAUSES, FUNCTIONS, AND OPERATORS

In this module, you learned how to create queries that retrieve data from a single table by constructing appropriate SELECT commands. In the next module, you learn how to create queries that retrieve data from multiple tables. The queries you created in this module used the clauses, functions, and operators shown in Figure 4-42.

CLAUSE OR OPERATOR	DESCRIPTION
AND operator	Specifies that all simple conditions must be true for the compound condition to be true
BETWEEN operator	Specifies a range of values in a condition
DESC operator	Sorts the query results in descending order based on the column name
DISTINCT operator	Ensures uniqueness in the condition by eliminating duplicate values
FROM clause	Indicates the table from which to retrieve the specified columns
GROUP BY clause	Groups rows based on the specified column
HAVING clause	Limits a condition to the groups that are included
IN operator	Finds a value in a group of values specified in the condition
IS NOT NULL operator	Finds rows that do not contain a null value in the specified column
IS NULL operator	Finds rows that contain a null value in the specified column
LIKE operator	Indicates a pattern of characters to find in a condition
NOT operator	Reverses the result of the original condition
OR operator	Specifies that the compound condition is true whenever any of the simple conditions is true
ORDER BY clause	Lists the query results in the specified order based on the column name
SELECT clause	Specifies the columns to retrieve in the query
WHERE clause	Specifies any conditions for the query

FIGURE 4-42   SQL query clauses and operators

Module Summary

- The basic form of the SQL SELECT command is SELECT-FROM-WHERE. Specify the columns to be listed after the word SELECT (or type an asterisk [*] to select all columns) and then specify the table name that contains these columns after the word FROM. Optionally, you can include one or more conditions after the word WHERE.

- Simple conditions are written in the following form: column name, comparison operator, column name or value. Simple conditions can involve any of the comparison operators: =, >, >=, <, <=, or <>.

- You can form compound conditions by combining simple conditions using the AND, OR, and NOT operators.

- Use the BETWEEN operator to indicate a range of values in a condition.

- Use computed columns in SQL commands by using arithmetic operators and writing the computation in place of a column name. You can assign a name to the computed column by following the computation with the word AS and then the desired name.

- To check for a value in a character column that is similar to a particular string of characters, use the LIKE operator. In MySQL, Oracle, and SQL Server, the percent (%) wildcard represents any collection of characters, and the underscore (_) wildcard represents any single character.

- To determine whether a column contains a value in a set of values, use the IN operator.

- Use an ORDER BY clause to sort data. List sort keys in order of importance. To sort in descending order, follow the sort key with the DESC operator.

- SQL processes the aggregate functions COUNT, SUM, AVG, MAX, and MIN. These calculations apply to groups of rows.

- To avoid duplicates in a query that uses an aggregate function, precede the column name with the DISTINCT operator.

- When one SQL query is placed inside another, it is called a subquery. The inner query (the subquery) is evaluated first.

- Use a GROUP BY clause to group data.

- Use a HAVING clause to restrict the output to certain groups.

- Use the IS NULL operator in a WHERE clause to find rows containing a null value in a particular column. Use the IS NOT NULL operator in a WHERE clause to find rows that do not contain a null value.

Key Terms

aggregate functions	LIKE
AND	major sort key
AND condition	MAX
AS	MIN
AVG	minor sort key
BETWEEN	NOT
compound condition	NOT condition
computed column	OR
COUNT	OR condition
DESC	ORDER BY clause
DISTINCT	primary sort key
FROM clause	query
GROUP BY clause	secondary sort key
grouping	SELECT clause
HAVING clause	simple condition
IN clause	sort key
IS NOT NULL	subquery
IS NULL	SUM
key	WHERE clause

Review Questions

Module Quiz

1. Describe the basic form of the SQL SELECT command.
2. How do you form a simple condition?
3. How do you form a compound condition?
4. In SQL, which operator do you use to determine whether a value is between two other values without using an AND condition?
5. How do you use a computed column in SQL? How do you name the computed column?
6. In which clause would you use a wildcard in a condition?
7. What wildcards are available in MySQL, and what do they represent?
8. How do you determine whether a column contains one of a particular set of values without using an AND condition?
9. How do you sort data?
10. How do you sort data on more than one sort key? What is the more important key called? What is the less important key called?

11.   How do you sort data in descending order?

12.   What are the SQL aggregate functions?

13.   How do you avoid including duplicate values in a query's results?

14.   What is a subquery?

15.   How do you group data in an SQL query?

16.   When grouping data in a query, how do you restrict the output to only those groups satisfying some condition?

17.   How do you find rows in which a particular column contains a null value?

Critical Thinking

1.   Use the Internet to research the SQL [charlist] wildcard that is available in Oracle and SQL Server. Using the information you find, complete the following SQL command to find all cities that begin with the letters "C" or "G."

```
SELECT CUSTOMER _ NAME, CITY
    FROM CUSTOMER
        WHERE CITY LIKE
```

Be sure to cite the URL(s) that provided the information.

Case Exercises

KimTay Pet Supplies

Use SQL and the KimTay Pet Supplies database (see Figure 1-2 in Module 1) to complete the following exercises. If directed to do so by your instructor, use the information provided with the Module 3 Exercises to print your output or save it to a document.

1.   List the item ID, description, and price for all items.

2.   List all rows and columns for the complete INVOICES table.

3.   List the first and last names of customers with credit limits of $1,000 or more.

4.   List the order number for each order placed by customer number 125 on 11/15/2021. (*Hint*: If you need help, use the discussion of the DATE data type in Figure 3-19 in Module 3.)

5.   List the number and name of each customer represented by sales rep 10 or sales rep 15.

6.   List the item ID and description of each item that is not in category HOR.

7.   List the item ID, description, and number of units on hand for each item that has between 10 and 30 units on hand, including both 10 and 30. Provide two alternate SQL statements to produce the same results.

8.   List the item ID, description, and on-hand value (units on hand * unit price) of each item in category CAT. (On-hand value is technically units on hand * cost, but there is no COST column in the ITEM table.) Assign the name ON_HAND_VALUE to the computed column.

9. List the item ID, description, and on-hand value for each item where the on-hand value is at least $1,500. Assign the name ON_HAND_VALUE to the computed column.

10. Use the IN operator to list the item ID and description of each item in category FSH or BRD.

11. Find the ID, first name, and last name of each customer whose first name begins with the letter "S."

12. List all details about all items. Order the output by description.

13. List all details about all items. Order the output by item ID within location. (That is, order the output by location and then by item ID.)

14. How many customers have balances that are more than their credit limits?

15. Find the total of the balances for all customers represented by sales rep 10 with balances that are less than their credit limits.

16. List the item ID, description, and on-hand value of each item whose number of units on hand is more than the average number of units on hand for all items. (*Hint*: Use a subquery.)

17. What is the price of the least expensive item in the database?

18. What is the item ID, description, and price of the least expensive item in the database? (*Hint*: Use a subquery.)

19. List the sum of the balances of all customers for each sales rep. Order and group the results by sales rep ID.

20. List the sum of the balances of all customers for each sales rep but restrict the output to those sales reps for which the sum is more than $150. Order the results by sales rep ID.

21. List the item ID of any item with an unknown description.

Critical Thinking

1. List the item ID and description of all items that are in the DOG or CAT category and contain the word "Small" in the description.

2. KimTay Pet Supplies is considering discounting the price of all items by 10 percent. List the item ID, description, and discounted price for all items. Use DISCOUNTED_PRICE as the name for the computed column.

StayWell Student Accommodation

Use SQL and the StayWell Student Accommodation database (Figures 1-4 through 1-9 in Module 1) to complete the following exercises. If directed to do so by your instructor, use the information provided with the Module 3 Exercises to print your output or save it to a document.

1. List the owner number, last name, and first name of every property owner.

2. List the complete PROPERTY table (all rows and all columns).

3. List the last name and first name of every owner who lives in Seattle.

4. List the last name and first name of every owner who does not live in Seattle.

5. List the property ID and office number for every property whose square footage is equal to or less than 1,400 square feet.

6. List the office number and address for every property with three bedrooms.

7. List the property ID for every property with two bedrooms that is managed by StayWell-Georgetown.

8. List the property ID for every property with a monthly rent that is between $1,350 and $1,750.

9. List the property ID for every property managed by StayWell-Columbia City whose monthly rent is less than $1,500.

10. Labor is billed at the rate of $35 per hour. List the property ID, category number, estimated hours, and estimated labor cost for every service request. To obtain the estimated labor cost, multiply the estimated hours by 35. Use the column name ESTIMATED_COST for the estimated labor cost.

11. List the owner number and last name for all owners who live in Nevada (NV), Oregon (OR), or Idaho (ID).

12. List the office number, property ID, square footage, and monthly rent for all properties. Sort the results by monthly rent within the square footage.

13. How many three-bedroom properties are managed by each office?

14. Calculate the total value of monthly rents for all properties.

Critical Thinking

1. There are two ways to create the query in Step 11. Write the SQL command that you used and then write the alternate command that also would obtain the correct result.

2. What WHERE clause would you use to find all service requests with the word "heating" anywhere in the description field?

MODULE **5**

MULTIPLE-TABLE QUERIES

OBJECTIVES

- Use joins to retrieve data from more than one table.
- Use the IN and EXISTS operators to query multiple tables.
- Use a subquery within a subquery.
- Use an alias.
- Join a table to itself.
- Perform set operations (union, intersection, and difference).
- Use the ALL and ANY operators in a query.
- Perform special operations (inner join, outer join, and product).

INTRODUCTION

In this module, you learn how to use SQL to retrieve data from two or more tables using one SQL command. You join tables together and examine how to obtain similar results using the SQL IN and EXISTS operators. Then you use aliases to simplify queries and join a table to itself. You also implement the set operations of union, intersection, and difference using SQL commands. You examine two related SQL operators: ALL and ANY. Finally, you perform inner joins, outer joins, and products.

QUERYING MULTIPLE TABLES

In Module 4, you learned how to retrieve data from a single table. Many queries require you to retrieve data from two or more tables. To retrieve data from multiple tables, you first must join the tables and then formulate a query using the same commands that you use for single-table queries.

> **HELPFUL HINT**
>
> In the following queries, your results might contain the same rows, but they might be listed in a different order. If order is important, you can include an ORDER BY clause in the query to ensure that the results are listed in the desired order.

Joining Two Tables

To retrieve data from more than one table, you must **join** the tables together by finding rows in the two tables that have identical values in matching columns. You can join tables by using a condition in the WHERE clause, as you see in Example 1.

EXAMPLE 1: List the ID, first name, and last name of each customer, together with the ID, first name, and last name of the sales rep who represents the customer.

Because the customer ID values and names are in the CUSTOMER table and the sales rep ID values and names are in the SALES_REP table, you need to include both tables in the SQL command so you can retrieve data from both tables. To join (or relate) the tables, you construct the SQL command as follows:

1.   In the SELECT clause, list all columns you want to display.
2.   In the FROM clause, list all tables involved in the query.
3.   In the WHERE clause, list the condition that restricts the data to be retrieved to only those rows from the two tables that match; that is, restrict it to the rows that have common values in matching columns.

As you learned in Module 2, it is often necessary to qualify a column name to specify the particular column you are referencing. Qualifying column names is especially important when joining tables because you must join tables on *matching* columns that frequently have identical column names. To qualify a column name, precede the name of the column with the name of the table, followed by a period. The matching columns in this example are both named REP_ID—there is a column in the SALES_REP table named REP_ID and a column in the CUSTOMER table that also is named REP_ID. The REP_ID column in the SALES_REP table is written as SALES_REP.REP_ID and the REP_ID column in the CUSTOMER table is written as CUSTOMER.REP_ID. The query and its results appear in Figure 5-1.

```
SELECT CUST_ID, CUSTOMER.FIRST_NAME, CUSTOMER.LAST_NAME, SALES_
       REP. REP_ID, SALES_REP.FIRST_NAME, SALES_REP.LAST_NAME
   FROM CUSTOMER, SALES_REP
       WHERE (CUSTOMER.REP_ID = SALES_REP.REP_ID);
```

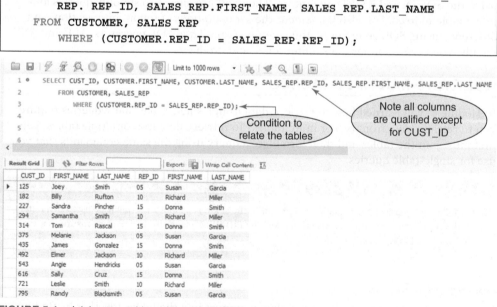

FIGURE 5-1   Joining two tables with a single SQL command

When there is potential ambiguity in listing column names, you *must* qualify the columns involved in the query. It is permissible to qualify other columns as well, even when there is no possible confusion. Some people prefer to qualify all column names; however, in this text, you qualify column names only when necessary. In Figure 5-1, all columns are qualified except for CUST_ID. Because there are FIRST_NAME and LAST_NAME columns in both the CUSTOMER and SALES_REP tables, qualifying is necessary.

Q & A

Question: In the first row of output in Figure 5-1, the customer ID is 125, the customer first name is Joey, and the customer last name is Smith. These values represent the first row of the CUSTOMER table. How do you know the first and last names of sales rep ID 05 is Susan Garcia?

Answer: In the CUSTOMER table, the sales rep ID for customer ID 125 is 05. (This indicates that customer ID 125 is *related* to sales rep ID 05.) In the SALES_REP table, the first name of sales rep 05 is Susan and the last name is Garcia.

EXAMPLE 2: List the ID, first name, and last name of each customer whose credit limit is $500, together with the ID, first name, and last name of the sales rep who represents the customer.

In Example 1, you used a condition in the WHERE clause only to relate a customer with a sales rep to join the tables. Although relating a customer with a sales rep is essential in this example as well, you also need to restrict the output to only those customers whose credit limits are $500. You can restrict the rows by using a compound condition, as shown in Figure 5-2.

```
SELECT CUST_ID, CUSTOMER.FIRST_NAME, CUSTOMER.LAST_NAME, SALES_
       REP. REP_ID, SALES_REP.FIRST_NAME, SALES_REP.LAST_NAME
   FROM CUSTOMER, SALES_REP
       WHERE (CUSTOMER.REP_ID = SALES_REP.REP_ID) AND (CREDIT_LIMIT
       = 500);
```

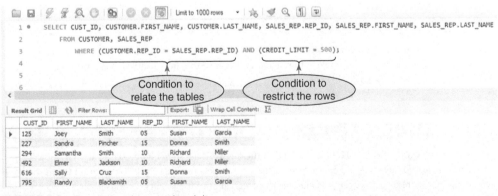

FIGURE 5-2   Restricting the rows in a join

EXAMPLE 3: For every item on an invoice, list the invoice number, item ID, description, quantity ordered, quoted price, and unit price.

An item is considered to be *on an invoice* when there is a row in the INVOICE_LINE table on which the item appears. You can find the invoice number, quantity ordered, and quoted price in the INVOICE_LINE table. To find the description and the unit price, however, you need to look in the ITEM table. Then you need to find rows in the INVOICE_LINE table and rows in the ITEM table that match (rows containing the same item ID). The query and its results appear in Figure 5-3.

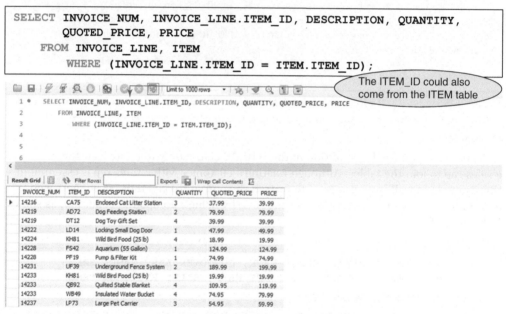

```
SELECT INVOICE_NUM, INVOICE_LINE.ITEM_ID, DESCRIPTION, QUANTITY,
       QUOTED_PRICE, PRICE
    FROM INVOICE_LINE, ITEM
       WHERE (INVOICE_LINE.ITEM_ID = ITEM.ITEM_ID);
```

The ITEM_ID could also come from the ITEM table

INVOICE_NUM	ITEM_ID	DESCRIPTION	QUANTITY	QUOTED_PRICE	PRICE
14216	CA75	Enclosed Cat Litter Station	3	37.99	39.99
14219	AD72	Dog Feeding Station	2	79.99	79.99
14219	DT12	Dog Toy Gift Set	4	39.99	39.99
14222	LD14	Locking Small Dog Door	1	47.99	49.99
14224	KH81	Wild Bird Food (25 lb)	4	18.99	19.99
14228	FS42	Aquarium (55 Gallon)	1	124.99	124.99
14228	PF19	Pump & Filter Kit	1	74.99	74.99
14231	UF39	Underground Fence System	2	189.99	199.99
14233	KH81	Wild Bird Food (25 lb)	1	19.99	19.99
14233	QB92	Quilted Stable Blanket	4	109.95	119.99
14233	WB49	Insulated Water Bucket	4	74.95	79.99
14237	LP73	Large Pet Carrier	3	54.95	59.99

FIGURE 5-3   Joining the INVOICE_LINE and ITEM tables

Q & A

Question: Can you use ITEM.ITEM_ID instead of INVOICE_LINE.ITEM_ID in the SELECT clause?
Answer: Yes. The values for these two columns match because they must satisfy the condition INVOICE_LINE.ITEM_ID = ITEM.ITEM_ID.

HELPFUL HINT

Remember the word DESCRIPTION was added to the keyword list in version 8.0.4 of MySQL; however, it is a non-reserved keyword and can be used. This is why the word DESCRIPTION is not blue in the command in Figure 5-3; however, it is blue in the screen shot of the results.

COMPARING JOINS, IN, AND EXISTS

You join tables in SQL by including a condition in the WHERE clause to ensure that matching columns contain equal values (for example, INVOICE_LINE.ITEM_ID = ITEM. ITEM_ID). You can obtain similar results by using either the IN operator (described in Module 4) or the EXISTS operator with a subquery. The choice is a matter of personal preference because either approach obtains the same results. The following examples illustrate the use of each operator.

EXAMPLE 4: Find the description of each item included in invoice number 14233.

Because this query also involves retrieving data from the INVOICE_LINE and ITEM tables (as illustrated in Example 3), you could approach it in a similar fashion. There are two basic differences, however, between Examples 3 and 4. First, the query in Example 4 does not require as many columns; second, it involves only invoice number 14233. Having fewer columns to retrieve means that there are fewer columns listed in the SELECT clause. You can restrict the query to a single invoice by adding the condition INVOICE_NUM = '14233' to the WHERE clause. The query and its results appear in Figure 5-4.

```
SELECT DESCRIPTION
    FROM INVOICE_LINE, ITEM
        WHERE (INVOICE_LINE.ITEM_ID = ITEM.ITEM_ID) AND (INVOICE_
            NUM = '14233');
```

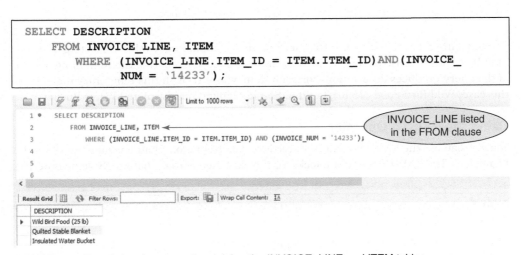

FIGURE 5-4   Restricting the rows when joining the INVOICE_LINE and ITEM tables

Notice that the INVOICE_LINE table is listed in the FROM clause, even though you do not need to display any columns from the INVOICE_LINE table. The WHERE clause contains columns from the INVOICE_LINE table, so it is necessary to include the table in the FROM clause.

Using the IN Operator

Another way to retrieve data from multiple tables in a query is to use the IN operator with a subquery. In Example 4, you first could use a subquery to find all item ID values in the INVOICE_LINE table that appear in any row on which the invoice number is 14233. Then you could find the description for any item whose item ID is in this list. The query and its results appear in Figure 5-5.

```
SELECT DESCRIPTION
    FROM ITEM
        WHERE ITEM_ID IN(SELECT ITEM_ID
                        FROM INVOICE_LINE
                            WHERE (INVOICE_NUM ='14233')
                );
```

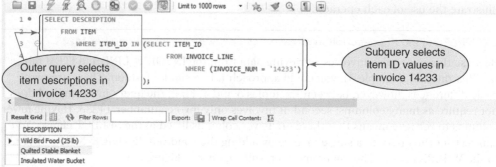

FIGURE 5-5   Using the IN operator instead of a join to query two tables

In Figure 5-5, evaluating the subquery produces a temporary table consisting of those item ID values that are present in invoice number 14233. Executing the remaining portion of the query produces descriptions for each item whose ID is in this temporary table; in this case, Wild Bird Food (25 lb), Quilted Stable Blanket, and Insulated Water Bucket.

Using the EXISTS Operator

You also can use the EXISTS operator to retrieve data from more than one table, as shown in Example 5. The **EXISTS** operator checks for the existence of rows that satisfy some criterion.

EXAMPLE 5: Find the invoice number and invoice date for each invoice that contains item ID KH81.

This query is similar to the one in Example 4, but this time the query involves the INVOICES table and not the ITEM table. In this case, you can write the query in either of the ways previously demonstrated. For example, you could use the IN operator with a subquery, as shown in Figure 5-6.

Using the EXISTS operator provides another approach to solving Example 5, as shown in Figure 5-7.

The subquery in Figure 5-7 is the first one you have seen that involves a table listed in the outer query. This type of subquery is called a **correlated subquery**. In this case, the INVOICES table, which is listed in the FROM clause of the outer query, is used in the subquery. For this reason, you need to qualify the INVOICE_NUM column in the subquery (INVOICES.INVOICE_NUM). You did not need to qualify the columns in the previous queries involving the IN operator.

The query shown in Figure 5-7 works as follows. For each row in the INVOICES table, the subquery is executed using the value of INVOICES.INVOICE_NUM that occurs in

```
SELECT INVOICE_NUM, INVOICE_DATE
    FROM INVOICES
        WHERE INVOICE_NUM IN (SELECT INVOICE_NUM
                              FROM INVOICE_LINE
                              WHERE (ITEM_ID ='KH81')
                              ) ;
```

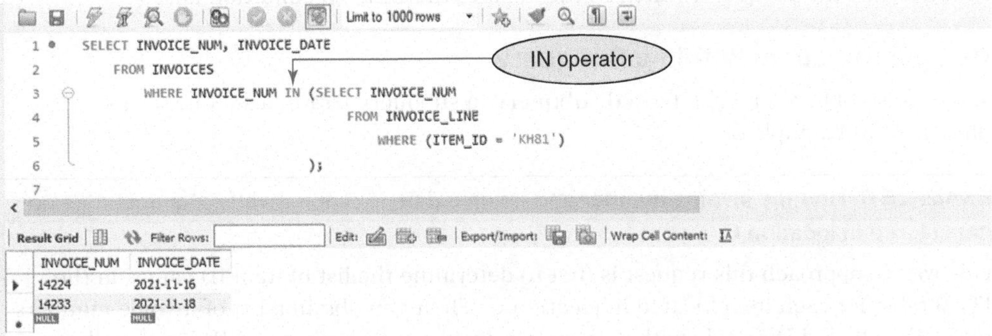

FIGURE 5-6   Using the IN operator to select invoice information

```
SELECT INVOICE_NUM, INVOICE_DATE
    FROM INVOICES
        WHERE EXISTS (SELECT*
                      FROM INVOICE_LINE
                      WHERE (INVOICES.INVOICE_NUM = INVOICE_
                          LINE.INVOICE_NUM) AND (ITEM_ID
                          =    'KH81')
                      ) ;
```

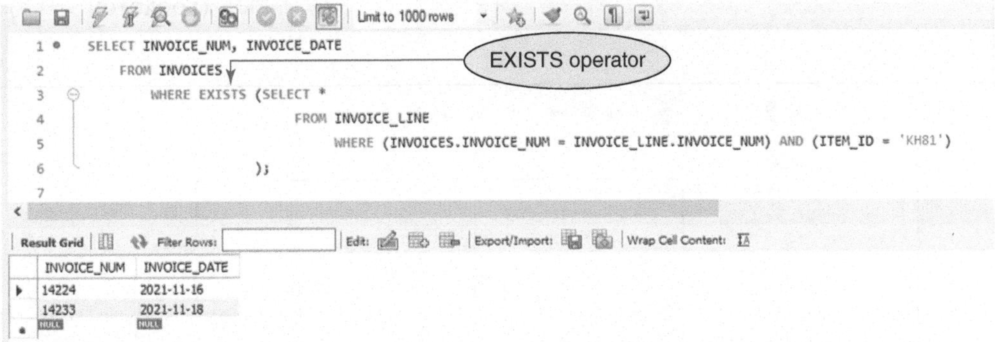

FIGURE 5-7   Using the EXISTS operator to select invoice information

that row. The inner query produces a list of all rows in the INVOICE_LINE table in which
INVOICE_LINE.INVOICE_NUM matches this value and in which ITEM_ID is equal to
KH81. You can precede a subquery with the EXISTS operator to create a condition that
is true if one or more rows are obtained when the subquery is executed; otherwise, the
condition is false.

To illustrate the process, consider invoice numbers 14224 and 14228 in the INVOICES table. Invoice number 14224 is included because a row exists in the INVOICE_LINE table with this invoice number and item ID KH81. When the subquery is executed, there is at least one row in the results, which in turn makes the EXISTS condition true. Invoice number 14228, however, is not included because no row exists in the INVOICE_LINE table with this invoice number and item ID KH81. There are no rows contained in the results of the subquery, which in turn makes the EXISTS condition false.

Using a Subquery Within a Subquery

You can use SQL to create a **nested subquery** (a subquery within a subquery), as illustrated in Example 6.

EXAMPLE 6: Find the invoice number and invoice date for each invoice that includes an item stored in location C.

One way to approach this request is first to determine the list of item ID values in the ITEM table for each item located in location C. Then you obtain a list of invoice numbers in the INVOICE_LINE table with a corresponding item ID in the item ID list. Finally, you retrieve those invoice numbers and invoice dates in the INVOICES table for which the invoice number is in the list of invoice numbers obtained during the second step. The query and its results appear in Figure 5-8.

```
SELECT INVOICE_NUM, INVOICE_DATE
    FROM INVOICES
        WHERE INVOICE_NUM IN(SELECT INVOICE_NUM
                             FROM INVOICE_LINE
                             WHERE ITEM_ID IN (SELECT ITEM_ID
                                               FROM ITEM
                                               WHERE (LOCATION = 'C')
                                               )
                            );
```

FIGURE 5-8   Nested subqueries (a subquery within a subquery)

As you might expect, SQL evaluates the queries from the innermost query to the out-ermost query. The query in this example is evaluated in three steps:

1. The innermost subquery is evaluated first, producing a temporary table of item ID values for those items stored in location C.

2. The next (intermediate) subquery is evaluated, producing a second temporary table with a list of invoice numbers. Each invoice number in this collection has a row in the INVOICE_LINE table for which the item ID is in the temporary table produced in Step 1.

3. The outer query is evaluated last, producing the desired list of invoice numbers and invoice dates. Only those invoices whose numbers are in the temporary table produced in Step 2 are included in the results.

Another approach to solving Example 6 involves joining the INVOICES, INVOICE_LINE, and ITEM tables. The query and its results appear in Figure 5-9.

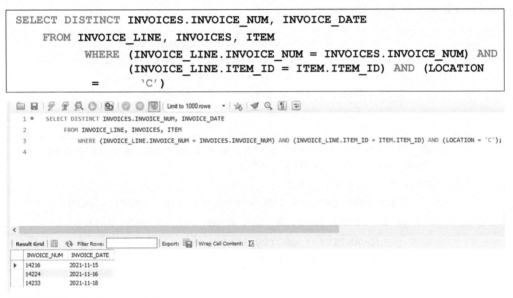

```
SELECT DISTINCT INVOICES.INVOICE_NUM, INVOICE_DATE
    FROM INVOICE_LINE, INVOICES, ITEM
        WHERE (INVOICE_LINE.INVOICE_NUM = INVOICES.INVOICE_NUM) AND
              (INVOICE_LINE.ITEM_ID = ITEM.ITEM_ID) AND (LOCATION
    =       'C')
```

FIGURE 5-9 Joining three tables

In this query, the following conditions join the tables:

```
INVOICE_LINE.INVOICE_NUM = INVOICES.INVOICE_NUM
INVOICE_LINE.ITEM_ID = ITEM.ITEM_ID
```

The condition LOCATION = 'C' restricts the output to only those items stored in location C.

The query results are correct regardless of which command you use. You can use whichever approach you prefer.

You might wonder whether one approach is more efficient than the other. SQL performs many built-in optimizations that analyze queries to determine the best way to

satisfy them. Given a good optimizer, it should not make much difference how you formulate the query—both set of results completed in less than 0.00 seconds in the computing
environment used for this text; however, your computing environment may show different results. It is expected that using nested subqueries (Figure 5-8) produces the results
in a slightly longer amount of time than joining the tables (Figure 5-9). If you are using a
DBMS without an optimizer, the way you write a query *can* make a difference in the speed
at which the DBMS executes the query. When you are working with a very large database
and efficiency is a prime concern, consult the DBMS's manual or try some timings yourself. Try running the same query both ways to see whether you notice a difference in the
speed of execution. In small databases, there should not be a significant time difference
between the two approaches.

A Comprehensive Example

The query used in Example 7 involves several of the features already presented. The query
illustrates all the major clauses that you can use in a SELECT command. It also illustrates
the order in which these clauses must appear.

**EXAMPLE 7: List the customer ID, invoice number, invoice date, and invoice total for each
invoice with a total that exceeds $250. Assign the column name INVOICE_TOTAL to the
column that displays invoice totals. Order the results by invoice number.**

The query and its results appear in Figure 5-10.

```
SELECT CUST_ID, INVOICES.INVOICE_NUM, INVOICE_DATE, SUM(QUANTITY *
       QUOTED_PRICE) AS INVOICE_TOTAL
   FROM INVOICES, INVOICE_LINE
      WHERE (INVOICES.INVOICE_NUM = INVOICE_LINE.INVOICE_NUM)
      GROUP BY INVOICES.INVOICE_NUM, CUST_ID, INVOICE_DATE
      HAVING SUM(QUANTITY * QUOTED_PRICE) > 250
      ORDER BY INVOICES.INVOICE_NUM;
```

FIGURE 5-10   Comprehensive example

In this query, the INVOICES and INVOICE_LINE tables are joined by listing both tables in the FROM clause and relating them in the WHERE clause. Selected data is sorted by invoice number using the ORDER BY clause. The GROUP BY clause indicates that the data is to be grouped by invoice number, customer ID, and invoice date. For each group, the SELECT clause displays the customer ID, invoice number, invoice date, and invoice total (SUM(QUANTITY * QUOTED_PRICE)). In addition, the total was renamed INVOICE_TOTAL. Not all groups are displayed, however. The HAVING clause displays only those groups whose SUM(NUM_ORDERED * QUOTED_PRICE) is greater than $250.

The invoice number, customer ID, and invoice date are unique for each invoice. Thus, it would seem that merely grouping by invoice number would be sufficient. SQL requires that both the customer ID and the invoice date be listed in the GROUP BY clause. Recall that a SELECT clause can include statistics calculated for only the groups or columns whose values are identical for each row in a group. By stating that the data is to be grouped by invoice number, customer ID, and invoice date, you tell SQL that the values in these columns must be the same for each row in a group.

Using an Alias

When tables are listed in the FROM clause, you can give each table an **alias**, or an alternate name, that you can use in the rest of the statement. You create an alias by typing the name of the table, pressing the Spacebar, and then typing the name of the alias. No commas or periods are necessary to separate the two names.

One reason for using an alias is simplicity. In Example 8, you assign the SALES_REP table the alias R and the CUSTOMER table the alias C. By doing this, you can type R instead of SALES_REP and C instead of CUSTOMER in the remainder of the query. The query in this example is simple, so you might not see the full benefit of this feature. When a query is complex and requires you to qualify the names, using aliases can simplify the process.

EXAMPLE 8: List the ID, first name, and last name for each sales rep together with the ID, first name, and last name for each customer the sales rep represents.

The query and its results using aliases appear in Figure 5-11.

HELPFUL HINT

Technically, it is unnecessary to qualify CUST_ID because it is included only in the CUSTOMER table. It is qualified in Figure 5-11 for illustration purposes only.

```
SELECT R.REP_ID, R.FIRST_NAME, R.LAST_NAME, C.CUST_ID, C.FIRST_NAME,
    C.LAST_NAME
    FROM SALES_REP R, CUSTOMER C
        WHERE (R.REP_ID = C.REP_ID);
```

REP_ID	FIRST_NAME	LAST_NAME	CUST_ID	FIRST_NAME	LAST_NAME
05	Susan	Garcia	125	Joey	Smith
10	Richard	Miller	182	Billy	Rufton
15	Donna	Smith	227	Sandra	Pincher
10	Richard	Miller	294	Samantha	Smith
15	Donna	Smith	314	Tom	Rascal
05	Susan	Garcia	375	Melanie	Jackson
15	Donna	Smith	435	James	Gonzalez
10	Richard	Miller	492	Elmer	Jackson
05	Susan	Garcia	543	Angie	Hendricks
15	Donna	Smith	616	Sally	Cruz
10	Richard	Miller	721	Leslie	Smith
05	Susan	Garcia	795	Randy	Blacksmith

FIGURE 5-11   Using aliases in a query

Joining a Table to Itself

A second situation for using an alias is to join a table to itself, called a **self-join**, as illustrated in Example 9.

EXAMPLE 9: For each pair of customers located in the same city, display the customer ID, first name, last name, and city.

If you had two separate tables for customers and the query requested customers in the first table having the same city as customers in the second table, you could use a normal join operation to find the answer. In this case, however, there is only *one* table (CUSTOMER) that stores all the customer information. You can treat the CUSTOMER table as if it were two tables in the query by creating an alias, as illustrated in Example 8. In this case, you use the following FROM clause:

```
FROM CUSTOMER F, CUSTOMER S
```

SQL treats this clause as a query of two tables: one that has the alias F (first), and another that has the alias S (second). The fact that both tables are really the same CUSTOMER table is not a problem. The query and its results appear in Figure 5-12.

```
SELECT F.CUST_ID, F.FIRST_NAME, F.LAST_NAME, S.CUST_ID, S.FIRST_NAME,
   S.LAST_NAME, F.CITY
    FROM CUSTOMER F, CUSTOMER S
        WHERE (F.CITY = S.CITY) AND (F.CUST_ID < S.CUST_ID)
        ORDER BY F.CUST_ID, S.CUST_ID;
```

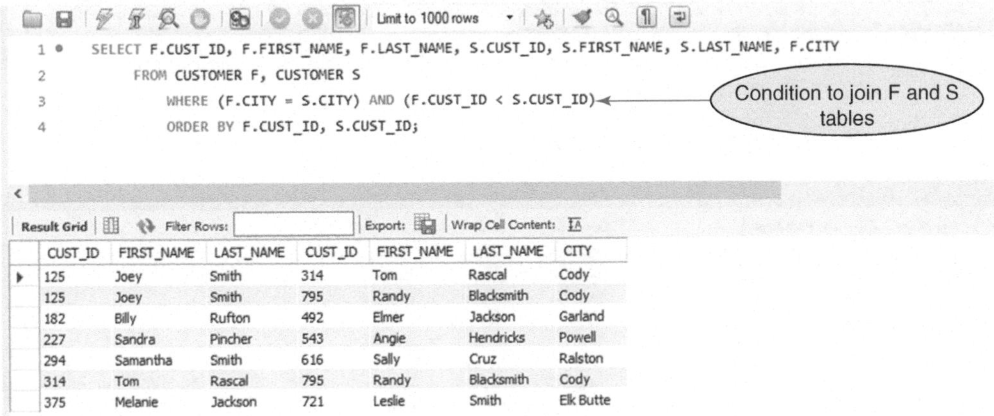

CUST_ID	FIRST_NAME	LAST_NAME	CUST_ID	FIRST_NAME	LAST_NAME	CITY
125	Joey	Smith	314	Tom	Rascal	Cody
125	Joey	Smith	795	Randy	Blacksmith	Cody
182	Billy	Rufton	492	Elmer	Jackson	Garland
227	Sandra	Pincher	543	Angie	Hendricks	Powell
294	Samantha	Smith	616	Sally	Cruz	Ralston
314	Tom	Rascal	795	Randy	Blacksmith	Cody
375	Melanie	Jackson	721	Leslie	Smith	Elk Butte

FIGURE 5-12 Using aliases for a self-join

You are requesting a customer ID, first name, and last name from the F table, followed by a customer ID, first name, and last name from the S table, and then the city. (Because the city in the first table must match the city in the second table, you can select the city from either table.) The WHERE clause contains two conditions: the cities must match, and the customer ID from the first table must be less than the customer ID from the second table. In addition, the ORDER BY clause ensures that the data is sorted by the first customer ID. For those rows with the same first customer ID, the data is further sorted by the second customer ID.

Q & A

Question: Why is the condition F.CUST_ID < S.CUST_ID important in the query?

Answer: If you did not include this condition, you would get the query results shown in Figure 5-13.

The first row is included because it is true that customer ID 125 (Joey Smith) in the F table has the same city as customer ID 125 (Joey Smith) in the S table. The second row indicates that customer ID 125 (Joey Smith) has the same city as customer number 314 (Tom Rascal). The tenth row, however, repeats the same information because customer number 314 (Tom Rascal) has the same city as customer ID 125 (Joey Smith). Of these three rows, the only row that should be included in the query results is the second row. The second row also is the only one of the three rows in which the first customer ID (125) is less than the second customer ID (314). This is why the query requires the condition F.CUST_ID < S.CUST_ID.

```
SELECT F.CUST_ID, F.FIRST_NAME, F.LAST_NAME, S.CUST_ID, S.FIRST_NAME,
   S.LAST_NAME, F.CITY
   FROM CUSTOMER F, CUSTOMER S
      WHERE (F.CITY = S.CITY)
      ORDER BY F.CUST_ID, S.CUST_ID;
```

FIGURE 5-13   Incorrect joining of a table to itself

Using a Self-Join on a Primary Key Column

Figure 5-14 shows some fields from an EMPLOYEE table whose primary key is EMP_ID. Another field in the table is MGR_EMP_ID, which represents the ID of the employee's manager, who also is an employee. If you look at the row for employee 217 (Lynn Thomas), you see that employee 182 (Edgar Davis) is Lynn's manager. By looking at the row for employee 182 (Edgar Davis), you see that his manager is employee 105 (Samantha Baker). In the row for employee 105 (Samantha Baker), the manager number is null, indicating that she has no manager.

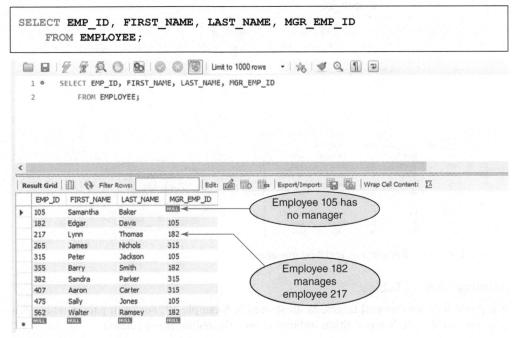

FIGURE 5-14   Employee and manager data

Suppose you need to list the employee ID, employee first name, and employee last name along with the ID, first name, and last name of each employee's manager. Just as in the previous self-join, you would list the EMPLOYEE table twice in the FROM clause with aliases.

The command shown in Figure 5-15 uses the letter E as an alias for the employee and the letter M as an alias for the manager. Thus, E.EMP_ID is the employee's ID and M.EMP_ID is the ID of the employee's manager. In the SQL command, M.EMP_ID is renamed as MGR_ID, M.FIRST_NAME is renamed as MGR_FIRST, and M.LAST_NAME is renamed as MGR_LAST. The condition in the WHERE clause ensures that E.MGR_EMP_ID (the ID of the employee's manager) matches M.EMP_ID (the employee ID on the manager's row in the table). Employee 105 is not included in the results because Samantha Baker has no manager (see Figure 5-14).

```
SELECT E.EMP_ID, E.FIRST_NAME, E.LAST_NAME, M.EMP_ID AS MGR_ID,
       M.FIRST_NAME AS MGR_FIRST, M.LAST_NAME AS MGR_LAST
   FROM EMPLOYEE E, EMPLOYEE M
        WHERE (E.MGR_EMP_ID = M.EMP_ID)
        ORDER BY E.EMP_ID;
```

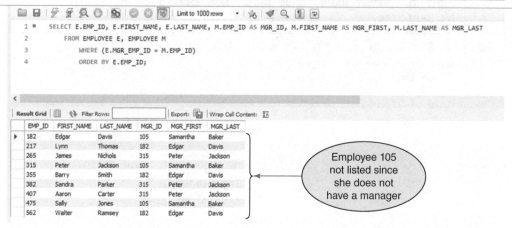

FIGURE 5-15   List of employees and their managers

Joining Several Tables

It is possible to join several tables, as illustrated in Example 10. For each pair of tables you join, you must include a condition indicating how the columns are related.

EXAMPLE 10: For each item on an invoice, list the item ID, quantity ordered, invoice number, invoice date, customer ID, customer first name, and customer last name, along with the last name of the sales rep who represents each customer.

As mentioned earlier, an item is on an invoice when it occurs on any row in the INVOICE_LINE table. The item ID, quantity ordered, and invoice number appear in the INVOICE_LINE table. If these requirements represent the entire query, you would write the query as follows:

```
SELECT ITEM_ID, QUANTITY, INVOICE_NUM
   FROM INVOICE_LINE;
```

This query is not sufficient, however. You also need the invoice date, which is in the INVOICES table; the customer ID, first name, and last name, which are in the CUSTOMER table; and the last name of the sales rep, which is in the SALES_REP table. Thus, you need to join *four* tables: INVOICE_LINE, INVOICES, CUSTOMER, and SALES_REP. The procedure for joining more than two tables is essentially the same as the one for joining two tables. The difference is that the condition in the WHERE clause becomes a compound condition. In this case, you write the WHERE clause as follows:

```
WHERE (INVOICES.INVOICE_NUM = INVOICE_LINE.INVOICE_NUM) AND
      (CUSTOMER.CUST_ID = INVOICES.CUST_ID) AND
      (SALES_REP.REP_ID = CUSTOMER.REP_ID)
```

Note the entire WHERE clause could be typed on one line; however, because a single line in the text-book would not accommodate the entire WHERE clause, it is logically broken up here. Because the condition is very long, this option also promotes readability. Remember you can type a statement in any manner, and the statement ends only with a semicolon. The same is true for the columns in the SELECT clause because they would also not fit on one line in the textbook. The indention is consistent and makes the statement more readable.

The first condition relates an invoice to an invoice line with a matching invoice number. The second condition relates the customer to the invoice with a matching customer ID. The final condition relates the sales rep to a customer with a matching sales rep ID.

For the complete query, you list all the desired columns in the SELECT clause and qualify any columns that appear in more than one table. In the FROM clause, you list the tables that are involved in the query. The query and its results appear in Figure 5-16.

```
SELECT ITEM_ID, QUANTITY, INVOICE_LINE.INVOICE_NUM, INVOICE_DATE,
       CUSTOMER.CUST_ID,CUSTOMER.FIRST_NAME, CUSTOMER.LAST_NAME,
    SALES_REP.LAST_NAME AS SALES_REP_LAST
    FROM INVOICE_LINE, INVOICES, CUSTOMER, SALES_REP
       WHERE (INVOICES.INVOICE_NUM = INVOICE_LINE.INVOICE_NUM) AND
             (CUSTOMER.CUST_ID = INVOICES.CUST_ID) AND
             (SALES_REP.REP_ID = CUSTOMER.REP_ID)
          ORDER BY ITEM_ID, INVOICE_LINE.INVOICE_NUM;
```

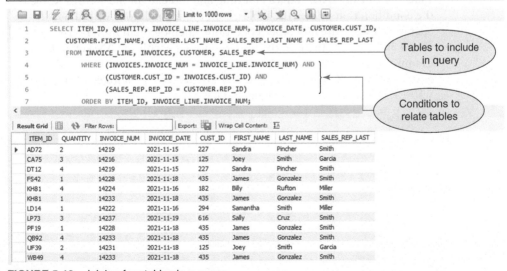

FIGURE 5-16   Joining four tables in a query

Q & A

Question: Why is the ITEM_ID column, which appears in the ITEM and INVOICE_LINE tables, not qualified in the SELECT clause?

Answer: Among the tables listed in the query, only one table contains a column named ITEM_ID, so it is not necessary to qualify the table. If the ITEM table also appeared in the FROM clause, you would need to qualify ITEM_ID to avoid confusion between the ITEM_ID columns in the ITEM and INVOICE_LINE tables.

The query shown in Figure 5-16 is more complex than many of the previous ones you have examined. You might think that SQL is not such an easy language to use after all. If you take it one step at a time, however, the query in Example 10 really is not that difficult. To construct a detailed query in a systematic fashion, do the following:

1. List in the SELECT clause all the columns that you want to display. If the name of a column appears in more than one table, precede the column name with the table name (that is, qualify the column name).

2. List in the FROM clause all the tables involved in the query. Usually you include the tables that contain the columns listed in the SELECT clause. Occasionally, however, there might be a table that does not contain any columns used in the SELECT clause but that does contain columns used in the WHERE clause. In this case, you also must list the table in the FROM clause. For example, if you do not need to list a customer ID or name, but you do need to list the sales rep name, you would not include any columns from the CUSTOMER table in the SELECT clause. The CUSTOMER table still is required, however, because you must include a column from it in the WHERE clause.

3. Take one pair of related tables at a time and indicate in the WHERE clause the condition that relates the tables. Join these conditions with the AND operator. If there are any other conditions, include them in the WHERE clause and connect them to the other conditions with the AND operator. For example, if you want to view items present on invoices placed by only those customers with $500 credit limits, you would add one more condition to the WHERE clause, as shown in Figure 5-17.

```
SELECT ITEM_ID, QUANTITY, INVOICE_LINE.INVOICE_NUM, INVOICE_DATE,
       CUSTOMER.CUST_ID, CUSTOMER.FIRST_NAME, CUSTOMER.LAST_NAME,
       SALES_REP.LAST_NAME AS SALES_REP_LAST
    FROM INVOICE_LINE, INVOICES, CUSTOMER, SALES_REP
       WHERE (INVOICES.INVOICE_NUM = INVOICE_LINE.INVOICE_NUM) AND
             (CUSTOMER.CUST_ID = INVOICES.CUST_ID) AND
             (SALES_REP.REP_ID = CUSTOMER.REP_ID) AND
             (CREDIT_LIMIT = 500)
          ORDER BY ITEM_ID, INVOICE_LINE.INVOICE_NUM;
```

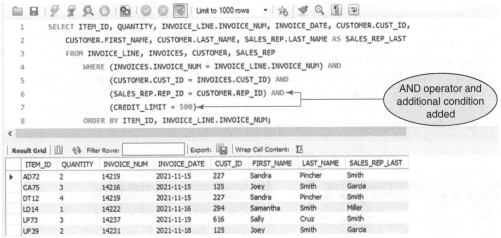

FIGURE 5-17   Restricting the rows when joining four tables

SET OPERATIONS

In SQL, you can use the set operations for taking the union, intersection, and difference of two tables. The **union** of two tables uses the **UNION** operator to create a temporary table containing every row that is in either the first table, the second table, or both tables. The **intersection** of two tables uses the **INTERSECT** operator to create a temporary table containing all rows that are in both tables. The **difference** of two tables uses the **MINUS** operator to create a temporary table containing the set of all rows that are in the first table but that are not in the second table.

For example, suppose that TEMP1 is a table containing the ID and names of each customer represented by sales rep 05. Further, suppose that TEMP2 is a table containing the ID and names of those customers that currently have invoices on file, as shown in Figure 5-18.

TEMP1

CUST_ID	FIRST_NAME	LAST_NAME
125	Joey	Smith
375	Melanie	Jackson
543	Angie	Hendricks
795	Randy	Blacksmith

TEMP2

CUST_ID	FIRST_NAME	LAST_NAME
125	Joey	Smith
182	Billy	Rufton
227	Sandra	Pincher
294	Samantha	Smith
435	James	Gonzalez
616	Sally	Cruz

FIGURE 5-18   Customers of sales rep 05 and customers with active invoices

The union of TEMP1 and TEMP2 (TEMP1 UNION TEMP2) consists of the ID and names of those customers that are represented by sales rep 05 *or* that currently have invoices on file, *or* both. The intersection of these two tables (TEMP1 INTERSECT TEMP2) contains those customers that are represented by sales rep 05 *and* that have invoices on file. The difference of these two tables (TEMP1 MINUS TEMP2) contains those customers that are represented by sales rep 05 but that *do not* have invoices on file. The results of these set operations are shown in Figure 5-19.

TEMP1 UNION TEMP2

CUST_ID	FIRST_NAME	LAST_NAME
125	Joey	Smith
182	Billy	Rufton
227	Sandra	Pincher
294	Samantha	Smith
375	Melanie	Jackson
435	James	Gonzalez
543	Angie	Hendricks
616	Sally	Cruz
795	Randy	Blacksmith

TEMP1 INTERSECT TEMP2

CUST_ID	FIRST_NAME	LAST_NAME
125	Joey	Smith

TEMP1 MINUS TEMP2

CUST_ID	FIRST_NAME	LAST_NAME
375	Melanie	Jackson
543	Angie	Hendricks
795	Randy	Blacksmith

FIGURE 5-19   Union, intersection, and difference of the TEMP1 and TEMP2 tables

There is a restriction on set operations. It does not make sense, for example, to talk about the union of the CUSTOMER table and the INVOICES table because these tables do not contain the same columns. What might rows in this union look like? The two tables in the union *must* have the same structure for a union to be appropriate; the formal term is *union compatible.* Two tables are **union compatible** when they have the same number of columns and their corresponding columns have identical data types and lengths.

Note that the definition of union compatible does not state that the columns of the two tables must be identical but rather that the columns must be of the same type. Thus, if one column is CHAR(20), the matching column also must be CHAR(20).

EXAMPLE 11: List the ID and names of each customer that is either represented by sales rep 10 or currently has invoices on file, or both.

You can create a temporary table containing the ID, first name, and last name of each customer that is represented by sales rep 10 by selecting the customer ID values and names from the CUSTOMER table for which the sales rep number is 10. Then you can create another temporary table containing the ID, first name, and last name of each customer that currently has invoices on file by joining the CUSTOMER and INVOICES tables. The two temporary tables created by this process have the same structure; that is, they both contain the CUST_ID, FIRST_NAME, and LAST_NAME columns. Because the temporary tables are union compatible, it is possible to take the union of these two tables. The query and its results appear in Figure 5-20.

```
SELECT CUST_ID, FIRST_NAME, LAST_NAME
    FROM CUSTOMER
        WHERE (REP_ID = '10')
UNION
SELECT CUSTOMER.CUST_ID, CUSTOMER.FIRST_NAME, CUSTOMER.LAST_NAME
    FROM CUSTOMER, INVOICES
        WHERE (CUSTOMER.CUST_ID = INVOICES.CUST_ID);
```

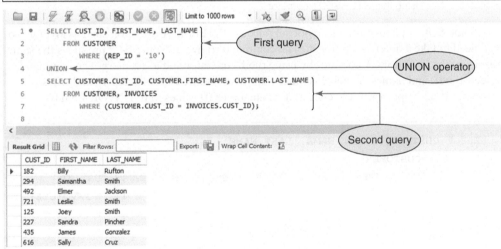

FIGURE 5-20   Using the UNION operator

Note the results of the query are not in order by CUST_ID as they were pictured in Figures 5-18 and 5-19. If you want your results in a particular order, you may use the ORDER BY clause. You would remove the semicolon from the second WHERE clause and add the following at the end of your statement:

```
ORDER BY CUST_ID;
```

If your SQL implementation truly supports the union operation, it removes any duplicate rows automatically. For example, any customer that is represented by sales rep 10 *and* that currently has invoices on file (such as customers 182 and 294 in this case) appears only once in the results. Oracle, Access, and SQL Server support the union operation and correctly remove duplicates.

EXAMPLE 12: List the ID and names of each customer that is represented by sales rep 10 and that currently has invoices on file.

The only difference between this query and the one in Example 11 is that the appropriate operator to use is INTERSECT, as shown in Figure 5-21. Note that MySQL does not support the INTERSECT operator, so there is no screen shot with the figure. If your version of SQL does support the INTERSECT operator, the statement would be as follows:

```
SELECT CUST_ID, FIRST_NAME, LAST_NAME
    FROM CUSTOMER
        WHERE (REP_ID = '10')                INTERSECT operator
INTERSECT
SELECT CUSTOMER.CUST_ID, CUSTOMER.FIRST_NAME, CUSTOMER.LAST_NAME
    FROM CUSTOMER, INVOICES
        WHERE (CUSTOMER.CUST_ID = INVOICES.CUST_ID);
```

FIGURE 5-21   Using the INTERSECT operator

Some SQL implementations do not support the INTERSECT operator, such as MySQL, so you need to take a different approach. The command shown in Figure 5-22 produces the same results as the INTERSECT operator by using the IN operator and a subquery. The command selects the ID and names of each customer that is represented by sales rep 10 and whose customer ID also appears in the collection of customer ID values in the INVOICES table.

```
SELECT CUST_ID, FIRST_NAME, LAST_NAME
    FROM CUSTOMER
        WHERE (REP_ID = '10') AND (CUST_ID IN (SELECT CUST_ID
                                                  FROM INVOICES));
```

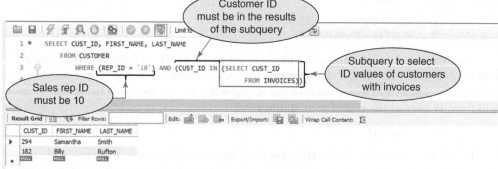

FIGURE 5-22   Performing an intersection without using the INTERSECT operator

HELPFUL HINT

Oracle and SQL Server support the INTERSECT operator.

HELPFUL HINT

Note that the parentheses are formatted differently for the subquery than those previously used in this module (for example, see Figure 5-6). Remember that your formatting is a matter of preference to support readability on your part. This example was used on purpose to draw attention to the difference.

EXAMPLE 13: List the ID and names of each customer that is represented by sales rep 10 but that does not have invoices currently on file.

The query uses the MINUS operator, as shown in Figure 5-23. Note that MySQL does not support the MINUS operator, so there is no screen shot with the figure. If your version of SQL does support the MINUS operator, the statement would be as follows:

```
SELECT CUST_ID, FIRST_NAME, LAST_NAME
    FROM CUSTOMER
        WHERE (REP_ID = '10')
MINUS
SELECT CUSTOMER.CUST_ID, CUSTOMER.FIRST_NAME, CUSTOMER.LAST_NAME
    FROM CUSTOMER, INVOICES
        WHERE (CUSTOMER.CUST_ID = INVOICES.CUST_ID);
```

MINUS operator

FIGURE 5-23 Using the MINUS operator

Just as with the INTERSECT operator, some SQL implementations do not support the MINUS operator. In such cases, you need to take a different approach, such as the one shown in Figure 5-24. This command produces the same results by selecting the ID and names of each customer that is represented by sales rep 10 and whose customer ID does *not* appear in the collection of customer ID values in the INVOICES table.

```
SELECT CUST_ID, FIRST_NAME, LAST_NAME
    FROM CUSTOMER
        WHERE (REP_ID = '10') AND (CUST_ID NOT IN (SELECT CUST_ID
                                                    FROM INVOICES));
```

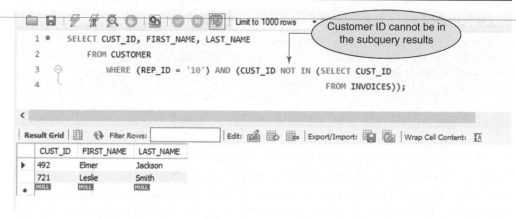

FIGURE 5-24   Performing a difference without using the MINUS operator

● ORACLE USER NOTE

Oracle supports the MINUS operator same as MySQL.

▶ SQL SERVER USER NOTE

Unlike Oracle and MySQL, SQL Server does not support the MINUS operator. SQL Server uses the EXCEPT operator instead of MINUS as in SQL Server Figure 5-1.

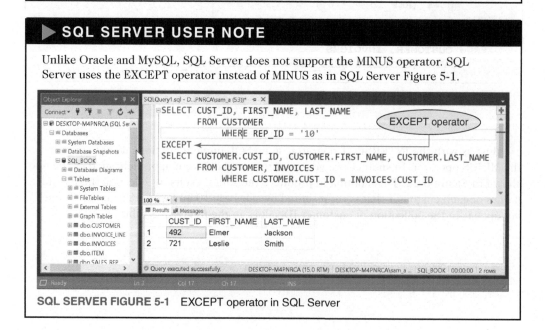

SQL SERVER FIGURE 5-1   EXCEPT operator in SQL Server

ALL AND ANY

You can use the ALL and ANY operators with subqueries to produce a single column of numbers. When you precede the subquery by the **ALL** operator, the condition is true only if it satisfies *all* values produced by the subquery. When you precede the subquery by the **ANY** operator, the condition is true if it satisfies *any* value (one or more) produced by the subquery. The following examples illustrate the use of these operators.

EXAMPLE 14: Find the customer ID, full name, current balance, and sales rep ID of each customer whose balance exceeds the maximum balance of all customers represented by sales rep 10.

You can find the maximum balance of the customers represented by sales rep 10 in a subquery and then find all customers whose balances are greater than this number. There is an alternative method that is simpler, however. You can use the ALL operator, as shown in Figure 5-25.

```
SELECT CUST_ID, FIRST_NAME, LAST_NAME, BALANCE, REP_ID
    FROM CUSTOMER
        WHERE (BALANCE > ALL (SELECT BALANCE
                              FROM CUSTOMER
                              WHERE REP_ID = '10'));
```

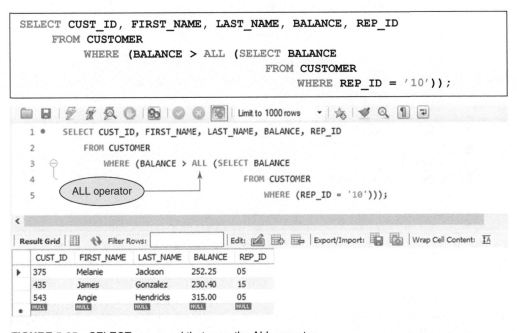

FIGURE 5-25   SELECT command that uses the ALL operator

To some users, the query shown in Figure 5-25 might seem more natural than finding the maximum balance in the subquery. For other users, the opposite might be true. You can use whichever approach you prefer.

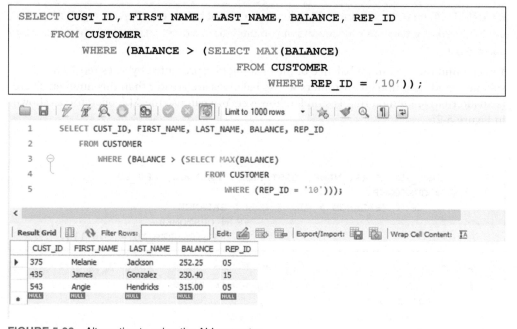

```
SELECT CUST_ID, FIRST_NAME, LAST_NAME, BALANCE, REP_ID
     FROM CUSTOMER
          WHERE (BALANCE > (SELECT MAX(BALANCE)
                            FROM CUSTOMER
                            WHERE REP_ID = '10'));
```

FIGURE 5-26 Alternative to using the ALL operator

EXAMPLE 15: Find the customer ID, full name, current balance, and sales rep ID of each customer whose balance is greater than the balance of at least one customer of sales rep 10.

You can find the minimum balance of the customers represented by sales rep 10 in a sub-query and then find all customers whose balance is greater than this number. To simplify the process, you can use the ANY operator, as shown in Figure 5-27.

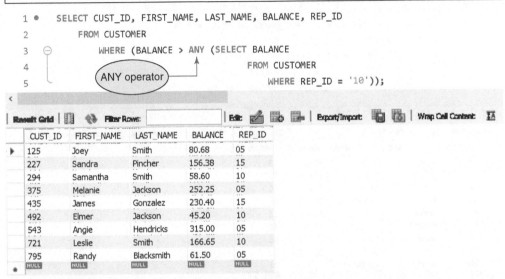

```
SELECT CUST_ID, FIRST_NAME, LAST_NAME, BALANCE, REP_ID
    FROM CUSTOMER
        WHERE (BALANCE > ANY(SELECT BALANCE
                                FROM CUSTOMER
                                    WHERE REP_ID = '10'));
```

FIGURE 5-27   SELECT command that uses the ALL operator

Q & A

Question: How would you get the same results without using the ANY operator?

Answer: You could select each customer whose balance is greater than the minimum balance of any customer of sales rep 10, as shown in Figure 5-28.

```
SELECT CUST_ID, FIRST_NAME, LAST_NAME, BALANCE, REP_ID
    FROM CUSTOMER
        WHERE (BALANCE > (SELECT MIN(BALANCE)
                            FROM CUSTOMER
                                WHERE REP_ID = '10')));
```

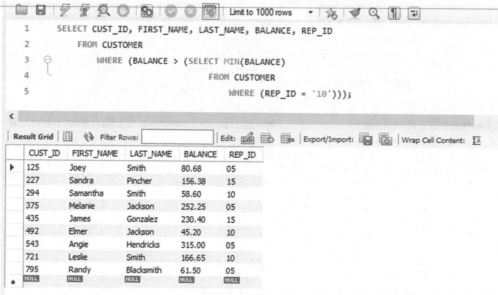

FIGURE 5-28   Alternative to using the ANY operator

SPECIAL OPERATIONS

You can perform special operations within SQL, such as the self-join that you already used. Three other special operations are the inner join, the outer join, and the product.

Inner Join

A join that compares the tables in a FROM clause and lists only those rows that satisfy the condition in the WHERE clause is called an **inner join**. The joins that you have performed so far in this text have been inner joins. Example 16 illustrates the inner join.

EXAMPLE 16: Display the ID, first name, and last name for each customer, along with the invoice number, and invoice date for each invoice. Sort the results by customer ID.

This example requires the same type of join that you have been using. The command is as follows:

```
SELECT CUSTOMER.CUST_ID, FIRST_NAME, LAST_NAME, INVOICE_NUM,
    INVOICE_DATE
```

```
FROM CUSTOMER, INVOICES
     WHERE (CUSTOMER.CUST_ID = INVOICES.CUST_ID)
     ORDER BY CUSTOMER.CUST_ID;
```

The previous approach should work in any SQL implementation. An update to the SQL standard approved in 1992, called SQL-92, provides an alternative way of performing an inner join, as shown in Figure 5-29.

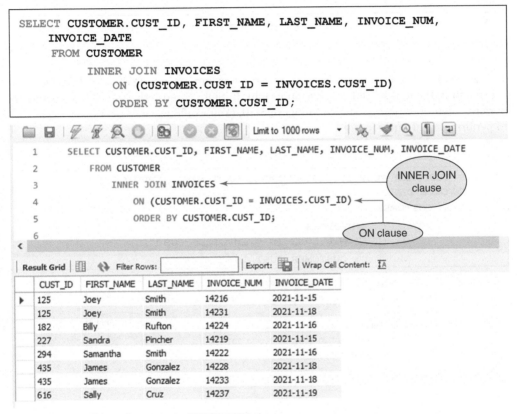

```
SELECT CUSTOMER.CUST_ID, FIRST_NAME, LAST_NAME, INVOICE_NUM,
    INVOICE_DATE
    FROM CUSTOMER
       INNER JOIN INVOICES
           ON (CUSTOMER.CUST_ID = INVOICES.CUST_ID)
           ORDER BY CUSTOMER.CUST_ID;
```

FIGURE 5-29   Query that uses an INNER JOIN clause

In the FROM clause, list the first table, and then include an INNER JOIN clause that includes the name of the second table. Instead of a WHERE clause, use an ON clause containing the same condition that you would have included in the WHERE clause.

Outer Join

Sometimes you need to list all the rows from one of the tables in a join, regardless of whether they match any rows in a second table. For example, you can perform the join of the CUSTOMER and INVOICES tables in the query for Example 16, but display all customers—even the ones without invoices. This type of join is called an **outer join**.

There are actually three types of outer joins. In a **left outer join**, all rows from the table on the left (the table listed first in the query) are included regardless of whether they match rows from the table on the right (the table listed second in the query). Rows from the table on the right are included only when they match. In a **right outer join**, all rows from the table on the right are included regardless of whether they match rows from the table on the left. Rows from the table on the left are included only when they match. In a **full outer join**, all rows from both tables are included regardless of whether they match rows from the other table. (The full outer join is rarely used.)

Example 17 illustrates the use of a left outer join.

EXAMPLE 17: Display the ID, first name, and last name for each customer, along with the invoice number, and invoice date for all invoices. Include all customers in the results. For customers that do not have invoices, omit the invoice number and invoice date.

To include all customers, you must perform an outer join. Assuming the CUSTOMER table is listed first, the join should be a left outer join. In SQL, you use the LEFT JOIN clause to perform a left outer join as shown in Figure 5-30. (You would use a RIGHT JOIN clause to perform a right outer join.)

```
SELECT CUSTOMER.CUST_ID, FIRST_NAME, LAST_NAME, INVOICE_NUM,
    INVOICE_DATE
    FROM CUSTOMER
        LEFT JOIN INVOICES
            ON (CUSTOMER.CUST_ID = INVOICES.CUST_ID)
            ORDER BY CUSTOMER.CUST_ID;
```

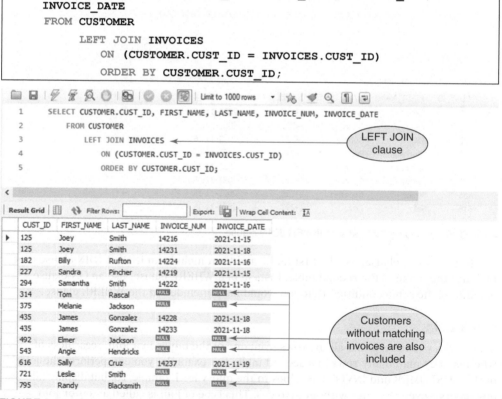

FIGURE 5-30   Query that uses a LEFT JOIN clause

All customers are included in the results. For customers without invoices, the invoice number and date are blank. Technically, these blank values are null.

In Oracle, not MySQL, there is another way to perform left and right outer joins. You write the join as you have been doing, with one exception. You include parentheses and a plus sign in the WHERE clause after the column in the table for which only matching rows are to be included. In this example, the plus sign would follow the CUST_ID column in the INVOICES table because only invoices that match customers are to be included. Because customers that do not have invoices are to be included in the results, there is no plus sign after the CUST_ID column in the CUSTOMER table. The correct query is as follows:

```
SELECT CUSTOMER.CUST_ID, FIRST_NAME, LAST_NAME, INVOICE_NUM,
INVOICE_DATE
        FROM CUSTOMER, INVOICES
                WHERE (CUSTOMER.CUST_ID = INVOICES.CUST_ID (+))
                ORDER BY CUSTOMER.CUST_ID;
```

Running this query produces the same results as shown in Figure 5-30 in Oracle.

Product

The **product** (formally called the **Cartesian product**) of two tables is the combination of all rows in the first table and all rows in the second table.

The product operation is not common. You need to be aware of it, however, because it is easy to create a product inadvertently by omitting the WHERE clause when you are attempting to join tables.

EXAMPLE 18: Form the product of the CUSTOMER and INVOICES tables. Display the customer ID, first name, and last name from the CUSTOMER table, along with the invoice number and invoice date from the INVOICES table.

Forming a product is actually very easy. You simply omit the WHERE clause, as shown in Figure 5-31.

```
SELECT CUSTOMER.CUST_ID, FIRST_NAME, LAST_NAME, INVOICE_NUM,
    INVOICE DATE
      FROM CUSTOMER, INVOICES;
```

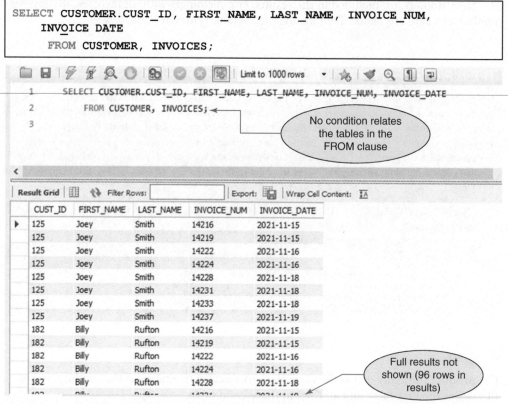

FIGURE 5-31   Query that produces a product of two tables

Q & A

Question: Figure 5-31 does not show all the rows in the result. How many rows are actually included?
Answer: The CUSTOMER table has 12 rows and the INVOICES table has eight rows. Because each of the 12 customer rows is matched with each of the eight invoice rows, there are 96 (12 × 8) rows in the result.

Module Summary

- To join tables, indicate in the SELECT clause all columns to display, list in the FROM clause all tables to join, and then include in the WHERE clause any conditions requiring values in matching columns to be equal.

- When referring to matching columns in different tables, you must qualify the column names to avoid confusion. You qualify column names using the following format: table name.column name.

- Use the IN or EXISTS operators with an appropriate subquery as an alternate way of performing a join.

- A subquery can contain another subquery. The innermost subquery is executed first.

- The name of a table in a FROM clause can be followed by an alias, which is an alternate name for a table. You can use the alias in place of the table name throughout the SQL command. By using two different aliases for the same table in a single SQL command, you can join a table to itself.

- The UNION operator creates a union of two tables (the collection of rows that are in either or both tables). The INTERSECT operator creates the intersection of two tables (the collection of rows that are in both tables). The MINUS operator creates the difference of two tables (the collection of rows that are in the first table but not in the second table). To perform any of these operations, the tables involved must be union compatible. Two tables are union compatible when they have the same number of columns and their corresponding columns have identical data types and lengths.

- When the ALL operator precedes a subquery, the condition is true only if it is satisfied by *all* values produced by the subquery.

- When the ANY operator precedes a subquery, the condition is true if it is satisfied by *any* value (one or more) produced by the subquery.

- In an inner join, only matching rows from both tables are included. You can use the INNER JOIN clause to perform an inner join.

- In a left outer join, all rows from the table on the left (the table listed first in the query) are included regardless of whether they match rows from the table on the right (the table listed second in the query). Rows from the table on the right are included only when they match. You can use the LEFT JOIN clause to perform a left outer join. In a right outer join, all rows from the table on the right are included regardless of whether they match rows from the table on the left. Rows from the table on the left are included only when they match. You can use the RIGHT JOIN clause to perform a right outer join.

- The product (Cartesian product) of two tables is the combination of all rows in the first table and all rows in the second table. To form a product of two tables, include both tables in the FROM clause and omit the WHERE clause.

Key Terms

alias	join
ALL	left outer join
ANY	MINUS
Cartesian product	nested subquery
correlated subquery	outer join
difference	product
EXISTS	right outer join
full outer join	self-join
inner join	union
INTERSECT	UNION
intersection	union compatible

Review Questions

Module Quiz

1. How do you join tables in SQL?

2. When must you qualify names in SQL commands? How do you qualify a column name?

3. List two operators that you can use with subqueries as an alternate way of performing joins.

4. What is a nested subquery? In which order does SQL evaluate nested subqueries?

5. What is an alias? How do you specify an alias in SQL? Why would you use an alias?

6. How do you join a table to itself in SQL?

7. What command would you use to show all rows of two tables? How would you use it? What command would you use to show only common rows between two tables? How would you use it?

8. What does it mean for two tables to be union compatible?

9. How do you use the ALL operator with a subquery?

10. How do you use the ANY operator with a subquery?

11. Which rows are included in an inner join? What clause can you use to perform an inner join in SQL?

12. Which rows are included in a left outer join? What clause can you use to perform a left outer join in SQL?

13. Which rows are included in a right outer join? What clause can you use to perform a right outer join in SQL?

14. What is the formal name for the product of two tables? How do you form a product in SQL?

Critical Thinking

1. Use the Internet to find definitions for the terms equi-join, natural join, and cross join. Write a short report that identifies how these terms relate to the terms join, inner join, and Cartesian product. Be sure to reference your online sources properly.

2. Use the Internet to find information on cost-based query optimizers. Write a short report that explains how cost-based query optimization works and what type(s) of queries benefit the most from cost-based query optimization. Be sure to reference your online sources properly.

Case Exercises

KimTay Pet Supplies

Use SQL and the KimTay Pet Supplies database (see Figure 1-2 in Module 1) to complete the following exercises. If directed to do so by your instructor, use the information provided with the Module 3 Exercises to print your output or save it to a document.

1. For each invoice, list the invoice number and invoice date along with the ID, first name, and last name of the customer for which the invoice was created.

2. For each invoice placed on November 15, 2021, list the invoice number along with the ID, first name, and last name of the customer for which the invoice was created.

3. For each invoice, list the invoice number, invoice date, item ID, quantity ordered, and quoted price for each invoice line that makes up the invoice.

4. Use the IN operator to find the ID, first name, and last name of each customer for which as invoice was created on November 15, 2021.

5. Repeat Exercise 4, but this time use the EXISTS operator in your answer.

6. Find the ID, first name, and last name of each customer for which an invoice was not created on November 15, 2021.

7. For each invoice, list the invoice number, invoice date, item ID, description, and category for each item that makes up the invoice.

8. Repeat Exercise 7, but this time order the rows by category and then by invoice number.

9. Use a subquery to find the sales rep ID, first name, and last name of each sales rep who represents at least one customer with a credit limit of $500. List each sales rep only once in the results.

10. Repeat Exercise 9, but this time do not use a subquery.

11. Find the ID, first name, and last name of each customer that currently has an invoice on file for Wild Bird Food (25 lb).

12. List the item ID, description, and category for each pair of items that are in the same category. (For example, one such pair would be item FS42 and item PF19, because the category for both items is FSH.)

13. List the invoice number and invoice date for each invoice created for the customer James Gonzalez.

14. List the invoice number and invoice date for each invoice that contains an invoice line for a Wild Bird Food (25 lb).

15. List the invoice number and invoice date for each invoice that either was created for James Gonzalez or that contains an invoice line for Wild Bird Food (25 lb).

16. List the invoice number and invoice date for each invoice that was created for James Gonzalez and that contains an invoice line for Wild Bird Food (25 lb).

17. List the invoice number and invoice date for each invoice that was created for James Gonzalez but that does not contain an invoice line for Wild Bird Food (25 lb).

18. List the item ID, description, unit price, and category for each item that has a unit price greater than the unit price of every item in category CAT. Use either the ALL or ANY operator in your query. (*Hint*: Make sure you select the correct operator.)

19. For each item, list the item ID, description, units on hand, invoice number, and quantity ordered. All items should be included in the results. For those items that are currently not on an invoice, the invoice number and quantity ordered should be left blank. Order the results by item ID.

Critical Thinking

1. If you used ALL in Exercise 18, repeat the exercise using ANY. If you used ANY, repeat the exercise using ALL, and then run the new command. What question does the new command answer?

2. For each sales rep, list the ID, first name, and last name for the customer, along with the sales rep first name, and sales rep last name. All reps should be included in the results. Order the results by rep ID. There are two SQL commands for this query that lists the same results. Create and run each SQL command.

StayWell Student Accommodation

Use SQL and the StayWell Student Accommodation database (see Figures 1-4 through 1-9 in Module 1) to complete the following exercises. If directed to do so by your instructor, use the information provided with the Module 3 Exercises to print your output or save it to a document.

1. For every property, list the management office number, address, monthly rent, owner number, owner's first name, and owner's last name.

2. For every completed or open service request, list the property ID, description, and status.

3. For every service request for furniture replacement, list the property ID, management office number, address, estimated hours, spent hours, owner number, and owner's last name.

4. List the first and last names of all owners who own a two-bedroom property. Use the IN operator in your query.

5. Repeat Exercise 4, but this time use the EXISTS operator in your query.

6. List the property IDs of any pair of properties that have the same number of bedrooms. For example, one pair would be property ID 2 and property ID 6, because they both have four bedrooms. The first property ID listed should be the major sort key and the second property ID should be the minor sort key.

7. List the square footage, owner number, owner last name, and owner first name for each property managed by the Columbia City office.

8. Repeat Exercise 7, but this time include only those properties with three bedrooms.

9. List the office number, address, and monthly rent for properties whose owners live in Washington state or own two-bedroom properties.

10. List the office number, address, and monthly rent for properties whose owners live in Washington state and own a two-bedroom property.

11. List the office number, address, and monthly rent for properties whose owners live in Washington state but do not own two-bedroom properties.

12. Find the service ID and property ID for each service request whose estimated hours are greater than the number of estimated hours of at least one service request on which the category number is 5.

13. Find the service ID and property ID for each service request whose estimated hours are greater than the number of estimated hours on every service request on which the category number is 5.

14. List the address, square footage, owner number, service ID, number of estimated hours, and number of spent hours for each service request on which the category number is 4.

15. Repeat Exercise 14, but this time be sure each property is included regardless of whether the property currently has any service requests for category 4.

16. Repeat Exercise 15 using a different SQL command to obtain the same result. What is the difference between the two commands?

UPDATING DATA

OBJECTIVES

- Create a new table from an existing table.
- Change data using the UPDATE command.
- Add new data using the INSERT command.
- Delete data using the DELETE command.
- Use nulls in an UPDATE command.
- Change the structure of an existing table.
- Use the COMMIT and ROLLBACK commands to make permanent data updates or to reverse updates.
- Understand transactions and the role of COMMIT and ROLLBACK in supporting transactions.
- Drop a table.

INTRODUCTION

In this module, you learn how to create a new table from an existing table and make changes to the data in a table. You use the UPDATE command to change data in one or more rows in a table and use the INSERT command to add new rows. You use the DELETE command to delete rows. You learn how to change the structure of a table in a variety of ways and use nulls in update operations. You use the COMMIT command to make changes permanent, use the ROLLBACK command to undo changes, and understand how to use these commands in transactions. Finally, you learn how to delete a table and its data.

CREATING A NEW TABLE FROM AN EXISTING TABLE

You can create a new table using data in an existing table, as illustrated in the following examples.

EXAMPLE 1: Create a new table named LEVEL1_CUSTOMER that contains the following columns from the CUSTOMER table: CUST_ID, FIRST_NAME, LAST_NAME, BALANCE, CREDIT_LIMIT, and REP_ID. The columns in the new LEVEL1_CUSTOMER table should have the same characteristics as the corresponding columns in the CUSTOMER table.

You describe the new table named LEVEL1_CUSTOMER by using the CREATE TABLE command shown in Figure 6-1.

```
CREATE TABLE LEVEL1_CUSTOMER
(
    CUST_ID CHAR(3) PRIMARY KEY,
    FIRST_NAME CHAR(20),
    LAST_NAME CHAR(20),
    BALANCE DECIMAL(7,2),
    CREDIT_LIMIT DECIMAL(7,2),
    REP_ID CHAR(2)
);
```

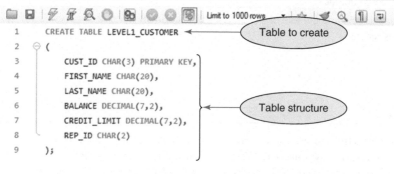

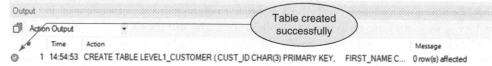

FIGURE 6-1   Creating the LEVEL1_CUSTOMER table

EXAMPLE 2: Insert into the LEVEL1_CUSTOMER table the customer ID, first name, last name, balance, credit limit, and rep ID for customers with credit limits of $500.

You can create a SELECT command to select the desired data from the CUSTOMER table, just as you did in Module 4. By placing this SELECT command in an INSERT command, you can add the query results to a table. The INSERT command appears in Figure 6-2; this command inserts six rows into the LEVEL1_CUSTOMER table. The same query can be used in SQL Server without parentheses around the SELECT statement.

```
INSERT INTO LEVEL1_CUSTOMER
    (SELECT CUST_ID, FIRST_NAME, LAST_NAME, BALANCE, CREDIT_LIMIT,
    REP_ID
        FROM CUSTOMER
            WHERE (CREDIT_LIMIT = 500)
    );
```

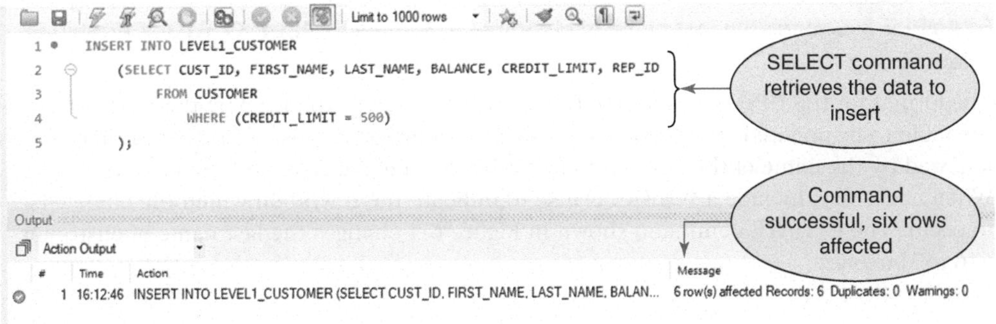

FIGURE 6-2   INSERT command to add data to the LEVEL1_CUSTOMER table

The SELECT command shown in Figure 6-3 displays the data in the LEVEL1_ CUSTOMER table. Notice that the data comes from the new table you just created (LEVEL1_CUSTOMER), and not from the CUSTOMER table.

```
SELECT *
    FROM LEVEL1_CUSTOMER;
```

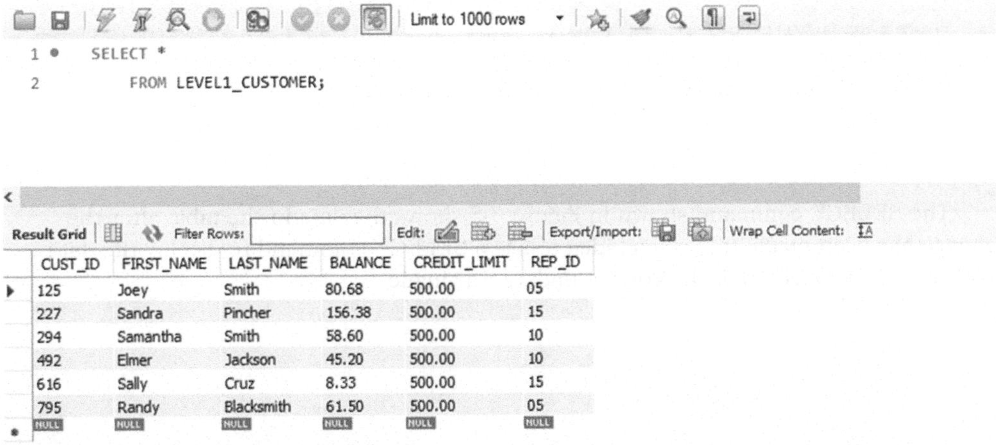

FIGURE 6-3   LEVEL1_CUSTOMER data

CHANGING EXISTING DATA IN A TABLE

The data stored in tables is subject to constant change; prices, addresses, commission amounts, and other data in a database change on a regular basis. To keep data current, you must be able to make these changes to the data in your tables. You can use the **UPDATE** command to change rows for which a specific condition is true.

EXAMPLE 3: Change the last name of customer 616 in the LEVEL1_CUSTOMER table to "Martinez."

The format for the UPDATE command is the word UPDATE, followed by the name of the table to be updated. The next portion of the command consists of the word SET, followed by the name of the column to be updated, an equal sign, and the new value. When necessary, include a WHERE clause to indicate the row(s) on which the change is to occur. The UPDATE command shown in Figure 6-4 changes the last name of customer 616 to Martinez.

```
UPDATE LEVEL1_CUSTOMER
    SET LAST_NAME = 'Martinez'
        WHERE (CUST_ID = '616');
```

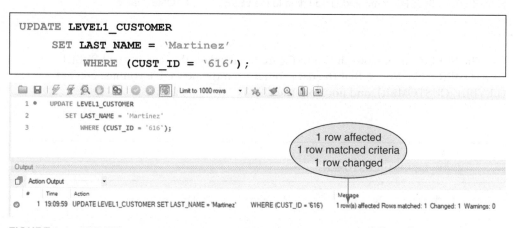

FIGURE 6-4   UPDATE command to change the last name of customer 616

The SELECT command shown in Figure 6-5 shows the data in the table after the change has been made. It is a good idea to use a SELECT command to display the data you changed to verify that the correct update was made.

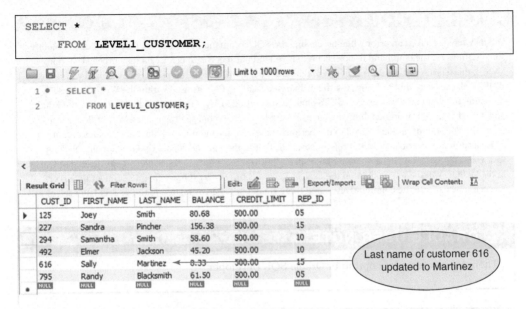

```
SELECT *
    FROM LEVEL1_CUSTOMER;
```

FIGURE 6-5   LEVEL1_CUSTOMER data after update

EXAMPLE 4: For each customer in the LEVEL1_CUSTOMER table that is represented by sales rep 15 and has a balance over $150, increase the customer's credit limit to $550.

The only difference between Examples 3 and 4 is that Example 4 uses a compound condition to identify the row(s) to be changed. The UPDATE command appears in Figure 6-6.

```
UPDATE LEVEL1_CUSTOMER
    SET CREDIT_LIMIT = 550
        WHERE (REP_ID = '15') AND (BALANCE > 150);
```

FIGURE 6-6   Using a compound condition in an update

HELPFUL HINT

You may have received an error when processing the SQL command in Figure 6-6. If so, you need to modify some settings for the command to be executed. If you did not receive an error, you may proceed. Within MySQL there is a setting that prevents an update from occurring unless the primary key is used within the WHERE clause (note that in Figure 6-4 the primary key, CUST_ID, was used within the WHERE clause; therefore, the command was executed). To change this setting in MySQL, you need to first select the Edit option in the MySQL Workbench menu. Once selected, you then choose Preferences. Within Preferences, select the SQL Editor options. Scroll to the bottom of the options and uncheck the Safe Updates options. In a visual summary it would be Edit, Preferences, SQL Editor, then uncheck Safe Updates. Finally, click OK to save your changes. The changes cannot take effect until you reconnect to the server. To do so, choose Query in the MySQL Workbench menu, and then select Reconnect to Server (Query then Reconnect to Server). You can now execute the command again and there should be no error related to the safe update preference.

● ORACLE USER NOTE

There is no safe update option in Oracle SQL Developer.

▶ SQL SERVER USER NOTE

There is no safe update option in SQL Server Management Studio.

The SELECT command shown in Figure 6-7 shows the table after the update.

```
SELECT *
    FROM LEVEL1_CUSTOMER;
```

```
1    SELECT *
2        FROM LEVEL1_CUSTOMER;
```

CUST_ID	FIRST_NAME	LAST_NAME	BALANCE	CREDIT_LIMIT	REP_ID
125	Joey	Smith	80.68	500.00	05
227	Sandra	Pincher	156.38	550.00	15
294	Samantha	Smith	58.60	500.00	10
492	Elmer	Jackson	45.20	500.00	10
616	Sally	Martinez	8.33	500.00	15
795	Randy	Blacksmith	61.50	500.00	05
NULL	NULL	NULL	NULL	NULL	NULL

Credit limit increased for customer ID 227

FIGURE 6-7   Credit limit increased for customer ID 227

You also can use the existing value in a column and a calculation to update a value. For example, when you need to increase the credit limit by 10 percent instead of changing it to a specific value, you can multiply the existing credit limit by 1.10. The following SET clause makes this change:

```
SET CREDIT_LIMIT = CREDIT_LIMIT * 1.10
```

ADDING NEW ROWS TO AN EXISTING TABLE

In Module 3, you used the INSERT command to add the initial rows to the tables in the database. You also can use the INSERT command to add additional rows to tables.

EXAMPLE 5: Add customer ID 837 to the LEVEL1_CUSTOMER table. The first name is Debbie, the last name is Thomas, the balance is zero, the credit limit is $500, and the sales rep ID is 15.

The appropriate INSERT command is shown in Figure 6-8.

```
INSERT INTO LEVEL1_CUSTOMER
    VALUES ('837', 'Debbie', 'Thomas', 0, 500, '15');
```

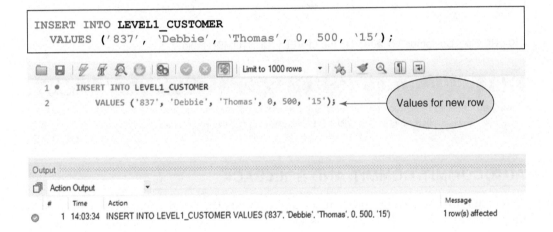

FIGURE 6-8   Inserting a row

The SELECT command in Figure 6-9 shows that the row was successfully added.

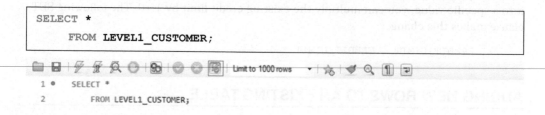

```
SELECT *
     FROM LEVEL1_CUSTOMER;
```

FIGURE 6-9   Customer 837 added to the LEVEL1_CUSTOMER table

HELPFUL HINT

Your output might be sorted in a different order from what is shown in Figure 6-9. If you need to sort the rows in a specific order, use an ORDER BY clause with the desired sort key(s).

AUTOCOMMIT, COMMIT, AND ROLLBACK

Autocommit is the default update mode and commits (makes permanent) each action query (INSERT, UPDATE, DELETE) as soon as the user executes the query. Although the Autocommit mode is fine for most action queries, there are times when the user needs better control over when a transaction is committed. This is particularly important in multi-user database applications when more than one person can update the database and in applications when users are running script files that contain multiple updates. When you need more control over when transactions are committed, you should disable the Autocommit feature by clearing its check box before executing a query. By default, MySQL runs with Autocommit mode enabled. In MySQL, the Auto-Commit Transactions option is located within the Query menu of the MySQL Workbench main menu.

● ORACLE USER NOTE

SQL Developer has an option to set Autocommit by navigating to Tools in the main menu, select Preferences, and expand Databases in the left pane. Then click Advanced and check or uncheck Autocommit as shown in Oracle Figure 6-1.

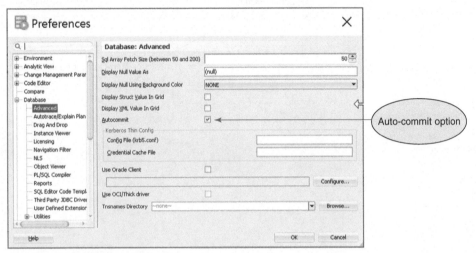

Source: Oracle Corporation

ORACLE FIGURE 6-1   Auto-Commit option in Oracle SQL Developer

▶ SQL SERVER USER NOTE

In Microsoft SQL Server, the Auto-Commit feature is IMPLICIT_TRANSACTION. When the IMPLICIT_TRANSACTION option is set as ON, there is no need to issue START TRANSACTION and COMMIT or ROLLBACK—all transactions (updates, inserts, and deletes) are committed if the statement is executed successfully. In order to set this feature on or off in SQL Server Management Studio, navigate to Tools and select Options. Expand Query Execution in the left pane and click ANSI, then check or uncheck IMPLICIT_TRANSACTION, as shown in SQL Server Figure 6-1.

(continued)

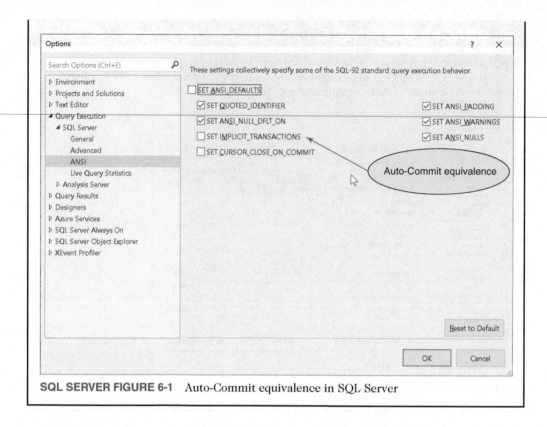

SQL SERVER FIGURE 6-1   Auto-Commit equivalence in SQL Server

If you disable the Autocommit feature, queries that include updates to table data are only temporary and you can reverse (cancel) them at any time during your current work session. Updates become permanent automatically when you exit from the DBMS. If you are not using Autocommit during your current work session, however, you can still **commit** (permanently save your changes) by executing the **COMMIT** command.

If you decide that you do not want to save the changes you have made during your current work session, you can **roll back** (reverse) the changes by executing the **ROLLBACK** command. Any updates made since you ran the most recent COMMIT command are reversed when you run the ROLLBACK command. If you have not run the COMMIT command at all during your session, executing the ROLLBACK command will reverse all updates made during the session. You should note that the ROLLBACK command only reverses changes made to the data; it does not reverse changes made to a table's structure. For example, if you change the length of a character column, you cannot use the ROLLBACK command to return the column length to its original state.

If you determine that an update was made incorrectly, you can use the ROLLBACK command to return the data to its original state. On the other hand, if you have verified that the update you made is correct, you can use the COMMIT command to make the update permanent. You do this by typing COMMIT after running the update. However, you should note that the COMMIT command is permanent; after executing a COMMIT command, running the ROLLBACK command cannot reverse the update.

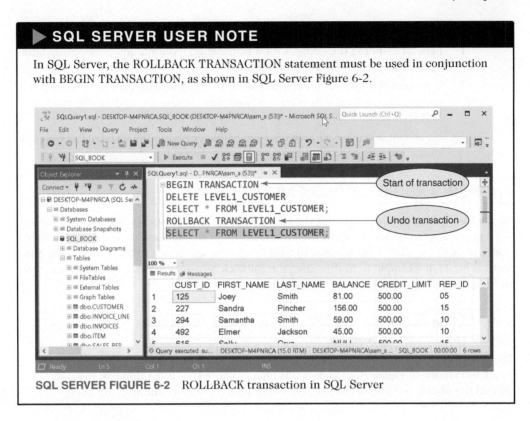

> ▶ **SQL SERVER USER NOTE**
>
> In SQL Server, the ROLLBACK TRANSACTION statement must be used in conjunction with BEGIN TRANSACTION, as shown in SQL Server Figure 6-2.

SQL SERVER FIGURE 6-2 ROLLBACK transaction in SQL Server

TRANSACTIONS

A **transaction** is a logical unit of work. You can think of a transaction as a sequence of steps that accomplish a single task. When discussing transactions, it is essential that the entire sequence be completed successfully.

For example, to enter an invoice, you must add the corresponding invoice to the INVOICES table, and then add each invoice line in the invoice to the INVOICE_LINE table. These multiple steps accomplish the *single* task of entering an invoice. Suppose you have added the invoice and the first invoice line, but you are unable to enter the second invoice line for some reason; perhaps the item on the invoice line does not exist. This problem would leave the invoice in a partially entered state, which is unacceptable. To prevent this problem, you would execute a rollback, thus reversing the insertion of the invoice and the first invoice line.

You can use the COMMIT and ROLLBACK commands to support transactions as follows:

1. Before beginning the updates for a transaction, commit any previous updates by executing the COMMIT command.

2. Complete the updates for the transaction. If any update cannot be completed, execute the ROLLBACK command and discontinue the updates for the current transaction.

3. If you can complete all updates successfully, execute the COMMIT command after completing the final update.

CHANGING AND DELETING EXISTING ROWS

As you learned in Module 3, you use the DELETE command to remove rows from a table. In Example 6, you change data and then use the DELETE command to delete a customer from the LEVEL1_CUSTOMER table. In Example 7, you execute a rollback to reverse the updates made in Example 6. In this case, the rollback returns the row to its previous state and reinstates the deleted record.

EXAMPLE 6: In the LEVEL1_CUSTOMER table, change the last name of customer 294 to "Jones," and then delete customer 795.

The first part of Example 6 requests a change of last name for customer 294; the command shown in Figure 6-10 makes this change. Note that in Example 6, the user cleared the check mark from the Autocommit check box before running the query.

FIGURE 6-10   Using an UPDATE command to change the last name of customer 294

The second part of Example 6 requires deleting customer 795; this command is shown in Figure 6-11. To delete data from the database, use the DELETE command. The format for the **DELETE** command is the word DELETE followed by the name of the table from which the row(s) is to be deleted. Next, use a WHERE clause with a condition to select the row(s) to delete. All rows satisfying the condition are deleted.

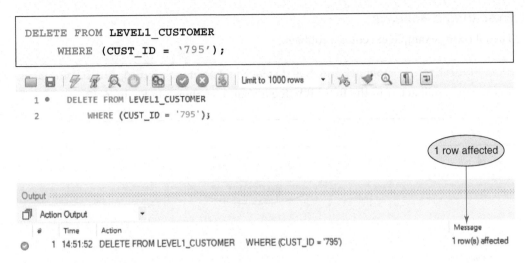

FIGURE 6-11   Using a DELETE command to delete customer 795

The command shown in Figure 6-12 displays the data in the table, verifying the change and the deletion.

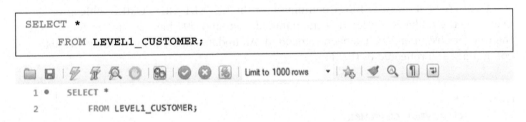

FIGURE 6-12   Results of update and delete commands

Q & A

Question: What happens when you run a DELETE command that does not contain a WHERE clause?
Answer: Without a condition to specify which row(s) to delete, the query deletes all rows from the table.

Executing a Rollback

The following example executes a rollback.

EXAMPLE 7: Execute a rollback and then display the data in the LEVEL1_CUSTOMER table.

To execute a rollback, run the ROLLBACK command, as shown in Figure 6-13.

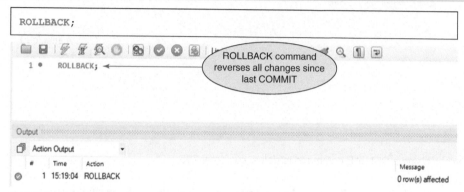

FIGURE 6-13   Executing a rollback

Figure 6-14 shows a SELECT command for the LEVEL1_CUSTOMER table after executing the rollback. Notice that the name of customer 294 has reverted to Smith and the row for customer 795 has been reinstated. All updates made prior to the previous commit are still reflected in the data.

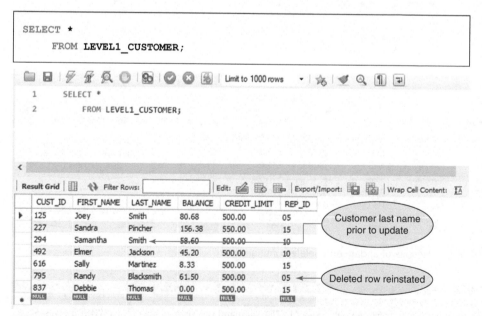

FIGURE 6-14   Data in the LEVEL1_CUSTOMER table after executing a rollback

CHANGING A VALUE IN A COLUMN TO NULL

There are some special issues involved when dealing with nulls. You already have seen how to add a row in which some of the values are null and how to select rows in which a given column is null. You also must be able to change the value in a column in an existing row to null, as shown in Example 8. Remember that to make this type of change, the affected column must accept nulls. If you specified NOT NULL for the column when you created the table, then changing a value in a column to null is prohibited.

EXAMPLE 8: Change the balance of customer 616 in the LEVEL1_CUSTOMER table to null.

The command for changing a value in a column to null is exactly what it would be for changing any other value. You simply use the value NULL as the replacement value, as shown in Figure 6-15. Notice that the value NULL is *not* enclosed in single quotation marks. If it were, the command would change the balance to the word NULL.

```
UPDATE LEVEL1_CUSTOMER
    SET BALANCE = NULL
        WHERE (CUST_ID = '616');
```

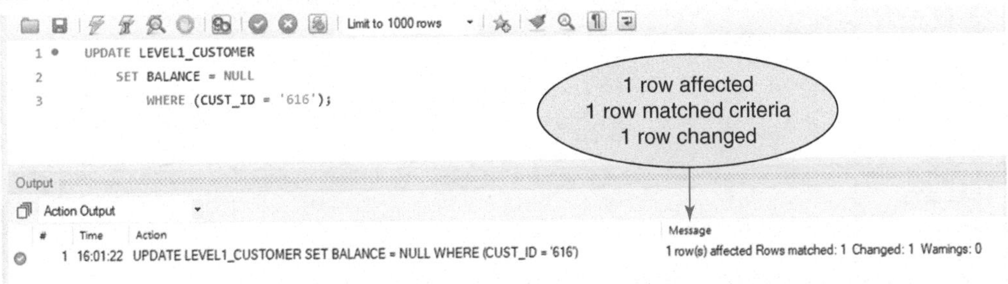

1 row affected
1 row matched criteria
1 row changed

FIGURE 6-15   Changing a value in a column to null

Figure 6-16 shows the data in the LEVEL1_CUSTOMER table after changing the BALANCE column value for customer 616 to null. In MySQL and SQL Server, this is represented as the word NULL inversely highlighted, as shown in Figure 6-16.

```
SELECT *
    FROM LEVEL1_CUSTOMER;
```

| | | | | | Limit to 1000 rows ▾ | | | | | | |

```
1 •   SELECT *
2         FROM LEVEL1_CUSTOMER;
```

Result Grid | | ↔ Filter Rows: [   ] | Edit: 🖉 🖩 🖩 | Export/Import: 🖩 🖩 | Wrap Cell Content: 𝕀̄A

	CUST_ID	FIRST_NAME	LAST_NAME	BALANCE	CREDIT_LIMIT	REP_ID	
▶	125	Joey	Smith	80.68	500.00	05	
	227	Sandra	Pincher	156.38	550.00	15	
	294	Samantha	Smith	58.60	500.00	10	
	492	Elmer	Jackson	45.20	500.00	10	
	616	Sally	Martinez	NULL	500.00	15	← Null value
	795	Randy	Blacksmith	61.50	500.00	05	
	837	Debbie	Thomas	0.00	500.00	15	
•	NULL	NULL	NULL	NULL	NULL	NULL	

FIGURE 6-16   BALANCE column for customer 616 in NULL

● ORACLE USER NOTE

A null value in Oracle is represented as shown in Oracle Figure 6-2.

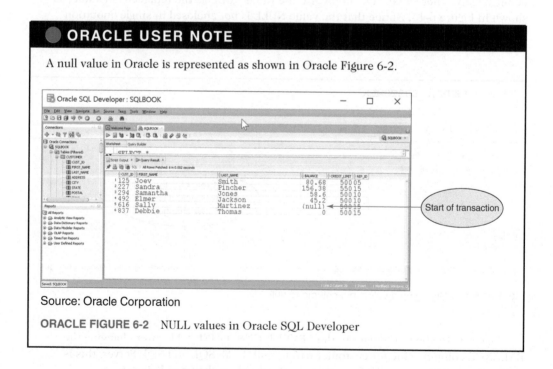

Source: Oracle Corporation

ORACLE FIGURE 6-2   NULL values in Oracle SQL Developer

> ▶ **SQL SERVER USER NOTE**
>
> A null value in SQL Server is represented with the word NULL as in MySQL.

CHANGING A TABLE'S STRUCTURE

One of the most useful features of a relational DBMS is the ease with which you can change table structures. In addition to adding new tables to the database and deleting tables that are no longer required, you can add new columns to a table and change the physical characteristics of existing columns. Next, you see how to accomplish these changes.

You can change a table's structure in SQL by using the **ALTER TABLE** command, as illustrated in the following examples.

EXAMPLE 9: KimTay Pet Supplies decides to maintain a customer type for each customer in the database. These types are R for regular customers, D for distributors, and S for special customers. Add this information in a new column named CUST_TYPE in the LEVEL1_CUSTOMER table.

To add a new column, use the **ADD clause** of the ALTER TABLE command. The format for the ALTER TABLE command is the words ALTER TABLE followed by the name of the table to be altered and an appropriate clause. The ADD clause consists of the word ADD followed by the name of the column to be added, followed by the characteristics of the column. Figure 6-17 shows the appropriate ALTER TABLE command for this example.

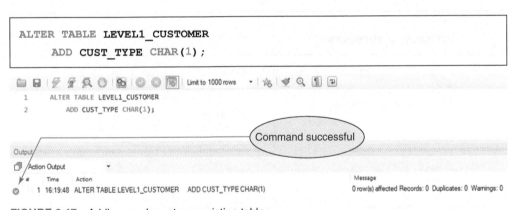

```
ALTER TABLE LEVEL1_CUSTOMER
    ADD CUST_TYPE CHAR(1);
```

FIGURE 6-17   Adding a column to an existing table

The LEVEL1_CUSTOMER table now contains a column named CUST_TYPE, a CHAR column with a length of 1. Any new rows added to the table must include values for the new column. Effective immediately, all existing rows also contain this new column. The data in any existing row will contain the new column the next time the row is updated. Any time a row is selected for any reason, however, the system treats the row as though the column is actually present. Thus, to the user, it seems as though the structure was changed immediately.

For existing rows, you must assign some value to the CUST_TYPE column. The simplest approach (from the point of view of the DBMS, not the user) is to assign the value NULL as a CUST_TYPE for all existing rows. This process requires the CUST_TYPE column to accept null values, and some systems actually insist on this. The default for MySQL, Oracle, and SQL Server is to accept null values.

To change the values in a new column that was added using an ALTER TABLE command, follow the ALTER TABLE command with an UPDATE command like the one shown in Figure 6-18, which sets the CUST_TYPE value for all rows to R.

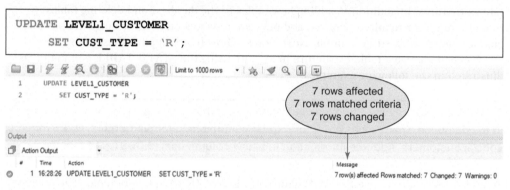

FIGURE 6-18   Making the same update for all rows

The SELECT command shown in Figure 6-19 verifies that the value in the CUST_TYPE column for all rows is R.

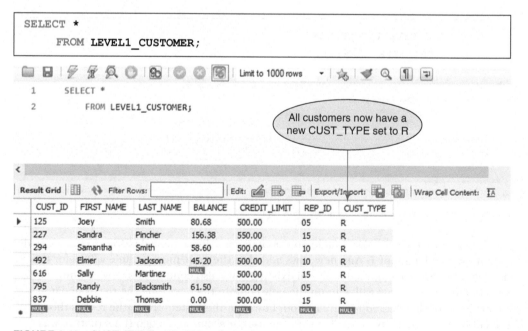

FIGURE 6-19   CUST_TYPE set to R for all rows

EXAMPLE 10: Two customers in the LEVEL1_CUSTOMER table have a type other than R. Change the types for customers 227 and 492 to S and D, respectively.

Example 9 used an UPDATE command to assign type R to every customer. To change individual types to something other than type R, use the UPDATE command. Figure 6-20 shows the UPDATE command to change customer 227 to customer type S.

```
UPDATE LEVEL1_CUSTOMER
    SET CUST_TYPE = 'S'
        WHERE (CUST_ID = '227');
```

```
1   UPDATE LEVEL1_CUSTOMER
2       SET CUST_TYPE = 'S'
3           WHERE (CUST_ID = '227');
```

1 row affected
1 row matched criteria
1 row changed

Output

Action Output

#	Time	Action	Message
1	16:50:16	UPDATE LEVEL1_CUSTOMER SET CUST_TYPE = 'S' WHERE (CUST_ID = '227')	1 row(s) affected Rows matched: 1 Changed: 1 Warnings: 0

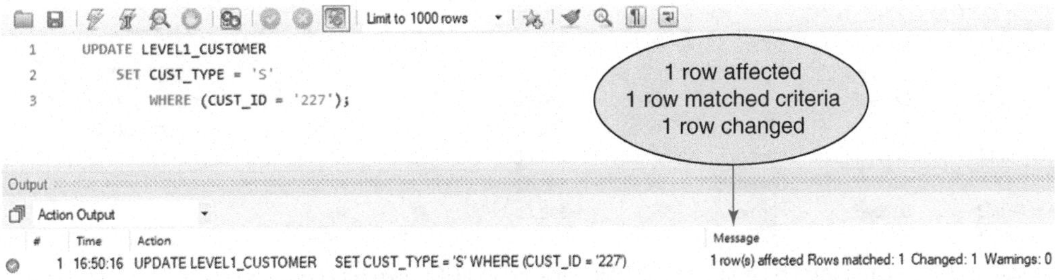

FIGURE 6-20   Updating customer 227 to customer type S

Figure 6-21 shows the UPDATE command to change customer 492 to customer type D.

```
UPDATE LEVEL1_CUSTOMER
    SET CUST_TYPE = 'D'
        WHERE (CUST_ID = '492');
```

```
1   UPDATE LEVEL1_CUSTOMER
2       SET CUST_TYPE = 'D'
3           WHERE (CUST_ID = '492');
```

1 row affected
1 row matched criteria
1 row changed

Output

Action Output

#	Time	Action	Message
1	16:54:21	UPDATE LEVEL1_CUSTOMER SET CUST_TYPE = 'D' WHERE (CUST_ID = '492')	1 row(s) affected Rows matched: 1 Changed: 1 Warnings: 0

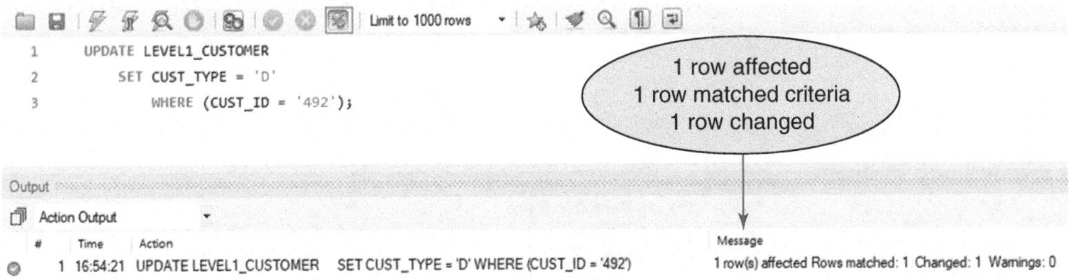

FIGURE 6-21   Updating customer 492 to customer type D

The SELECT command shown in Figure 6-22 shows the results of these UPDATE commands. The customer type for customer 227 is S and the type for customer 492 is D. The type for all other customers is R.

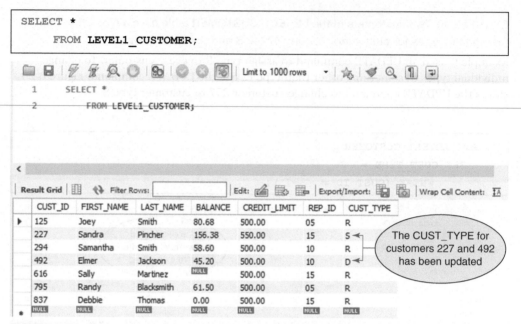

FIGURE 6-22   Customer types in the LEVEL1_CUSTOMER table after updates

Figure 6-23 uses the DESCRIBE command to display the structure of the LEVEL1_CUSTOMER table, which now includes the CUST_TYPE column.

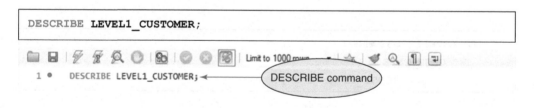

FIGURE 6-23   Structure of the LEVEL1_CUSTOMER table

EXAMPLE 11: The length of the LAST_NAME column in the LEVEL1_CUSTOMER table is too short. Increase its length to 30 characters. In addition, change the CREDIT_LIMIT column so it cannot accept nulls.

You can change the characteristics of existing columns by using the **MODIFY clause** of the ALTER TABLE command. Figure 6-24 shows the ALTER TABLE command that changes the length of the LAST_NAME column from 20 to 30 characters.

```
ALTER TABLE LEVEL1_CUSTOMER
    MODIFY LAST_NAME CHAR(30);
```

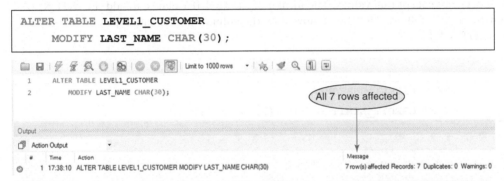

FIGURE 6-24   Changing the length of the LAST_NAME column in the LEVEL1_CUSTOMER table

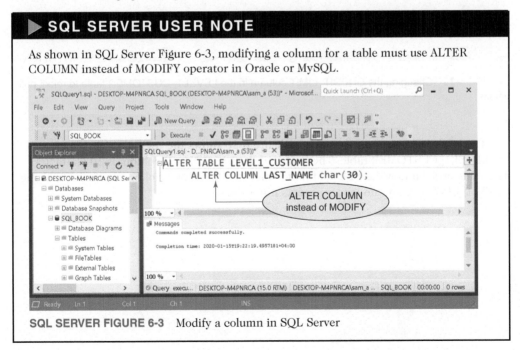

SQL SERVER FIGURE 6-3   Modify a column in SQL Server

HELPFUL HINT

You also can decrease the length of columns, but you might lose some data currently in the column. For example, if you decrease the length of the LAST_NAME column from 20 to 10 characters, only the first 10 characters of the current customer last names will be included. Any characters from position 11 on will be lost. Thus, you should only decrease column lengths when you are positive that you will not lose any data stored in the column.

You can change the length of DECIMAL columns in the same manner that you change the length of CHAR columns.

Figure 6-25 shows the ALTER TABLE command to change the CREDIT_LIMIT column so it does not accept null values. The format of the MODIFY clause to add the NOT NULL constraint is as follows: MODIFY, followed by the column name, data type of the column, and NOT NULL.

```
ALTER TABLE LEVEL1_CUSTOMER
     MODIFY CREDIT_LIMIT DECIMAL(7,2) NOT NULL;
```

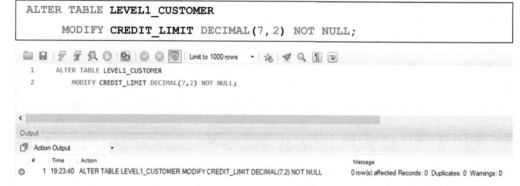

FIGURE 6-25 Changing the CREDIT_LIMIT column in the LEVEL1_CUSTOMER table to reject null values

The DESCRIBE command shown in Figure 6-26 shows the revised structure of the LEVEL1_CUSTOMER table. The length of the LAST_NAME column is 30 characters. The value of NO under the Null column for the CREDIT_LIMIT column indicates that the CREDIT_LIMIT column no longer accepts null values.

```
DESCRIBE LEVEL1_CUSTOMER;
```

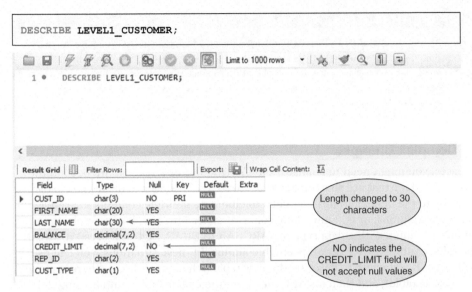

Length changed to 30 characters

NO indicates the CREDIT_LIMIT field will not accept null values

FIGURE 6-26   Revised structure of the LEVEL1_CUSTOMER table

▶ **SQL SERVER USER NOTE**

SQL Server Figure 6-4 shows a column description IS_NULLABLE; YES value indicates that the column can have NULL value and NO that the column requires a value.

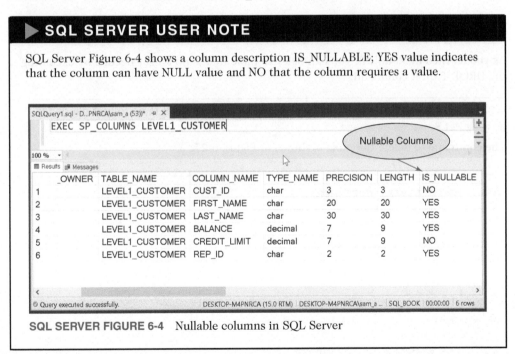

SQL SERVER FIGURE 6-4   Nullable columns in SQL Server

HELPFUL HINT

You also can use the MODIFY clause of the ALTER TABLE command to change a column that currently rejects null values so that it accepts null values by using NULL in place of NOT NULL in the ALTER TABLE command.

Making Complex Changes

In some cases, you might need to change a table's structure in ways that are beyond the capabilities of SQL or that are so complex that it would take longer to make the changes than to re-create the table. Perhaps you need to eliminate multiple columns, rearrange the order of several columns, or combine data from two tables into one. For example, if you try to change a column with a data type of VARCHAR to CHAR, SQL still uses VARCHAR when the table contains other variable-length columns. In these situations, you can use a CREATE TABLE command to describe the new table (which must use a different name than the existing table), and then insert values from the existing table into it using the INSERT command combined with an appropriate SELECT command.

DROPPING A TABLE

As you learned in Module 3, you can delete a table that is no longer needed by executing the DROP TABLE command.

EXAMPLE 12: Delete the LEVEL1_CUSTOMER table because it is no longer needed in the KimTay Pet Supplies database.

The command to delete the table is shown in Figure 6-27.

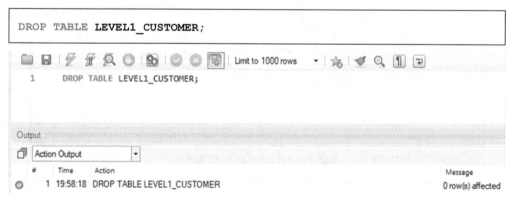

```
DROP TABLE LEVEL1_CUSTOMER;
```

FIGURE 6-27   DROP TABLE command to delete the LEVEL1_CUSTOMER table

When the command shown in Figure 6-27 is executed, the LEVEL1_CUSTOMER table and all its data are permanently removed from the database.

Module Summary

- To create a new table from an existing table, first create the new table by using the CREATE TABLE command. Then use an INSERT command containing a SELECT command to select the desired data to be included from the existing table.

- Use the UPDATE command to change existing data in a table.

- Use the INSERT command to add new rows to a table.

- Use the DELETE command to delete existing rows from a table.

- Use the COMMIT command to make updates permanent; use the ROLLBACK command to reverse any updates that have not been committed.

- To change all values in a column to null, use the SET clause followed by the column name, an equal sign, and the word NULL. To change a specific value in a column to null, use a condition to select the row.

- To add a column to a table, use the ALTER TABLE command with an ADD clause.

- To change the characteristics of a column, use the ALTER TABLE command with a MODIFY clause.

- Use the DROP TABLE command to delete a table and all its data.

Key Terms

ADD clause	MODIFY clause
ALTER TABLE	roll back
Autocommit	ROLLBACK
commit	transaction
COMMIT	UPDATE
DELETE	

Review Questions

Module Quiz

1. Which command creates a new table?
2. Which command and clause adds an individual row to a table?
3. How do you add data from an existing table to another table?
4. Which command changes data in a table?
5. Which command removes rows from a table?
6. Which command makes updates permanent?
7. Which command reverses updates? Which updates are reversed?
8. How do you use the COMMIT and ROLLBACK commands to support transactions?
9. What is the format of the SET clause that changes the value in a column to null in an UPDATE command?

10. Which command and clause adds a column to an existing table?

11. Which command and clause changes the characteristics of an existing column in a table?

12. Which command deletes a table and all its data?

Case Exercises

KimTay Pet Supplies

Use SQL to make the following changes to the KimTay Pet Supplies database (see Figure 1-2 in Module 1). After each change, execute an appropriate query to show that the change was made correctly. If directed to do so by your instructor, use the information provided with the Module 3 Exercises to print your output or to save it to a document.

1. Create a NONCAT table with the structure shown in Figure 6-28.

NONCAT

COLUMN	TYPE	LENGTH	DECIMAL PLACES	NULLS ALLOWED?	DESCRIPTION
ITEM_ID	CHAR	4		No	Item ID (primary key)
DESCRIPTION	CHAR	30			Item description
ON_HAND	DECIMAL	4	0		Number of units on hand
CATEGORY	CHAR	3			Item category
PRICE	DECIMAL	6	2		Unit price

FIGURE 6-28   NONCAT table layout

2. Insert into the NONCAT table the item ID, description, number of units on hand, category, and unit price from the ITEM table for each item that is *not* in category CAT.

3. In the NONCAT table, change the description of item ID DT12 to "Dog Toy Gift Bonanza."

4. In the NONCAT table, increase the price of each item in category BRD by 5 percent. (*Hint*: Multiply each price by 1.05.)

5. Add the following item to the NONCAT table: item ID: FF17; description: Premium Fish Food; number of units on hand: 10; category: FSH; and price: 11.95.

6. Delete every item in the NONCAT table for which the category is HOR.

7. In the NONCAT table, change the category for item UF39 to null.

8. Add a column named ON_HAND_VALUE to the NONCAT table. The on-hand value is a seven-digit number with two decimal places that represents the product of the number of units on hand and the price. Then set all values of ON_HAND_VALUE to ON_HAND * PRICE.

9. In the NONCAT table, increase the length of the DESCRIPTION column to 40 characters.

10. Remove the NONCAT table from the KimTay Pet Supplies database.

Critical Thinking

1. Use the Internet to find the SQL command to delete a column in a table in MySQL. Write the SQL command to delete the ON_HAND_VALUE column from the NONCAT table. Be sure to cite your references.

StayWell Student Accommodation

Use SQL to make the following changes to the StayWell Student Accommodation database (Figures 1-4 through 1-9 in Module 1). After each change, execute an appropriate query to show that the change was made correctly. If directed to do so by your instructor, use the information provided with the Module 3 Exercises to print your output or to save it to a document.

1. Create a LARGE_PROPERTY table with the structure shown in Figure 6-29. (*Hint:* If you have trouble creating the primary key, see Figure 3-36 in Module 3.)

COLUMN	TYPE	LENGTH	DECIMAL PLACES	NULLS ALLOWED?	DESCRIPTION
OFFICE_NUM	DECIMAL	2	0	No	Management office number (primary key)
ADDRESS	CHAR	25		No	Address of property (primary key)
BDRMS	DECIMAL	2	0		Number of bedrooms
FLOORS	DECIMAL	2	0		Number of floors
MONTHLY_RENT	DECIMAL	6	2		Monthly rent
OWNER_NUM	CHAR	5			Number of Property owner

FIGURE 6-29   LARGE_PROPERTY table layout

2. Insert into the LARGE_PROPERTY table the office number, address, bedrooms, baths, monthly rent, and owner number for those properties whose square footage is greater than 1,500 square feet.

3. StayWell has increased the monthly rent of each large property by $150. Update the monthly rents in the LARGE_PROPERTY table accordingly.

4. After increasing the monthly rent of each large property by $150 (Exercise 3), StayWell decides to decrease the monthly rent of any property whose monthly fee is more than $1750 by 1 percent. Update the monthly rents in the LARGE_PROPERTY table accordingly.

5. Insert a row into the LARGE_PROPERTY table for a new property. The office number is 1, the address is 2643 Lugsi Dr, the number of bedrooms is 3, the number of floors is 2, the monthly rent is $775, and the owner number is MA111.

6. Delete all properties in the LARGE_PROPERTY table for which the owner number is BI109.

7. The property in managed by Columbia City with the address 105 North Illinois Rd is in the process of being remodeled and the number of bedrooms is unknown. Change the bedrooms value in the LARGE_PROPERTY table to null.

8. Add to the LARGE_PROPERTY table a new character column named OCCUPIED that is one character in length. (This column indicates whether the property is currently occupied.) Set the value for the OCCUPIED column on all rows to Y.

9. Change the OCCUPIED column in the LARGE_PROPERTY table to N for property ID 9.

10. Change the MONTHLY_RENT column in the LARGE_PROPERTY table to reject nulls.

11. Delete the LARGE_PROPERTY table from the database.

Critical Thinking

1. Use the Internet to research another data type that you can use in Oracle for numeric values that store only whole numbers, and then re-write the SQL command to create the LARGE_PROPERTY table using the other data type. Be sure to cite your references.

MODULE **7**

DATABASE ADMINISTRATION

OBJECTIVES

- Understand, create, and drop views.
- Recognize the benefits of using views.
- Use a view to update data.
- Grant and revoke users' database privileges.
- Understand the purpose, advantages, and disadvantages of using an index.
- Create, use, and drop an index.
- Understand and obtain information from the system catalog.
- Use integrity constraints to control data entry.

INTRODUCTION

There are some special issues involved in managing a database. This process, often called **database administration**, is especially important when more than one person uses the database. In a business organization, a person or an entire group known as the **database administrator** is charged with managing the database.

In Module 6, you learned about one function of the database administrator: changing the structure of a database. In this module, you see how the database administrator can give each user his or her own view of the database. You use the GRANT and REVOKE commands to assign different database privileges to different users. You use indexes to improve database performance. You learn how a DBMS stores information about the database structure in an object called the system catalog and how to access that information. Finally, you learn how to specify integrity constraints that establish rules for the data in the database.

CREATING AND USING VIEWS

Most DBMSs support the creation of views. A **view** is a program's or an individual user's picture of the database. The existing, permanent tables in a relational database are called **base tables**. A view is a derived table because the data in it comes from one or more base tables. To the user, a view appears to be an actual table, but it is not. In many cases, a user can examine table data using a view. Because a view usually includes less information than the full database, its use can represent a great simplification. Views also provide a measure of security, because omitting sensitive tables or columns from a view renders them unavailable to anyone accessing the database through the view.

To help you understand the concept of a view, suppose that Martina is interested in the item ID, description, units on hand, and unit price of items in category DOG. She is not interested in any other columns in the ITEM table, nor is she interested in any rows that correspond to items in other categories. Viewing this data would be simpler for Martina if the other rows and columns were not even present. Although you cannot change the structure of the ITEM table and omit some of its rows just for Martina, you can do the next best thing. You can provide her with a view that consists of only the rows and columns that she needs to access.

A view is defined by creating a **defining query**, which indicates the rows and columns to include in the view. The SQL command (or the defining query) to create the view for Martina is illustrated in Example 1.

EXAMPLE 1: Create a view named DOGS that consists of the item ID, description, units on hand, and unit price of each item in category DOG.

To create a view, use the **CREATE VIEW** command, which includes the words CREATE VIEW, followed by the name of the view, the word AS, and then a query. The CREATE VIEW command shown in Figure 7-1 creates a view of the ITEM table that contains only the specified columns.

```
CREATE VIEW DOGS AS
     (SELECT ITEM_ID, DESCRIPTION, ON_HAND, PRICE
          FROM ITEM
               WHERE (CATEGORY = 'DOG')
     );
```

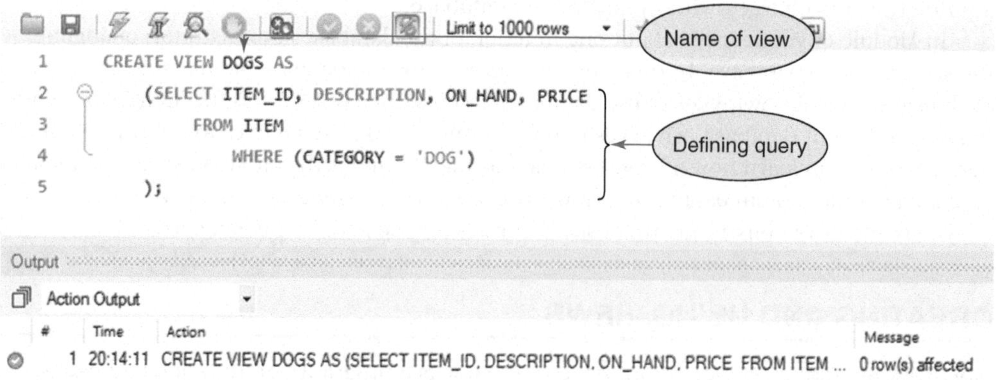

FIGURE 7-1   Creating the DOGS view

Given the current data in the KimTay Pet Supplies database, the DOGS view contains the data shown in Figure 7-2.

DOGS

ITEM_ID	DESCRIPTION	ON_HAND	PRICE
AD72	Dog Feeding Station	12	$79.99
DT12	Dog Toy Gift Set	27	$39.99
LD14	Locking Small Dog Door	14	$49.99
LP73	Large Pet Carrier	23	$59.99
UF39	Underground Fence System	7	$119.99

FIGURE 7-2   Creating the DOGS query

The data does not actually exist in this form, nor will it *ever* exist in this form. It is tempting to think that when Martina uses this view, the query is executed and produces some sort of temporary table, named DOGS, that Martina can access, but this is *not* what actually happens. Instead, the query acts as a sort of *window* into the database, as shown in Figure 7-3. As far as Martina is concerned, the entire database is just the amber shaded portion of the ITEM table. Martina can see any change that affects the amber portion of the ITEM table, but she is unaware of any other changes that are made in the database.

ITEM

ITEM_ID	DESCRIPTION	ON_HAND	CATEGORY	LOCATION	PRICE
AD72	Dog Feeding Station	12	DOG	B	$79.99
BC33	Feathers Bird Cage (12×24×18)	10	BRD	B	$79.99
CA75	Enclosed Cat Litter Station	15	CAT	C	$39.99
DT12	Dog Toy Gift Set	27	DOG	B	$39.99
FM23	Fly Mask with Ears	41	HOR	C	$24.95
FS39	Folding Saddle Stand	12	HOR	C	$39.99
FS42	Aquarium (55 Gallon)	5	FSH	A	$124.99
KH81	Wild Bird Food (25 lb)	24	BRD	C	$19.99
LD14	Locking Small Dog Door	14	DOG	A	$49.99
LP73	Large Pet Carrier	23	DOG	B	$59.99
PF19	Pump & Filter Kit	5	FSH	A	$74.99
QB92	Quilted Stable Blanket	32	HOR	C	$119.99
SP91	Small Pet Carrier	18	CAT	B	$39.99
UF39	Underground Fence System	7	DOG	A	$199.99
WB49	Insulated Water Bucket	34	HOR	C	$79.99

FIGURE 7-3   Martina's view of the ITEM table

When you create a query that involves a view, the DBMS changes the query to one that selects data from the table(s) in the database that created the view. For example, suppose Martina creates the query shown in Figure 7-4.

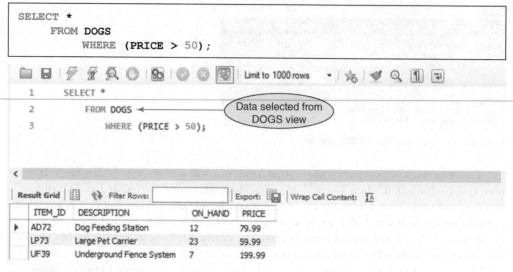

FIGURE 7-4   Using the DOGS view

The DBMS does not execute the query in this form. Instead, it merges the query Martina entered with the query that creates the DOGS view to form the query that is actually executed. When the DBMS merges the query that creates the view with Martina's query to select rows on which the PRICE value is greater than 50, the query that the DBMS actually executes is the following:

```
SELECT ITEM_ID, DESCRIPTION, ON_HAND, PRICE
    FROM ITEM
        WHERE (CATEGORY = 'DOG') AND (PRICE > 50);
```

In the query that the DBMS executes, the FROM clause lists the ITEM table rather than the DOGS view, the SELECT clause lists columns from the ITEM table instead of * to select all columns from the DOGS view, and the WHERE clause contains a compound condition to select only those items in the DOG category (as Marina sees in the DOGS view) and only those items with PRICE values of greater than 50. This new query is the one that the DBMS actually executes.

Martina, however, is unaware that this activity is taking place. To Martina, it seems that she is using a table named DOGS. One advantage of this approach is that because the DOGS view never exists in its own right, any update to the ITEM table is *immediately* available in the DOGS view. If the DOGS view were really a table, this immediate update would not be possible.

You also can assign column names that are different from those in the base table, as illustrated in the next example.

EXAMPLE 2: Create a view named DGS that consists of the item ID, description, units on hand, and unit price of all items in category DOG. In this view, change the names of the ITEM_ID, DESCRIPTION, ON_HAND, and PRICE columns to ID, DESC, OH, and PRCE, respectively.

When renaming columns, you include the new column names in parentheses following the name of the view, as shown in Figure 7-5. In this case, anyone accessing the DGS view will refer to ITEM_ID as ID, to DESCRIPTION as DESC, to ON_HAND as OH, and to PRICE as PRCE.

```
CREATE VIEW DGS (ID, DSC, OH, PRCE) AS
    (SELECT ITEM_ID, DESCRIPTION, ON_HAND, PRICE
        FROM ITEM
            WHERE (CATEGORY = 'DOG')
    );
```

FIGURE 7-5   Renaming columns when creating a view

If you select all columns from the DGS view, the output displays the new column names, as shown in Figure 7-6.

```
SELECT *
    FROM DGS;
```

ID	DSC	OH	PRCE
AD72	Dog Feeding Station	12	79.99
DT12	Dog Toy Gift Set	27	39.99
LD14	Locking Small Dog Door	14	49.99
LP73	Large Pet Carrier	23	59.99
UF39	Underground Fence System	7	199.99

FIGURE 7-6   Data in the DGS view

The DGS view is an example of a **row-and-column subset view** because it consists of a subset of the rows and columns in a base table—in this case, in the ITEM table. Because the defining query can be any valid SQL query, a view also can join two or more tables or involve statistics. The next example illustrates a view that joins two tables.

EXAMPLE 3: Create a view named REP_CUST consisting of the sales rep ID (named RID), sales rep first name (named RFIRST), sales rep last name (named RLAST), customer ID (named CID), customer first name (named CFIRST), and customer last name (named CLAST), for all sales reps and matching customers in the SALES_REP and CUSTOMER tables. Sort the records by rep ID and customer ID.

The command to create this view appears in Figure 7-7.

```
CREATE VIEW REP_CUST (RID, RFIRST, RLAST, CID, CFIRST, CLAST) AS
    (SELECT SALES_REP.REP_ID, SALES_REP.FIRST_NAME,
    SALES_REP.LAST_NAME, CUST_ID, CUSTOMER.FIRST_NAME,
    CUSTOMER.LAST_NAME
        FROM SALES_REP, CUSTOMER
            WHERE (SALES_REP.REP_ID = CUSTOMER.REP_ID)
                ORDER BY SALES_REP.REP_ID, CUST_ID
    );
```

```
1    CREATE VIEW REP_CUST (RID, RFIRST, RLAST, CID, CFIRST, CLAST) AS
2        (SELECT SALES_REP.REP_ID, SALES_REP.FIRST_NAME, SALES_REP.LAST_NAME, CUST_ID, CUSTOMER.FIRST_NAME, CUSTOMER.LAST_NAME
3            FROM SALES_REP, CUSTOMER
4                WHERE (SALES_REP.REP_ID = CUSTOMER.REP_ID)
5                    ORDER BY SALES_REP.REP_ID, CUST_ID
6        );
```

Output

Action Output   ▾

#	Time	Action	Message
⊘ 1	12:36:13	CREATE VIEW REP_CUST (RID, RFIRST, RLAST, CID, CFIRST, CLAST) AS (SELECT SALES_...	0 row(s) affected

FIGURE 7-7   Creating the REP_CUST view

● ORACLE USER NOTE

In Oracle, the ORDER BY clause in the CREATE VIEW statement results in an error; therefore, it must be removed.

► SQL SERVER USER NOTE

In SQL Server, the ORDER BY clause in the CREATE VIEW statement results in an error; therefore, it must be removed.

Given the current data in the KimTay Pet Supplies database, the REP_CUST view contains the data shown in Figure 7-8.

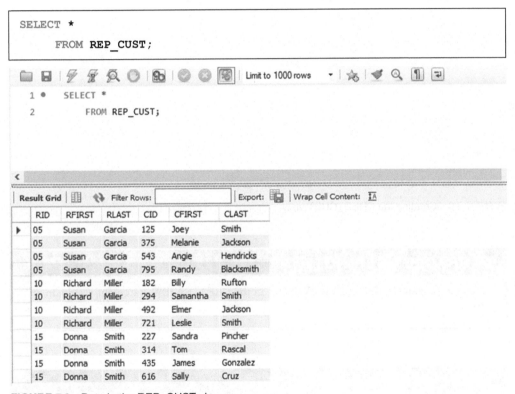

FIGURE 7-8 Data in the REP_CUST view

A view also can involve statistics, as illustrated in Example 4.

EXAMPLE 4: Create a view named CRED_CUST that consists of each credit limit (CREDIT_LIMIT) and the number of customers having this credit limit (NUM_ CUSTOMERS). Sort the credit limits in ascending order.

The command shown in Figure 7-9 creates this view.

```
CREATE VIEW CRED_CUST (CREDIT_LIMIT, NUM_CUSTOMERS) AS
    (SELECT CREDIT_LIMIT, COUNT (*)
        FROM CUSTOMER
            GROUP BY CREDIT_LIMIT
            ORDER BY CREDIT_LIMIT
    );
```

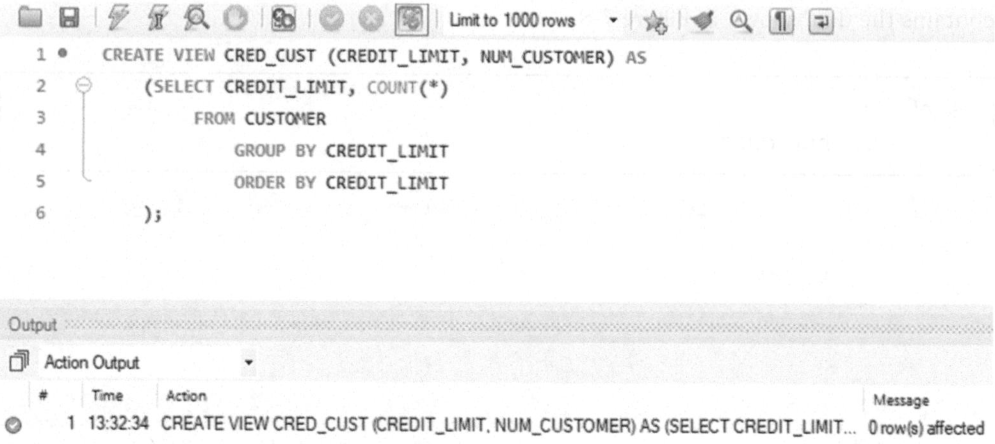

```
1 •    CREATE VIEW CRED_CUST (CREDIT_LIMIT, NUM_CUSTOMER) AS
2 ⊖        (SELECT CREDIT_LIMIT, COUNT(*)
3              FROM CUSTOMER
4                  GROUP BY CREDIT_LIMIT
5                  ORDER BY CREDIT_LIMIT
6          );
```

Output

Action Output ▾

#	Time	Action	Message
⊘ 1	13:32:34	CREATE VIEW CRED_CUST (CREDIT_LIMIT, NUM_CUSTOMER) AS (SELECT CREDIT_LIMIT...	0 row(s) affected

FIGURE 7-9 Creating the CRED_CUST view

● ORACLE USER NOTE

As stated previously, the ORDER BY clause in the CREATE VIEW statement results in an error.

▶ SQL SERVER USER NOTE

As stated previously, the ORDER BY clause in the CREATE VIEW statement results in an error.

The SELECT command shown in Figure 7-10 displays the current data in the KimTay Pet Supplies database for this view.

```
SELECT *
    FROM CRED_CUST;
```

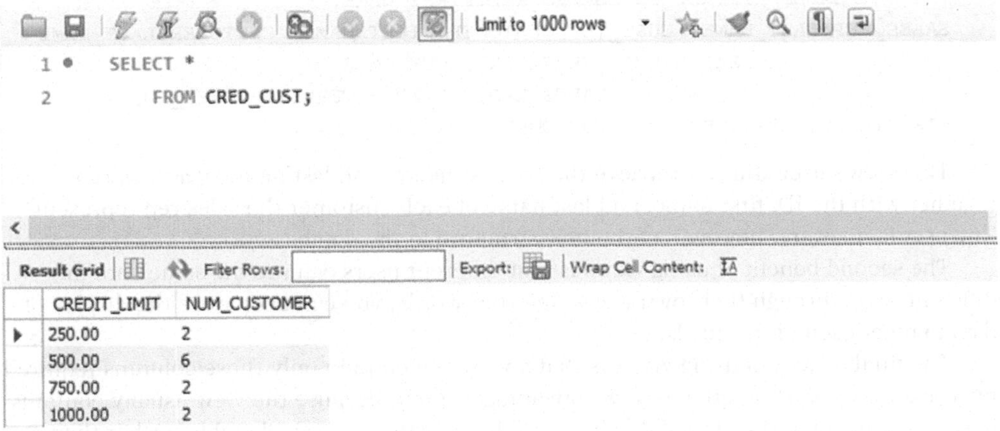

```
1 •   SELECT *
2           FROM CRED_CUST;
```

CREDIT_LIMIT	NUM_CUSTOMER
250.00	2
500.00	6
750.00	2
1000.00	2

FIGURE 7-10 Data in the CRED_CUST view

The use of views provides several benefits. First, views provide data independence. When the database structure changes (by adding columns or changing the way objects are related, for example) in such a way that the view still can be derived from existing data, the user can access and use the same view. If adding extra columns to tables in the database is the only change, and these columns are not required by the view's user, the defining query might not even need to be changed for the user to continue using the view. If table relationships are changed, the defining query might be different, but because users are not aware of the defining query, they are unaware of this difference. Users continue accessing the database through the same view, as though nothing has changed. For example, suppose customers are assigned to territories, each territory is assigned to a single sales rep, a sales rep can have more than one territory, and a customer is represented by the sales rep who covers the customer's assigned territory. To implement these changes, you might choose to restructure the database as follows:

```
SALES_REP(REP_ID, FIRST_NAME, LAST_NAME, ADDRESS, CITY,
    STATE, POSTAL, CELL_PHONE, COMMISSION, RATE)
TERRITORY(TERRITORY_ID, DESCRIPTION, REP_ID)
CUSTOMER(CUST_ID, FIRST_NAME, LAST_NAME, ADDRESS, CITY,
    STATE, POSTAL, EMAIL, BALANCE, CREDIT_LIMIT, TERRITORY_ID)
```

Assuming the REP_CUST view shown in Figure 7-8 is still required, you could change the defining query as follows:

```
CREATE VIEW REP_CUST (RID, RFIRST, RLAST, CID, CFIRST, CLAST) AS
(SELECT SALES_REP.REP_ID, SALES_REP.FIRST_NAME,
SALES_REP.LAST_NAME, CUST_ID, CUSTOMER.FIRST_NAME, CUSTOMER.LAST_NAME
             FROM SALES_REP, TERRITORY, CUSTOMER
                  WHERE (SALES_REP.REP_ID = TERRITORY.REP_ID) AND
(TERRITORY.TERRITORY_ID = CUSTOMER.TERRITORY_ID) );
```

This view's user still can retrieve the ID, first name, and last name of a sales rep together with the ID, first name, and last name of each customer the sales rep represents. The user is unaware, however, of the new structure in the database.

The second benefit of using views is that different users can see the same data in different ways through their own views. In other words, you can customize the display of data to meet each user's needs.

The final benefit of using views is that a view can contain only those columns required by a given user. This practice has two advantages. First, because the view usually contains fewer columns than the overall database and is conceptually a single table, rather than a collection of tables, a view greatly simplifies the user's perception of the database. Second, views provide a measure of security. Columns that are not included in the view are not accessible to the view's user. For example, omitting the BALANCE column from a view ensures that the view's user cannot access any customer's balance. Likewise, rows that are not included in the view are not accessible. A user of the DOGS view, for example, cannot obtain any information about items in the CAT or FSH categories.

USING A VIEW TO UPDATE DATA

The benefits of using views hold true only when views are used for retrieval purposes. When updating the database, the issues involved in updating data through a view depend on the type of view, as you see next.

Updating Row-and-Column Subset Views

Consider the row-and-column subset view for the DOGS view. There are columns in the underlying base table (ITEM) that are not present in the view. If you attempt to add a row with the data ('DB42', 'Dog Biscuit Basket',15,24.95), the DBMS must determine how to enter the data in those columns from the ITEM table that are not included in the DOGS view (CATEGORY and LOCATION). In this case, it is clear what data to enter in the CATEGORY column—according to the view definition, all rows are category DOG—but it is not clear what data to enter in the LOCATION column. The only possibility would be NULL. Therefore, if every column not included in a view can accept nulls, you can add new rows using the INSERT command. There is another problem, however. Suppose the user attempts to add a row to the DOGS view containing the data ('AD72', 'Dog Bowl Set', 7,49.95). Because item number AD72 already exists in the ITEM table, the system *must* reject this attempt. Because this item is not in category DOG (and therefore is not in the DOGS view), this rejection certainly will seem strange to the user, because there is no such item in the user's view.

On the other hand, updates or deletions cause no particular problem in this view. If the description of item number DT12 changes from Dog Toy Gift Set to Dog Toy Gift Bonanza, this change is made in the ITEM table. If item number DT12 is deleted, this deletion occurs in the ITEM table. One surprising change could take place, however. Suppose that the CATEGORY column is included in the DOGS view and a user changes the category of item number DT12 from DOG to CAT. Because this item would no longer satisfy the criterion for being included in the DOGS view, item number DT12 would disappear from the user's view!

Although there are problems to overcome when updating row-and-column subset views, it seems possible to update the database through the DOGS view. This does not mean that *any* row-and-column subset view is updatable, however. Consider the REP_CRED view shown in Figure 7-11. (The DISTINCT operator is used to omit duplicate rows from the view.)

```
CREATE VIEW REP_CRED AS
    (SELECT DISTINCT CREDIT_LIMIT, REP_ID
        FROM CUSTOMER
            ORDER BY CREDIT_LIMIT, REP_ID
    ) ;
```

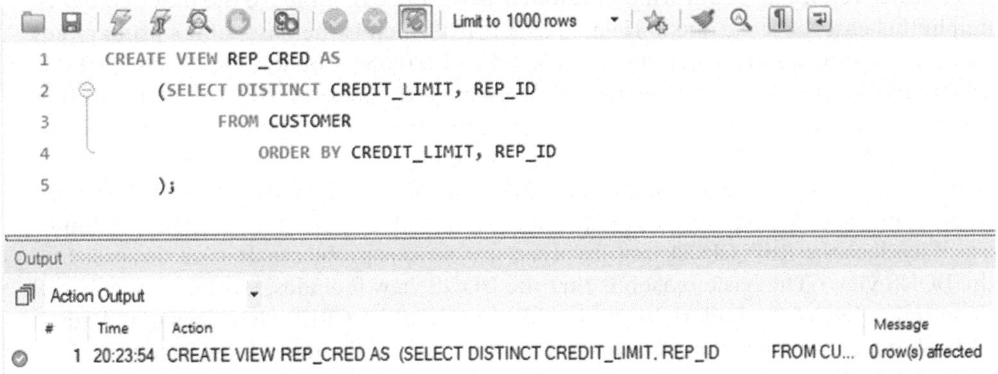

FIGURE 7-11   Creating the REP_CRED view

Figure 7-12 shows the data in the REP_CRED view.

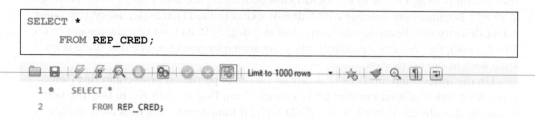

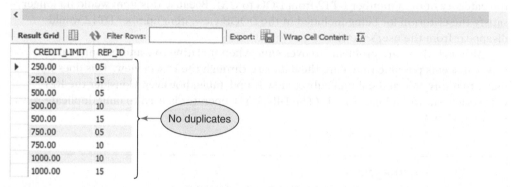

FIGURE 7-12   Data in the REP_CRED view

How would you add the row 1000,'05' to this view? In the underlying base table (CUSTOMER), at least one customer must be added whose credit limit is $1,000 and whose sales rep ID is 05, but which customer is it? You cannot leave the other columns null in this case, because one of them is CUST_ID, which is the base table's primary key. What would it mean to change the row 750,05 to 1000,05? Would it mean changing the credit limit to $1,000 for each customer represented by sales rep ID 05 that currently has a credit limit of $750? Would it mean changing the credit limit of one of these customers and deleting the rest? What would it mean to delete the row 750,05? Would it mean deleting all customers with credit limits of $750 and represented by sales rep ID 05, or would it mean assigning these customers a different sales rep or a different credit limit?

Why does the REP_CRED view involve a few serious problems that are not present in the DOGS view? The basic reason is that the DOGS view includes, as one of its columns, the primary key of the underlying base table, but the REP_CRED view does not. A row-and-column subset view that contains the primary key of the underlying base table is updatable (subject, of course, to some of the concerns already discussed).

Updating Views Involving Joins

In general, views that involve joins of base tables can cause problems when updating data. Consider the relatively simple REP_CUST view, for example, described earlier (see Figures 7-7 and 7-8). The fact that some columns in the underlying base tables are not included in this view presents some of the same problems discussed earlier. Assuming you can overcome these problems by using nulls, there are more serious problems when attempting to update the database through this view. On the surface, changing the row ('05', 'Susan', 'Garcia', '125', 'Joey', 'Smith') to ('05', 'Anna', 'Garcia', '125', 'Joey', 'Smith') might not appear to pose any problems other than some inconsistency in the data. (In the new version of the row, the name of sales rep 05 is Anna Garcia; whereas in the second row in the table, the name of sales rep 05, *the same sales rep*, is Susan Garcia.)

The problem is actually more serious than that—making this change is not possible. The name of a sales rep is stored only once in the underlying REP table. Changing the name of sales rep 15 from Susan Garcia to Anna Garcia in this one row of the view causes the change to be made to the single row for sales rep 15 in the SALES_REP table. Because the view simply displays data from the base tables, for each row on which the sales rep ID is 15, the sales rep name is now Anna Garcia. In other words, it appears that the same change has been made in the other rows. In this case, this change ensures consistency in the data. In general, however, the unexpected changes caused by an update are not desirable.

Before concluding the topic of views that involve joins, you should note that all joins do not create the preceding problem. When two base tables have the same primary key and the primary key is used as the join column, updating the database using the view is not a problem. For example, suppose the database contains two tables (REP_DEMO and REP_FIN) instead of one table (SALES_REP). The REP_DEMO table contains the demographic data (names, address, phone, etc.) for the sales rep, while the REP_FIN table contains the financial data (commission and rate) for the sales rep. Figure 7-13 shows the data in the REP_DEMO table.

```
SELECT *
    FROM REP_DEMO;
```

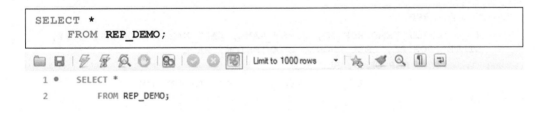

REP_ID	FIRST_NAME	LAST_NAME	ADDRESS	CITY	STATE	POSTAL	CELL_PHONE
05	Susan	Garcia	42 Mountain Ln	Cody	WY	82414	307-824-1245
10	Richard	Miller	87 Pikes Dr	Ralston	WY	82440	307-406-4321
15	Donna	Smith	312 Oak Rd	Powell	WY	82440	307-982-8401
20	Daniel	Jackson	19 Lookout Dr	Elk Butte	WY	82433	307-833-9481
NULL	NULL	NULL	NULL	NULL	NULL	NULL	NULL

FIGURE 7-13 Data in the REP_DEMO view

Figure 7-14 shows the data in the REP_FIN table.

```
SELECT *
    FROM REP_FIN;
```

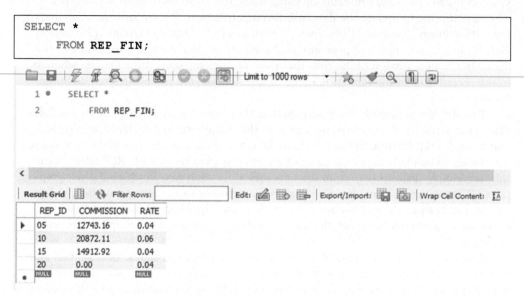

FIGURE 7-14   Data in the REP_FIN view

What was once a single table in the original KimTay Pet Supplies design has been divided into two separate tables. Users who need to see the sales rep data in a single table can use a view named REP that joins these two tables using the REP_ID column. The defining query for the REP view appears in Figure 7-15.

```
CREATE VIEW REP AS
    (SELECT REP_DEMO.REP_ID, FIRST_NAME, LAST_NAME, ADDRESS, CITY,
    STATE, POSTAL, CELL_PHONE, COMMISSION, RATE
        FROM REP_DEMO, REP_FIN
            WHERE (REP_DEMO.REP_ID = REP_FIN.REP_ID)
    );
```

FIGURE 7-15   Creating the REP view

HELPFUL HINT

Notice the name of the view is REP, and not SALES_REP. Because we already have one object in the database named SALES_REP (the table containing the data for each sales rep), we cannot create another object in the database with the same name.

The data in the REP view appears in Figure 7-16.

```
SELECT *
    FROM REP;
```

REP_ID	FIRST_NAME	LAST_NAME	ADDRESS	CITY	STATE	POSTAL	CELL_PHONE	COMMISSION	RATE
05	Susan	Garcia	42 Mountain Ln	Cody	WY	82414	307-824-1245	12743.16	0.04
10	Richard	Miller	87 Pikes Dr	Ralston	WY	82440	307-406-4321	20872.11	0.06
15	Donna	Smith	312 Oak Rd	Powell	WY	82440	307-982-8401	14912.92	0.04
20	Daniel	Jackson	19 Lookout Dr	Elk Butte	WY	82433	307-833-9481	0.00	0.04

FIGURE 7-16   Data in the REP view

It is easy to update the REP view. To add a row, use an INSERT command to add a row to each underlying base table. To update data in a row, make the change in the appropriate base table. To delete a row from the view, delete the corresponding rows from both underlying base tables.

Q & A

Question: How would you add the row ('03', 'Jack', 'Peterson', '142 Plyer Dr', 'Cody', 'WY', '82414', '307-824-9926',1750.25,0.05) to the REP view?
Answer: Use an INSERT command to add the row ('03', 'Jack', 'Peterson', '142 Plyer Dr', 'Cody', 'WY', '82414', '307-824-9926') to the REP_DEMO table, and then use another INSERT command to add the row ('03', 1750.25,0.05) to the REP_FIN table.

Q & A

Question: How would you change the name of sales rep 10 to Thomas Miller?
Answer: Use an UPDATE command to change the name in the REP_DEMO table.

Q & A

Question: How would you change Thomas's commission rate to 0.07?
Answer: Use an UPDATE command to change the rate in the REP_FIN table.

Updates (additions, changes, or deletions) to the REP view do not cause any problems. The main reason that the REP view is updatable—and that other views involving joins might not be updatable—is that this view is derived from joining two base tables *on the primary key of each table*. In contrast, the REP_CUST view is created by joining two tables by matching the primary key of one table with a column that is *not* the primary key in the other table. When neither of the join columns in a view is a primary key column, users encounter even more severe problems when attempting to make updates.

Updating Views Involving Statistics

A view that involves statistics calculated from one or more base tables is the most troublesome view when attempting to update data. Consider the CRED_CUST view, for example (see Figure 7-10). How would you add the row 600,3 to indicate that there are three customers that have credit limits of $600 each? Likewise, changing the row 250,2 to 250,4 means you are adding two new customers with credit limits of $250 each, for a total of four customers. Clearly these are impossible tasks; you cannot add rows to a view that includes calculations.

DROPPING A VIEW

When a view is no longer needed, you can remove it using the **DROP VIEW** command.

EXAMPLE 5: The DGS view is no longer necessary, so delete it.

The command to delete a view is DROP VIEW, as shown in Figure 7-17.

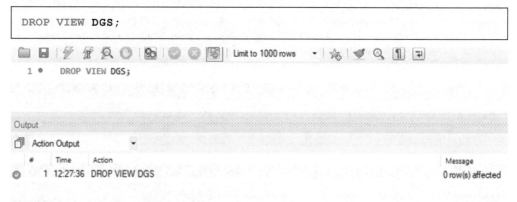

FIGURE 7-17   Dropping a view

SECURITY

Security is the prevention of unauthorized access to a database. Within an organization, the database administrator determines the types of access various users need to the database. Some users might need to retrieve and update anything in the database. Other users might need to retrieve any data from the database but not make any changes to it. Still other users might need to access only a portion of the database. For example, Bailey might need to retrieve and update customer data, but does not need to access data about sales reps, invoices, invoice lines, or items. Victor might need to retrieve item data and nothing else. Samantha might need to retrieve and update data on items in the DOG category but does not need to retrieve data in any other categories.

After the database administrator has determined the access different users of the database need, the DBMS enforces these access rules by whatever security mechanism the DBMS supports. You can use SQL to enforce two security mechanisms. You already have seen that views furnish a certain amount of security; when users are accessing the database through a view, they cannot access any data that is not included in the view. The main mechanism for providing access to a database, however, is the **GRANT** command.

The basic idea of the GRANT command is that the database administrator can grant different types of privileges to users and then revoke them later, if necessary. These privileges include the right to select, insert, update, and delete table data. You can grant and revoke user privileges using the GRANT and REVOKE commands. The following examples illustrate various uses of the GRANT command when the named users already exist in the database.

HELPFUL HINT

Do not execute the commands in this section unless your instructor asks you to do so.

EXAMPLE 6: User Johnson must be able to retrieve data from the SALES_REP table.

The following GRANT command permits a user named Johnson to execute SELECT commands for the REP table:

```
GRANT SELECT ON SALES_REP TO JOHNSON;
```

EXAMPLE 7: Users Smith and Brown must be able to add new items to the ITEM table.

The following GRANT command permits two users named Smith and Brown to execute INSERT commands for the ITEM table. Notice that a comma separates the usernames:

```
GRANT INSERT ON ITEM TO SMITH, BROWN;
```

EXAMPLE 8: User Anderson must be able to change the names and full address of customers.

The following GRANT command permits a user named Anderson to execute UPDATE commands involving the FIRST_NAME, LAST_NAME, ADDRESS, CITY, STATE, and

POSTAL columns in the CUSTOMER table. Notice that the SQL command includes the column names in parentheses before the ON clause:

```
GRANT UPDATE (FIRST_NAME, LAST_NAME, ADDRESS, CITY, STATE, POSTAL) ON
CUSTOMER TO ANDERSON;
```

EXAMPLE 9: User Thompson must be able to delete invoice lines.

The following GRANT command permits a user named Thompson to execute DELETE commands for the INVOICE_LINE table:

```
GRANT DELETE ON INVOICE_LINE TO THOMPSON;
```

EXAMPLE 10: Every user must be able to retrieve item ID values, descriptions, and categories.

The GRANT command to indicate that all users can retrieve data using a SELECT command includes the word PUBLIC, as follows:

```
GRANT SELECT (ITEM_ID, DESCRIPTION, CATEGORY) ON ITEM TO PUBLIC;
```

EXAMPLE 11: User Roberts must be able to create an index on the SALES_REP table.

You learn about indexes and their uses in the next section. The following GRANT command permits a user named Roberts to create an index on the SALES_REP table:

```
GRANT INDEX ON SALES_REP TO ROBERTS;
```

EXAMPLE 12: User Thomas must be able to change the structure of the CUSTOMER table.

The following GRANT command permits a user named Thomas to execute ALTER commands for the CUSTOMER table so he can change the table's structure:

```
GRANT ALTER ON CUSTOMER TO THOMAS;
```

EXAMPLE 13: User Wilson must have all privileges for the SALES_REP table.

The GRANT command to indicate that a user has all privileges includes the ALL privilege, as follows:

```
GRANT ALL ON SALES_REP TO WILSON;
```

The privileges that a database administrator can grant are SELECT to retrieve data, UPDATE to change data, DELETE to delete data, INSERT to add new data, INDEX to create an index, and ALTER to change the table structure. The database administrator usually assigns privileges. Normally, when the database administrator grants a privilege to a user, the user cannot pass that privilege along to other users. When the user needs to be able to pass the privilege to other users, the GRANT command must include the **WITH GRANT OPTION** clause. This clause grants the indicated privilege to the user and permits the user to grant the same privileges (or a subset of them) to other users.

The database administrator uses the **REVOKE** command to revoke privileges from users. The format of the REVOKE command is essentially the same as that of the GRANT command, but with two differences: the word GRANT is replaced by the word REVOKE, and the word TO is replaced by the word FROM. In addition, the clause WITH GRANT OPTION obviously is not meaningful as part of a REVOKE command. Incidentally, the revoke cascades, so if Johnson is granted privileges WITH GRANT OPTION and then Johnson grants these same privileges to Smith, revoking the privileges from Johnson revokes Smith's privileges at the same time. Example 14 illustrates the use of the REVOKE command.

EXAMPLE 14: User Johnson is no longer allowed to retrieve data from the SALES_REP table.

The following REVOKE command revokes the SELECT privilege for the SALES_REP table from the user named Johnson:

```
REVOKE SELECT ON SALES_REP FROM JOHNSON;
```

The database administrator can also apply the GRANT and REVOKE commands to views to restrict access to only certain rows within tables.

INDEXES

When you query a database, you are usually searching for a row (or collection of rows) that satisfies some condition. Examining every row in a table to find the ones you need often takes too much time to be practical, especially in tables with thousands of rows. Fortunately, you can create and use an index to speed up the searching process significantly. An index in SQL is similar to an index in a book. When you want to find a discussion of a given topic in a book, you could scan the entire book from start to finish, looking for references to the topic you need. More than likely, however, you would not have to resort to this technique. If the book has a good index, you could use it to identify the pages on which your topic is discussed.

In a DBMS, the main mechanism for increasing the efficiency with which data is retrieved from the database is the **index**. Conceptually, these indexes are very much like the index in a book. Consider Figure 7-18, for example, which shows the CUSTOMER table for KimTay Pet Supplies together with one extra column named ROW_NUMBER. This extra column gives the location of the row in the table (customer 125 is the first row in the table and is on row 1, customer 182 is on row 2, and so on). The DBMS—not the user—automatically assigns and uses these row numbers, and that is why you do not see them.

CUSTOMER

ROW_NUM	CUST_ID	FIRST_NAME	LAST_NAME	ADDRESS	CITY	STATE	POSTAL	EMAIL	BALANCE	CREDIT_LIMIT	REP_ID
1	125	Joey	Smith	17 Fourth St	Cody	WY	82414	jsmith17@example.com	$80.68	$500.00	05
2	182	Billy	Rufton	21 Simple Cir	Garland	WY	82435	billyruff@example.com	$43.13	$750.00	10
3	227	Sandra	Pincher	53 Verde Ln	Powell	WY	82440	spinch2@example.com	$156.38	$500.00	15
4	294	Samantha	Smith	14 Rock Ln	Ralston	WY	82440	ssmith5@example.com	$58.60	$500.00	10
5	314	Tom	Rascal	1 Rascal Farm Rd	Cody	WY	82414	trascal3@example.com	$17.25	$250.00	15
6	375	Melanie	Jackson	42 Blackwater Way	Elk Butte	WY	82433	mjackson5@example.com	$252.25	$250.00	05
7	435	James	Gonzalez	16 Rockway Rd	Wapiti	WY	82450	jgonzo@example.com	$230.40	$1,000.00	15
8	492	Elmer	Jackson	22 Jackson Farm Rd	Garland	WY	82435	ejackson4@example.com	$45.20	$500.00	10
9	543	Angie	Hendricks	27 Locklear Ln	Powell	WY	82440	ahendricks7@example.com	$315.00	$750.00	05
10	616	Sally	Cruz	199 18th Ave	Ralston	WY	82440	scruz5@example.com	$8.33	$500.00	15
11	721	Leslie	Smith	123 Sheepland Rd	Elk Butte	WY	82433	lsmith12@example.com	$166.65	$1,000.00	10
12	795	Randy	Blacksmith	75 Stream Rd	Cody	WY	82414	rblacksmith6@example.com	$61.50	$500.00	05

FIGURE 7-18   CUSTOMER table with row numbers

To access a customer's row using its customer number, you might create and use an index, as shown in Figure 7-19. The index has two columns: The first column contains a customer number, and the second column contains the number of the row on which the

CUST_ID Index

CUST_ID	ROW_NUMBER
125	1
182	2
227	3
294	4
314	5
375	6
435	7
492	8
543	9
616	10
721	11
795	12

FIGURE 7-19   Index for the CUSTOMER table on the CUST_ID column

customer number is found. To find a customer, look up the customer's number in the first column in the index. The value in the second column indicates which row to retrieve from the CUSTOMER table, then the row for the desired customer is retrieved.

Because customer numbers are unique, there is only a single row number in this index. This is not always the case, however. Suppose you need to access all customers with a specific credit limit or all customers represented by a specific sales rep. You might choose to create and use an index on the CREDIT_LIMIT column and an index on the REP_ID column, as shown in Figure 7-20. In the CREDIT_LIMIT index, the first column contains a credit limit and the second column contains the numbers of *all* rows on which that credit limit appears. The REP_ID index is similar, except that the first column contains a sales rep ID.

CREDIT_LIMIT Index

CREDIT_LIMIT	ROW_NUMBER
$250.00	5, 6
$500.00	1, 3, 4, 8, 10, 12
$750.00	2, 9
$1,000.00	7, 11

REP_ID Index

REP_ID	ROW_NUMBER
05	1, 6, 9, 12
10	2, 4, 8, 11
15	3, 5, 7, 10

FIGURE 7-20   Index for the CUSTOMER table on the CREDIT_LIMIT and REP_ID columns

Q & A

Question: How would you use the index shown in Figure 7-20 to find every customer with a $750 credit limit?

Answer: Look up $750 in the CREDIT_LIMIT index to find a collection of row numbers (2 and 9). Use these row numbers to find the corresponding rows in the CUSTOMER table (Billy Rufton and Angie Hendricks).

Q & A

Question: How would you use the index shown in Figure 7-20 to find every customer represented by sales rep 10?

Answer: Look up 10 in the REP_ID index to find a collection of row numbers (2, 4, 8, and 11). Use these row numbers to find the corresponding rows in the CUSTOMER table (Billy Rufton, Samantha Smith, Elmer Jackson, and Leslie Smith).

The actual structure of an index is more complicated than what is shown in the figures. Fortunately, you do not have to worry about the details of manipulating and using indexes because the DBMS manages them for you—your only job is to determine the columns on which to build the indexes. Typically, you can create and maintain an index for any column or combination of columns in any table. After creating an index, the DBMS uses it to speed up data retrieval.

As you would expect, the use of any index has advantages and disadvantages. An important advantage was already mentioned: An index makes certain types of retrieval more efficient.

There are two disadvantages when using indexes. First, an index occupies storage space. Using this space for an index, however, is technically unnecessary because any retrieval that you can make using an index also can be made without the index; the index just speeds up the retrieval. The second disadvantage is that the DBMS must update the index whenever corresponding data in the database is updated. Without the index, the DBMS would not need to make these updates. The main question that you must ask when considering whether to create a given index is this: Do the benefits derived during retrieval outweigh the additional storage required and the extra processing involved in update operations? In a very large database, you might find that indexes are essential to decrease the time required to retrieve records. In a small database, however, an index might not provide any significant benefits.

You can add and drop indexes as necessary. You can create an index after the database is built; it does not need to be created at the same time as the database. Likewise, when an existing index is no longer necessary, you can drop it.

Creating an Index

Suppose some users at KimTay Pet Supplies need to display customer records ordered by balance. Other users need to access a customer's name using the customer's ID. In addition, some users need to produce a report in which customer records are listed by credit limit in descending order. Within the group of customers having the same credit limit, the customer records must be ordered by last name.

Each of the previous requirements is carried out more efficiently when you create the appropriate index. The command used to create an index is **CREATE INDEX**, as illustrated in Example 15.

EXAMPLE 15: Create an index named BALIND on the BALANCE column in the CUSTOMER table. Create an index named REP_NAME on the combination of the LAST_NAME and FIRST_NAME columns in the SALES_REP table. Create an index named CRED_LASTNAME on the combination of the CREDIT_LIMIT and LAST_NAME columns in the CUSTOMER table, with the credit limits listed in descending order.

The CREATE INDEX command to create the index named BALIND appears in Figure 7-21. The command lists the name of the index and the table name on which the index is to be created. The column on which to create the index—BALANCE—is listed in parentheses.

```
CREATE INDEX BALIND ON CUSTOMER (BALANCE);
```

```
1    CREATE INDEX BALIND ON CUSTOMER(BALANCE);
```

Limit to 1000 rows

Output

Action Output

#	Time	Action	Message
1	19:27:51	CREATE INDEX BALIND ON CUSTOMER(BALANCE)	0 row(s) affected Records: 0 Duplicates: 0 Warnings: 0

FIGURE 7-21   Creating the BALIND index on the BALANCE column

The CREATE INDEX command to create the index named REP_NAME on the combination of the LAST_NAME and FIRST_NAME columns in the SALES_REP table appears in Figure 7-22.

```
CREATE INDEX REP_NAME ON SALES_REP(LAST_NAME, FIRST_NAME);
```

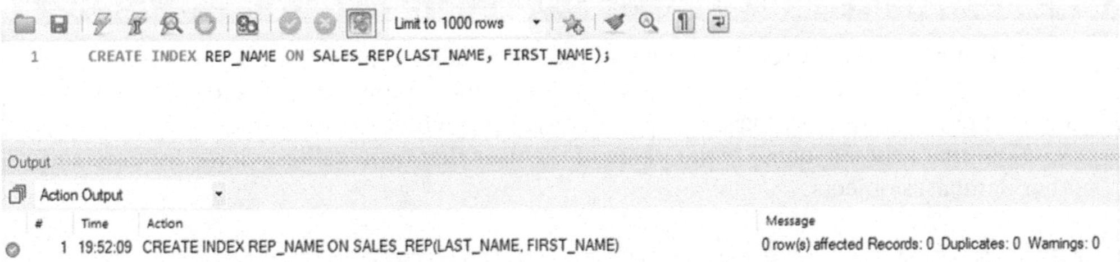

FIGURE 7-22   Creating the REP_NAME index on the LAST_NAME and FIRST_NAME columns

The CREATE INDEX command to create the index named CRED_LASTNAME on the combination of the CREDIT_LIMIT and LAST_NAME columns in the CUSTOMER table appears in Figure 7-23. When you need to index a column in descending order, the column name is followed by the DESC operator.

```
CREATE INDEX CRED_LASTNAME ON CUSTOMER(CREDIT_LIMIT DESC, LAST_NAME);
```

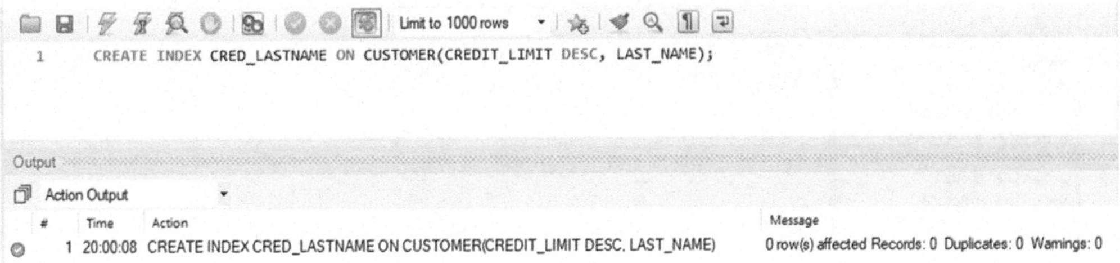

FIGURE 7-23   Creating the CRED_NAME index on the CREDIT_LIMIT and LAST_NAME columns

When customers are listed using the CRED_LASTNAME index, the records appear in descending order by credit limit. Within any credit limit, the customers are listed alphabetically by last name.

Dropping an Index

The command used to drop (delete) an index is **DROP INDEX**, which consists of the words DROP INDEX, followed by the name of the index, the keyword ON, and the table name. To delete the CRED_LASTNAME index on the CUSTOMER table, for example, the command is the following:

```
DROP INDEX CRED_LASTNAME ON CUSTOMER;
```

The DROP INDEX command permanently deletes the index. CRED_LASTNAME was the index the DBMS used when listing customer records in descending order by credit limit and then by customer last name within credit limit. The DBMS still can list customers in this order; however, it cannot do so as efficiently without the index.

● ORACLE USER NOTE

Oracle Figure 7-1 illustrates dropping an index in Oracle. Typically, the syntax to drop an index is DROP INDEX [schema_name.]index_name; in this case, schema_name is not required because the user logged in as the owner of the index is the same.

Note that schema_name is the name of the user that owns tables, views, indexes and other databases objects.

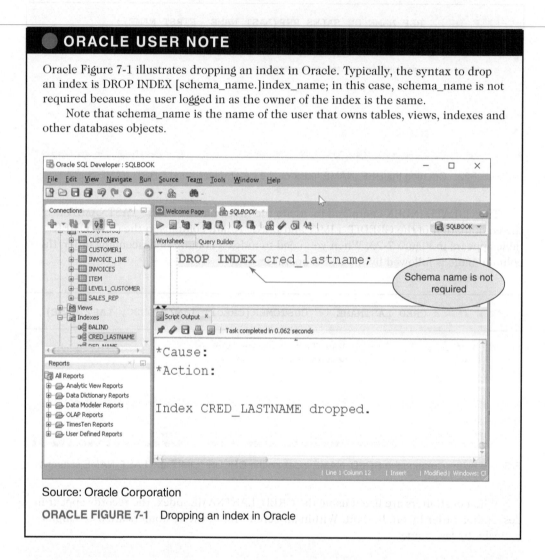

Source: Oracle Corporation

ORACLE FIGURE 7-1   Dropping an index in Oracle

▶ SQL SERVER USER NOTE

In SQL Server, dropping an index follows the same syntax as MySQL.

Creating Unique Indexes

When you specify a table's primary key, the DBMS automatically ensures that the values entered in the primary key column(s) are unique. For example, the DBMS rejects an attempt to add a second customer whose number is 125 in the CUSTOMER table because customer 125 already exists. Thus, you do not need to take any special action to make sure that values in the primary key column are unique; the DBMS does it for you.

Occasionally, a nonprimary key column might store unique values. For example, in the SALES_REP table, the primary key is REP_ID. If the REP table also contains a column for Social Security numbers, the values in this column also must be unique because no two people can have the same Social Security number. Because the Social Security number column is not the table's primary key, however, you need to take special action for the DBMS to ensure that there are no duplicate values in this column.

To ensure the uniqueness of values in a nonprimary key column, you can create a **unique index** by using the **CREATE UNIQUE INDEX** command. To create a unique index named SSN on the SOC_SEC_NUM column in the SALES_REP table, for example, the command is as follows:

```
CREATE UNIQUE INDEX SSN ON SALES_REP (SOC_SEC_NUM);
```

This unique index has all the properties of indexes already discussed, along with one additional property: The DBMS rejects any update that causes a duplicate value in the SOC_SEC_NUM column. In this case, the DBMS rejects the addition of a rep whose Social Security number is the same as that of another rep already in the database.

SYSTEM CATALOG

Information about the tables in the database is kept in the **system catalog (catalog)** or the **data dictionary**. In MySQL, this information is known as the **INFORMATION_SCHEMA**. INFORMATION_SCHEMA provides access to database metadata, information about the MySQL server such as the name of a database or table, the data type of a column, or access privileges. Each version of SQL is unique in the design and naming conventions of the system catalog. This section describes the types of items kept in the catalog and the way in which you can query it to access information about the database structure.

The DBMS automatically maintains the system catalog, which contains several tables. The catalog tables you consider in this basic introduction are **SYSTABLES** (information about the tables known to SQL), **SYSCOLUMNS** (information about the columns within these tables), and **SYSVIEWS** (information about the views that have been created). Individual SQL implementations might use different names for these tables. In MySQL, as mentioned previously, this information is accessed through the INFORMATION_SCHEMA. More specifically, it is accessed through the INFORMATION_ SCHEMA TABLES table, INFORMATION_SCHEMA COLUMNS table, and INFORMATION_ SCHEMA VIEWS table.

The system catalog is a relational database of its own. Consequently, you can use the same types of queries to retrieve information that you can use to retrieve data in a relational database. You can obtain information about the tables in a relational database, the columns they contain, and the views built on them from the system catalog. The following examples illustrate this process.

HELPFUL HINT

Most users need privileges to view system catalog data, so you might not be able to execute these commands.

● ORACLE USER NOTE

Oracle provides extensive views of the catalog which is referred to as the Data Dictionary. USER views provide all created tables, views, indexes and other objects owned by the schema owner. For example, a user named SCOTT can display all objects owned by him using USER_OBJECTS as shown in Oracle Figure 7-2. To display all tables owned by SCOTT, execute SELECT * FROM USER_TABLES. Refer to the Oracle documentation for complete list of USER views and descriptions. Similar to MySQL Oracle offers DBA_TABLES, DBA_TAB_COLUMNS, and DBA_VIEWS containing information about all tables, columns of tables, and views created in the database.

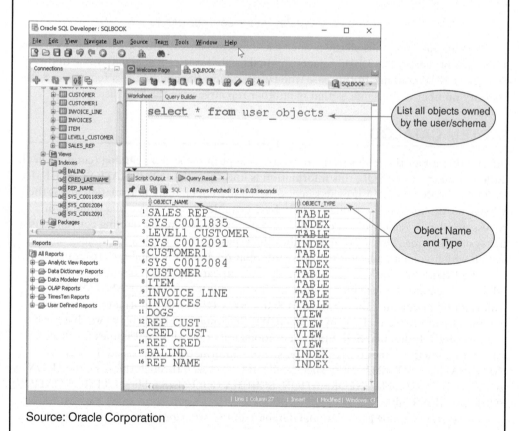

Source: Oracle Corporation

ORACLE FIGURE 7-2   Viewing all objects owned by schema owner in Oracle

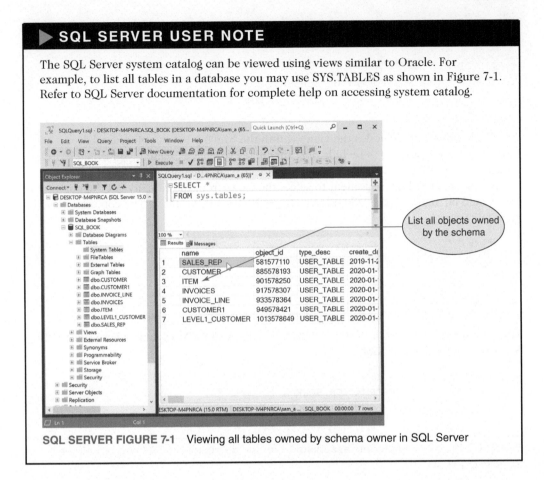

> ## ▶ SQL SERVER USER NOTE
>
> The SQL Server system catalog can be viewed using views similar to Oracle. For example, to list all tables in a database you may use SYS.TABLES as shown in Figure 7-1. Refer to SQL Server documentation for complete help on accessing system catalog.

SQL SERVER FIGURE 7-1   Viewing all tables owned by schema owner in SQL Server

---

EXAMPLE 16: List the tables associated with the database KIMTAY.

The command to list the tables in the system catalog associated with the KIMTAY database is as follows:

```
SELECT *
        FROM INFORMATION_SCHEMA.TABLES
                WHERE (TABLE_SCHEMA = 'KIMTAY');
```

The WHERE clause restricts the tables to only those in the KIMTAY database. In response to this command, MySQL produces a list of all the appropriate tables.

EXAMPLE 17: List the views associated with the database KIMTAY.

If you were able to run the command in the previous example, you noticed that the list of tables not only included tables you have created in the KimTay Pet Supplies database, but also includes the views you have created. This is because internally MySQL includes the views in the INFORMATION_SCHEMA TABLES table. If you want to list only the views, you may further define the query to include only the views by including an additional condition as follows:

```
SELECT *
        FROM INFORMATION_SCHEMA.TABLES
                WHERE (TABLE_SCHEMA = 'KIMTAY') AND (TABLE_TYPE =
'VIEW');
```

The list now only includes the views within the KimTay Pet Supplies database. Conversely, if you wanted to include only the tables you have created, you would search for a TABLE_TYPE of 'BASE TABLE' instead of 'VIEW' in the condition.

An alternate MySQL statement to select the views from the KimTay Pet Supplies database would be to search the INFORMATION_SCHEMA VIEWS table. The command would be as follows:

```
SELECT *
        FROM INFORMATION_SCHEMA.VIEWS
                WHERE (TABLE_SCHEMA = 'KIMTAY');
```

EXAMPLE 18: List the columns associated with the database KIMTAY.

This command selects from INFORMATION_SCHEMA COLUMNS table where the TABLE_SCHEMA, or database, is KIMTAY:

```
SELECT *
        FROM INFORMATION_SCHEMA.COLUMNS
                WHERE (TABLE_SCHEMA = 'KIMTAY');
```

EXAMPLE 19: List the columns associated with the database KIMTAY whose column name is CUST_ID.

In this case, the COLUMN_NAME column is used in the WHERE clause to restrict the rows to those on which the column name is CUST_ID within the KimTay Pet Supplies database. The command is the following:

```
SELECT *
        FROM INFORMATION_SCHEMA.COLUMNS
                WHERE (TABLE_SCHEMA = 'KIMTAY') AND (COLUMN_NAME =
'CUST_ID');
```

Update of the System Catalog

When users create, alter, or drop tables or create or drop indexes, the DBMS updates the system catalog automatically to reflect these changes. Users should not execute SQL queries to update the catalog directly because this might produce inconsistent information. For example, when a user deletes the CUST_ID column in the INFORMATION_SCHEMA.COLUMNS table, the DBMS would no longer have any knowledge of this column, which is the CUSTOMER table's primary key, yet all the rows in the CUSTOMER table would still contain a customer ID. The DBMS might now treat those customer ID values as names, because as far as the DBMS is concerned, the column named FIRST_NAME is the first column in the CUSTOMER table.

INTEGRITY CONSTRAINTS IN SQL

An **integrity constraint** is a rule for the data in the database. Examples of integrity constraints in the KimTay Pet Supplies database are as follows:

- A sales rep's ID must be unique.
- The sales rep ID for a customer must match the ID of a sales rep currently in the database. For example, because there is no sales rep ID 11, a customer cannot be assigned to sales rep 11.
- Categories for items must be BRD, CAT, DOG, FSH, or HOR, because these are the only valid categories.

If a user enters data in the database that violates any of these integrity constraints, the database develops serious problems. For example, two sales reps with the same ID, a customer with a nonexistent sales rep, or an item in a nonexistent category would compromise the integrity of data in the database. To manage these types of problems, SQL provides **integrity support**, the process of specifying and enforcing integrity constraints for a database. SQL has clauses to support three types of integrity constraints that you can specify within a CREATE TABLE or an ALTER TABLE command. The only difference between these two commands is that an ALTER TABLE command is followed by the word ADD to indicate that you are adding the constraint to the list of existing constraints. To change an integrity constraint after it has been created, just enter the new constraint, which immediately takes the place of the original.

The types of constraints supported in SQL are primary keys, foreign keys, and legal values. In most cases, you specify a table's primary key when you create the table. To add a primary key after creating a table, you can use the **ADD PRIMARY KEY** clause of the ALTER TABLE command. For example, to indicate that REP_ID is the primary key for the SALES_REP table, the ALTER TABLE command is as follows:

```
ALTER TABLE SALES_REP
  ADD PRIMARY KEY (REP_ID);
```

The PRIMARY KEY clause is PRIMARY KEY followed by the column name that makes up the primary key in parentheses. When the primary key contains more than one column, use commas to separate the column names.

A **foreign key** is a column in one table whose values match the primary key in another table. (One example is the CUST_ID column in the INVOICES table. Values in this column are required to match those of the primary key in the CUSTOMER table.)

EXAMPLE 20: Specify the CUST_ID column in the INVOICES table as a foreign key that must match the CUSTOMER table.

When a table contains a foreign key, you identify it using the **ADD FOREIGN KEY** clause of the ALTER TABLE command. In this clause, you specify the column that is a foreign key and the table it matches. The general form for assigning a foreign key is FOREIGN KEY, the column name(s) of the foreign key, the **REFERENCES** clause, and then the table name and column that the foreign key must match, as shown in Figure 7-24.

```
ALTER TABLE INVOICES
    ADD FOREIGN KEY (CUST_ID) REFERENCES CUSTOMER (CUST_ID);
```

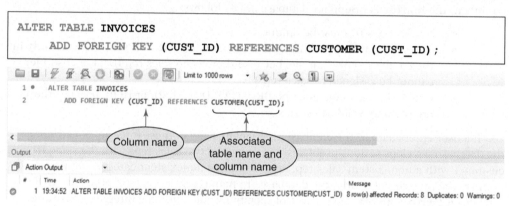

FIGURE 7-24   SQL adding a foreign key to an existing table

After creating a foreign key, the DBMS rejects any update that violates the foreign key constraint. For example, the DBMS rejects the INSERT command shown in Figure 7-25 because it attempts to add an order for which the customer ID (198) does not match any customer in the CUSTOMER table.

```
INSERT INTO INVOICES
    VALUES ('14239', '2021-11-20', '198');
```

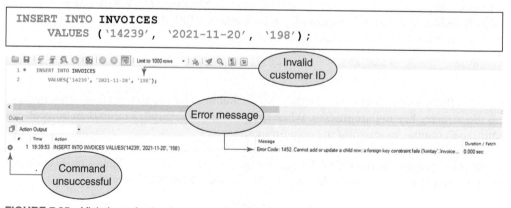

FIGURE 7-25   Violating a foreign key constraint when adding a row

The DBMS also rejects the DELETE command in Figure 7-26 because it attempts to delete customer ID 227; rows in the INVOICES table for which the customer ID is 227 would no longer match any row in the CUSTOMER table.

```
DELETE FROM CUSTOMER
     WHERE (CUST_ID = '227');
```

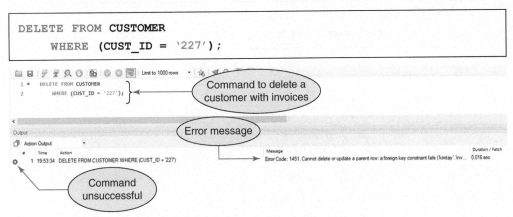

FIGURE 7-26 Violating a foreign key constraint when deleting a row

Note that the error messages shown in Figures 7-25 and 7-26 include the words *parent* and *child*. When you specify a foreign key, the table containing the foreign key is the **child**, and the table referenced by the foreign key is the **parent**. For example, the CUST_ID column in the INVOICES table is a foreign key that references the CUSTOMER table. For this foreign key, the CUSTOMER table is the parent, and the INVOICES table is the child. The error message shown in Figure 7-25 indicates that there is no parent for the invoice (there is no customer number 198). The error message shown in Figure 7-26 indicates that there are child records (rows) for customer 227 (customer 227 has invoices). The DBMS rejects both updates because they violate referential integrity.

EXAMPLE 21: Specify the valid categories for the ITEM table as BRD, CAT, DOG, FSH, and HOR.

You use the **CHECK** clause of the ALTER TABLE command to ensure that only legal values satisfying a particular condition are allowed in a given column. The general form of the CHECK clause is the word CHECK followed by a condition. If a user enters data that violates the condition, the DBMS rejects the update automatically. For example, to ensure that the only legal values for the CATEGORY column are BRD, CAT, DOG, FSH, or HOR, use one of the following versions of the CHECK clause:

```
CHECK (CATEGORY IN ('BRD', 'CAT', 'DOG', 'FSH', 'HOR') )
```

or

```
CHECK ( (CATEGORY = 'BRD') OR (CATEGORY = 'CAT') OR (CATEGORY = 'DOG')
OR (CATEGORY = 'FSH') OR (CATEGORY = 'HOR') )
```

The ALTER TABLE command shown in Figure 7-27 uses the first version of the CHECK clause.

```
ALTER TABLE ITEM
       ADD CHECK (CATEGORY IN ('BRD','CAT', 'DOG', 'FSH', 'HOR'));
```

FIGURE 7-27   Adding an integrity constraint to an existing table

Now the DBMS rejects the update shown in Figure 7-28 because the command attempts to change the category for an item to XYZ, which is an illegal value.

```
UPDATE ITEM
       SET CATEGORY = 'XYZ'
           WHERE (ITEM_ID = 'LP73');
```

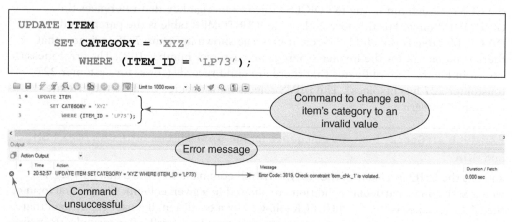

FIGURE 7-28   Update that violates an integrity constraint

Module Summary

- A view contains data that is derived from existing base tables when users attempt to access the view.

- To create a view, use the CREATE VIEW command, which includes a defining query that describes the portion of the database included in the view. When a user retrieves data from the view, the DBMS merges the query entered by the user with the defining query and produces the query that the DBMS actually executes.

- Views provide data independence, allow database access control, and simplify the database structure for users.

- You cannot update views that involve statistics and views with joins of nonprimary key columns. Updates for these types of views must be made in the base table.

- Use the DROP VIEW command to delete a view.

- Use the GRANT command to give users access privileges to data in the database.

- Use the REVOKE command to terminate previously granted privileges.

- You can create and use an index to make data retrieval more efficient. Use the CREATE INDEX command to create an index. Use the CREATE UNIQUE INDEX command to enforce a rule so only unique values are allowed in a nonprimary key column.

- Use the DROP INDEX command to delete an index.

- The DBMS, not the user, chooses which index to use to accomplish a given task.

- The DBMS maintains information about the tables, columns, indexes, and other system elements in the system catalog (catalog) or data dictionary. Information about tables is kept in the SYSTABLES table, information about columns is kept in the SYSCOLUMNS table, and information about views is kept in the SYSVIEWS table. In Oracle, these same tables are named DBA_TABLES, DBA_TAB_COLUMNS, and DBA_VIEWS.

- Use the SELECT command to obtain information from the system catalog. The DBMS updates the system catalog automatically whenever changes are made to the database. SQL Server uses stored procedures to obtain information about Tables, Columns, and other objects created in the database.

- Integrity constraints are rules that the data in the database must follow to ensure that only legal values are accepted in specified columns and that primary and foreign key values match between tables. To specify a general integrity constraint, use the CHECK clause. You usually specify primary key constraints when you create a table, but you can specify them later using the ADD PRIMARY KEY clause. To specify a foreign key, use the ADD FOREIGN KEY clause.

Key Terms

ADD FOREIGN KEY	CHECK
ADD PRIMARY KEY	child
base table	CREATE INDEX

CREATE UNIQUE INDEX	integrity support
CREATE VIEW	parent
data dictionary	REFERENCES
database administration	REVOKE
database administrator	row-and-column subset view
defining query	security
DROP INDEX	SYSCOLUMNS
DROP VIEW	SYSTABLES
foreign key	system catalog (catalog)
GRANT	SYSVIEWS
index	unique index
INFORMATION_SCHEMA	view
integrity constraint	WITH GRANT OPTION

Review Questions

Module Quiz

1. What is a view?
2. Which command creates a view?
3. What is a defining query?
4. What happens when a user retrieves data from a view?
5. What are three advantages of using views?
6. Which types of views cannot be updated?
7. Which command deletes a view?
8. Which command gives users access privileges to various portions of the database?
9. Which command terminates previously granted privileges?
10. What is the purpose of an index?
11. How do you create an index? How do you create a unique index? What is the difference between an index and a unique index?
12. Which command deletes an index?
13. Does the DBMS or the user make the choice of which index to use to accomplish a given task?
14. Describe the information the DBMS maintains in the system catalog. What are the generic names for three tables in the catalog?
15. The CUSTOMER table contains a foreign key, REP_ID, that must match the primary key of the SALES_REP table. What type of update(s) to the CUSTOMER table would violate the foreign key constraint?

16. What is the INFORMATION_SCHEMA in MySQL?

17. How is the system catalog updated?

18. What are integrity constraints?

19. How do you specify a general integrity constraint?

20. When would you usually specify primary key constraints? List two alternative methods to create a primary key?

21. How do you specify a foreign key in MySQL?

Critical Thinking

1. Use the Internet to find information about referential integrity. Write two or three paragraphs that describe what referential integrity is and include an example of how referential integrity is used in the KimTay Pet Supplies database. Be sure to cite the URLs that you use.

2. Use the Internet to find information about a data dictionary. Write a one-page paper that describes other types of information that can be stored in a data dictionary. Be sure to cite the URLs that you use.

Case Exercises

KimTay Pet Supplies

Use SQL to make the following changes to the KimTay Pet Supplies database (see Figure 1-2 in Module 1). After each change, execute an appropriate query to show that the change was made correctly. If directed to do so by your instructor, use the information provided with the Module 3 Exercises to print your output or save it to a document. For any exercises that use commands not supported by your version of SQL, write the command to accomplish the task.

1. Create a view named MAJOR_CUSTOMER. It consists of the customer ID, first name, last name, balance, credit limit, and rep ID for every customer whose credit limit is $500 or less.

   a. Write and execute the CREATE VIEW command to create the MAJOR_CUSTOMER view.

   b. Write and execute the command to retrieve the customer ID, first name, and last name of each customer in the MAJOR_CUSTOMER view with a balance that exceeds the credit limit.

   c. Write and execute the query that the DBMS actually executes.

   d. Does updating the database through this view create any problems? If so, what are they? If not, why not?

2. Create a view named ITEM_INVOICE. It consists of the item ID, description, price, invoice number, invoice date, number ordered, and quoted price for all invoice lines currently on file.

    a. Write and execute the CREATE VIEW command to create the ITEM_INVOICE view.

    b. Write and execute the command to retrieve the item ID, description, invoice number, and quoted price for all invoices in the ITEM_INVOICE view for items with quoted prices that exceed $100.

    c. Write and execute the query that the DBMS actually executes.

    d. Does updating the database through this view create any problems? If so, what are they? If not, why not?

3. Create a view named INVOICE_TOTAL. It consists of the invoice number and invoice total for each invoice currently on file. (The invoice total is the sum of the number of units ordered multiplied by the quoted price on each invoice line for each invoice.) Sort the rows by invoice number. Use TOTAL_AMOUNT as the name for the invoice total.

    a. Write and execute the CREATE VIEW command to create the INVOICE_TOTAL view.

    b. Write and execute the command to retrieve the invoice number and invoice total for only those orders totaling more than $250.

    c. Write and execute the query that the DBMS actually executes.

    d. Does updating the database through this view create any problems? If so, what are they? If not, why not?

4. Write, but do not execute, the commands to do the following with the system catalog:

    a. List all the tables contained within the system catalog.

    b. List all the columns contained within the system catalog.

    c. List all the views contained within the system catalog.

5. Write, but do not execute, the command to display only tables within the system catalog that are of the type BASE TABLE.

6. Perform the following tasks:

    a. Create an index named ITEM_INDEX1 on the ITEM_ID column in the INVOICE_LINE table.

    b. Create an index named ITEM_INDEX2 on the CATEGORY column in the ITEM table.

    c. Create an index named ITEM_INDEX3 on the CATEGORY and LOCATION columns in the ITEM table.

    d. Create an index named ITEM_INDEX4 on the CATEGORY and LOCATION columns in the ITEM table. List categories in descending order.

7. Delete the index named ITEM_INDEX3.

8. Write the commands to obtain the following information from the system catalog. Do not execute these commands unless your instructor asks you to do so.

    a. List every table that you have created thus far.

    b. List every column in the ITEM table and its associated data type.

9. Add the INVOICE_NUM column as a foreign key in the INVOICE_LINE table.

10. Ensure that the only legal values for the CREDIT_LIMIT column are 250, 500, 750, and 1000.

Critical Thinking

1. Samantha Smith currently has a credit limit of $500. Because Samantha Smith has an excellent credit rating, KimTay Pet Supplies is increasing her credit limit to $1000. If you run the SQL query in Exercise 1 after the credit limit has been increased, would Samantha Smith still be included in the view? Why or why not?

StayWell Student Accommodation

Use SQL to make the following changes to StayWell Student Accommodation database (Figures 1-4 through 1-9 in Module 1). After each change, execute an appropriate query to show that the change was made correctly. If directed to do so by your instructor, use the information provided with the Module 3 Exercises to print your output or save it to a document. For any exercises that use commands not supported by your version of SQL, write the command to accomplish the task.

1. Create a view named SMALL_PROPERTY. It consists of the property ID, office number, bedrooms, floor, monthly rent, and owner number for every property whose square footage is less than 1,250 square feet.

   a. Write and execute the CREATE VIEW command to create the SMALL_PROPERTY view.

   b. Write and execute the command to retrieve the office number, property ID, and monthly rent for every property in the SMALL_PROPERTY view with a monthly rent of $1150 or more.

   c. Write and execute the query that the DBMS actually executes.

   d. Does updating the database through this view create any problems? If so, what are they? If not, why not?

2. Create a view named PROPERTY_OWNERS. It consists of the property ID, office number, square footage, bedrooms, floors, monthly rent, and owner's last name for every property in which the number of bedrooms is three.

   a. Write and execute the CREATE VIEW command to create the PROPERTY_OWNERS view.

   b. Write and execute the command to retrieve the property ID, office number, monthly rent, square footage, and owner's last name for every property in the PROPERTY_OWNERS view with a monthly rent of less than $1675.

   c. Write and execute the query that the DBMS actually executes.

   d. Does updating the database through this view create any problems? If so, what are they? If not, why not?

3. Create a view named MONTHLY_RENTS. It consists of two columns: The first is the number of bedrooms, and the second is the average monthly rent for all properties in the PROPERTY table that have that number of bedrooms. Use AVERAGE_RENT as

the column name for the average monthly rent. Group and order the rows by number of bedrooms.

    a.   Write and execute the CREATE VIEW command to create the MONTHLY_RENTS view.

    b.   Write and execute the command to retrieve the square footage and average fee for each square footage for which the average fee is greater than $1,100.

    c.   Write and execute the query that the DBMS actually executes.

    d.   Does updating the database through this view create any problems? If so, what are they? If not, why not?

4.   Write, but do not execute, the commands to grant the following privileges:

    a.   User Oliver must be able to retrieve data from the PROPERTY table.

    b.   Users Crandall and Perez must be able to add new owners and properties to the database.

    c.   Users Johnson and Klein must be able to change the monthly rent of any unit.

    d.   All users must be able to retrieve the office number, monthly rent, and owner number for every property.

    e.   User Klein must be able to add and delete service categories.

    f.   User Adams must be able to create an index on the SERVICE_REQUEST table.

    g.   Users Adams and Klein must be able to change the structure of the PROPERTY table.

    h.   User Klein must have all privileges on the OFFICE, OWNER, and PROPERTY tables.

5.   Write, but do not execute, the command to revoke all privileges from user Adams.

6.   Create the following indexes:

    a.   Create an index named OWNER_INDEX1 on the STATE column in the OWNER table.

    b.   Create an index named OWNER_INDEX2 on the LAST_NAME column in the OWNER table.

    c.   Create an index named OWNER_INDEX3 on the STATE and CITY columns in the OWNER table. List the states in descending order.

7.   Delete the OWNER_INDEX 3 index from the OWNER table.

8.   Write the commands to obtain the following information from the system catalog. Do not execute these commands unless your instructor specifically asks you to do so.

    a.   List every column in the PROPERTY table and its associated data type.

    b.   List every table that contains a column named OWNER_NUM.

9.   Add the OWNER_NUM column as a foreign key in the PROPERTY table.

10.   Ensure that the only legal values for the BDRMS column in the PROPERTY table are 1, 2, or 3.

Critical Thinking

1.   In Question 9, you added owner number as a foreign key in the PROPERTY table. Identify all foreign keys in the StayWell Student Accommodation database and write the corresponding SQL commands.

FUNCTIONS, PROCEDURES, AND TRIGGERS

OBJECTIVES

- Understand how to use functions in queries.
- Use the UPPER and LOWER functions with character data.
- Use the ROUND and FLOOR functions with numeric data.
- Add a specific number of months or days to a date.
- Calculate the number of days between two dates.
- Use concatenation in a query.
- Embed SQL commands in MySQL, PL/SQL, and T-SQL procedures.
- Retrieve single rows using embedded SQL.
- Update a table using embedded INSERT, UPDATE, and DELETE commands.
- Use cursors to retrieve multiple rows in embedded SQL.
- Manage errors in procedures containing embedded SQL commands.
- Use triggers.

INTRODUCTION

You already have used functions that apply to groups (such as SUM and AVG). In this module, you learn to use functions that apply to values in individual rows. Specifically, you see how to use functions with characters or text, numbers, and dates. You learn how to concatenate values in a query. You embed SQL commands in MySQL, PL/SQL, and T-SQL procedures to retrieve rows and update data. You examine the different ways to manage errors in procedures. Finally, you learn how to create and use cursors and triggers.

USING SQL IN A PROGRAMMING ENVIRONMENT

SQL is a powerful **nonprocedural language** in which you submit requests to the computer using simple commands. As in other nonprocedural languages, you can accomplish many tasks using a single command. Although SQL and other nonprocedural languages are well equipped to store and query data, sometimes you might need to complete tasks that are beyond the capabilities of SQL. In such cases, you need to use a procedural language.

A **procedural language** is one in which you must give the computer the systematic process for accomplishing a task. MySQL procedural language was introduced in version 5 as an extension of SQL. MySQL procedural language allows developers to embed SQL statements to perform complex tasks that could not be done by SQL alone. These tasks can be saved within the database as stored procedures to be executed at anytime.

This module uses MySQL, Oracle PL/SQL, and Microsoft T-SQL to illustrate how to use SQL in a programming environment by **embedding** SQL commands in another language. The examples in this module illustrate how to use embedded SQL commands to retrieve a single row, insert new rows, update and delete existing rows, and retrieve multiple rows. In the process, you create stored procedures that are saved and are available for use at any time.

 ORACLE USER NOTE

PL/SQL, which stands for Procedural Language Structured Query Language, is a procedural language well-integrated with SQL, which was developed by Oracle. PL/SQL, like MySQL and others, features programming constructs such as conditions and loops and other programming languages structures.

▶ **SQL SERVER USER NOTE**

T-SQL, which stands for **Transact-SQL**, is another extension of SQL. T-SQL is the procedural language that SQL Server uses. You can perform tasks, such as retrieving a single row, inserting new rows, and retrieving multiple rows, using T-SQL in SQL Server. Although the language syntax is slightly different in T-SQL when compared to MySQL and PL/SQL, the functionality and the results are the same.

HELPFUL HINT

This module assumes that you have some programming background and does not cover programming basics. To understand the first part of this module, you should be familiar with variables, declaring variables, and creating procedural code, including IF statements and loops.

USING FUNCTIONS

You have used aggregate functions to perform calculations based on groups of records. For example, SUM(BALANCE) calculates the sum of the balances on all records that satisfy the condition in the WHERE clause. When you use a GROUP BY clause, the DBMS calculates the sum for each record in a group.

SQL also includes functions that affect single records. Some functions affect character data and others let you manipulate numeric data. The supported SQL functions vary among SQL implementations. This section illustrates some common functions. For additional information about the functions your SQL implementation supports, consult the program's documentation.

Character Functions

SQL includes several functions that affect character data. Example 1 illustrates the use of the UPPER function.

EXAMPLE 1: List the sales rep ID and last name for each sales rep. Display the last name in uppercase letters.

The **UPPER** function displays a value in uppercase letters; for example, the function UPPER(LAST_NAME) displays the last name Garcia as GARCIA. (Note that the UPPER function simply displays the last name in uppercase letters; it does not change the last name stored in the table to uppercase letters.) The item in parentheses (LAST_NAME) is called the **argument** for the function. The value produced by the function is the result of displaying all lowercase letters in the value stored in the LAST_NAME column as uppercase letters. The query and its results are shown in Figure 8-1.

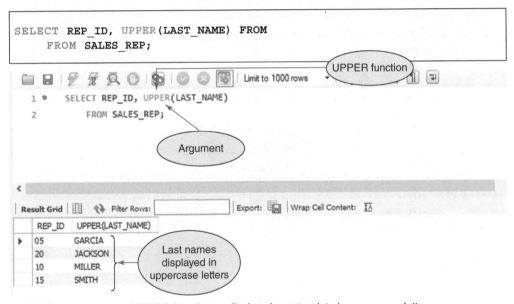

FIGURE 8-1   Using the UPPER function to display character data in uppercase letters

You can use functions in WHERE clauses as well. For example, the condition UPPER(LAST_NAME) = 'GARCIA' would be true for names like Garcia, GARCIA, and GaRcIA, because the result of applying the UPPER function to any of these values would result in the value GARCIA.

To display a value in lowercase letters, you can use the **LOWER** function.

> ▶ **SQL SERVER USER NOTE**
>
> SQL Server supports both the UPPER and LOWER function.

Number Functions

SQL also includes functions that affect numeric data. The **ROUND** function, which rounds values to a specified number of decimal places, is illustrated in Example 2.

EXAMPLE 2: List the item ID and price for all items. Round the price to the nearest whole dollar amount.

A function can have more than one argument. The ROUND function, which rounds a numeric value to a desired number of decimal places, has two arguments. The first argument is the value to be rounded; the second argument indicates the number of decimal places to which to round the result. For example, ROUND(PRICE,0) rounds the values in the PRICE column to zero decimal places (a whole number). If a price is 24.95, the result will be 25. On the other hand, if the price is 24.25, the result will be 24. Figure 8-2 shows the query and results to round values in the PRICE column to zero decimal places. The computed column ROUND(PRICE,0) is named ROUNDED_PRICE.

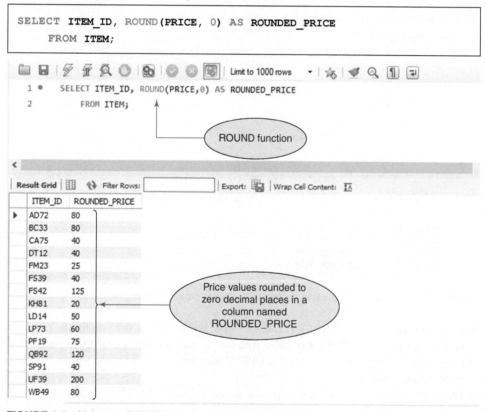

FIGURE 8-2 Using the ROUND function to round numeric values

Rather than rounding (using the ROUND function), you might need to truncate (remove) everything to the right of the decimal point. To do so, use the **FLOOR** function, which has only one argument. If a price is 24.95, for example, ROUND(PRICE,0) would result in 25, whereas FLOOR(PRICE) would result in 24.

● ORACLE USER NOTE

The UPPER, LOWER, ROUND, and FLOOR functions are available in Oracle. In Oracle these functions have the same use and functionality as in MySQL.

▶ SQL SERVER USER NOTE

Similar to MySQL and Oracle, SQL Server offers the UPPER, LOWER, ROUND, and FLOOR functions with the same functionality behavior.

Working with Dates

SQL uses functions and calculations for manipulating dates. To add a specific number of days, months, or years to a date, you can use the **DATE_ADD** function as illustrated in Example 3. This specific example adds one month to a date.

EXAMPLE 3: For each invoice, list the invoice number and the date that is one month after the invoice date. Name this date NEXT_MONTH.

The DATE_ADD function has two arguments. The first argument is the date to which you want to add a specific interval to, and the second argument is the interval value and specific component (whether days, months, or years). To add one month to the invoice date, for example, the expression is DATE_ADD(INVOICE_DATE, INTERVAL 1 MONTH) as illustrated in Figure 8-3. Note if the interval value was negative, the number of months would be decreased by the interval value.

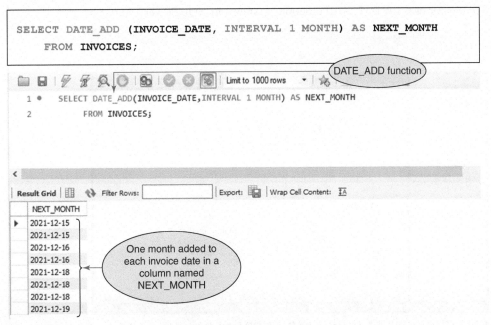

```
SELECT DATE_ADD (INVOICE_DATE, INTERVAL 1 MONTH) AS NEXT_MONTH
    FROM INVOICES;
```

FIGURE 8-3 Using the DATE_ADD function to add a month to a date

● ORACLE USER NOTE

Oracle uses the **ADD_MONTHS** function to attain same NEXT_MONTH result as in previous query as shown in Oracle Figure 8-1.

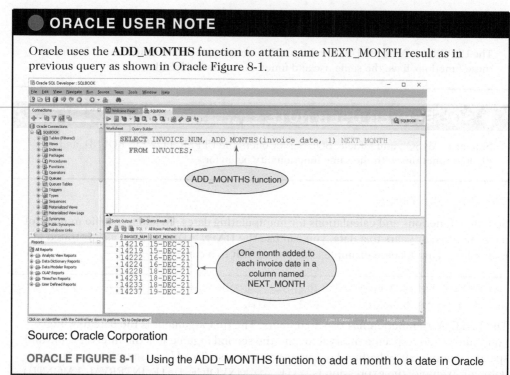

Source: Oracle Corporation

ORACLE FIGURE 8-1   Using the ADD_MONTHS function to add a month to a date in Oracle

▶ SQL SERVER USER NOTE

SQL Server uses the DATEADD function, as shown in SQL Server Figure 8-1.

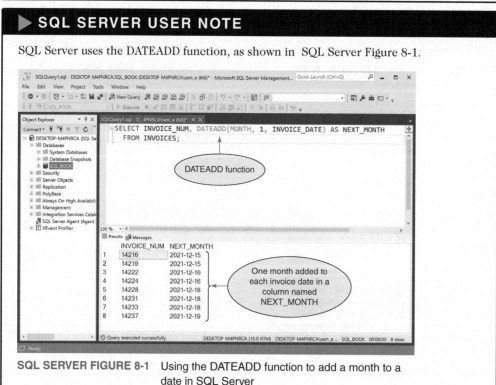

SQL SERVER FIGURE 8-1   Using the DATEADD function to add a month to a date in SQL Server

EXAMPLE 4: For each invoice, list the invoice number and the date that is seven days after the invoice date. Name this date NEXT_WEEK.

To add a specific number of days to a date, you do not need a function. You can add the number of days to the invoice date as illustrated in Figure 8-4. (You can also subtract dates in the same way.) This method works in MySQL, Oracle, and SQL Server.

```
SELECT INVOICE_NUM, INVOICE_DATE + 7 AS NEXT_WEEK
     FROM INVOICES;
```

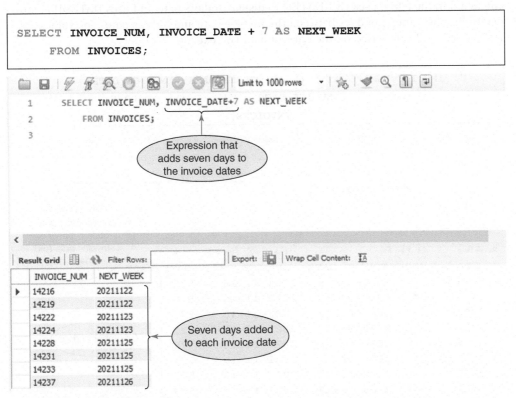

FIGURE 8-4   Adding days to dates

▶ SQL SERVER USER NOTE

SQL Server uses the same DATEADD function with WEEK as an interval like the following: DATEADD(WEEK, 1, INVOICE_DATE).

EXAMPLE 5: For each invoice, list the invoice number, today's date, the invoice date, and the number of days between the invoice date and today's date. Name today's date TODAYS_DATE and name the number of days between the invoice date and today's date DAYS_PAST.

You can use the **CURDATE()** function to obtain today's date, as shown in Figure 8-5. The command in the figure uses CURDATE() to display today's date and uses DATEDIFF() to determine the number of days between the invoice date and today's date. The values for DAYS_PAST will vary based on the current date you execute the query.

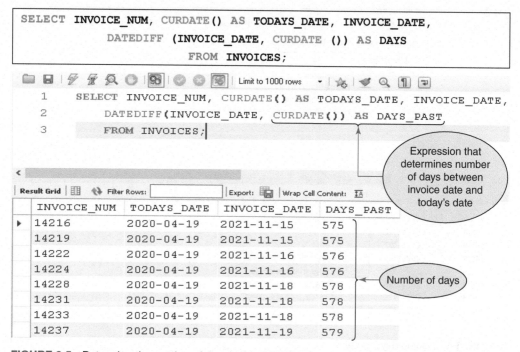

FIGURE 8-5   Determine the number of days using DATEDIFF

● ORACLE USER NOTE

Similar to MySQL, Oracle uses **SYSDATE** to obtain current date as shown in Oracle Figure 8-2. Note that the ROUND function is used to round the results to days; otherwise, the results show decimal numbers indicating a fraction of the day.

(continued)

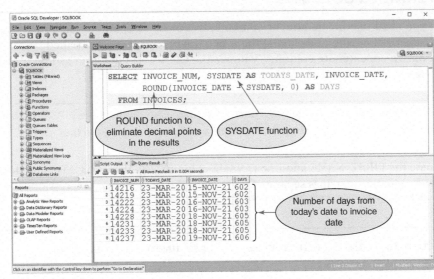

Source: Oracle Corporation

ORACLE FIGURE 8-2   Using SYSDATE in Oracle

▶ **SQL SERVER USER NOTE**

SQL Server uses the GETDATE() function to retrieve current date and the DATEDIFF() function to retrieve the number of days, weeks, months, or years between two dates as illustrated in SQL Server Figure 8-2.

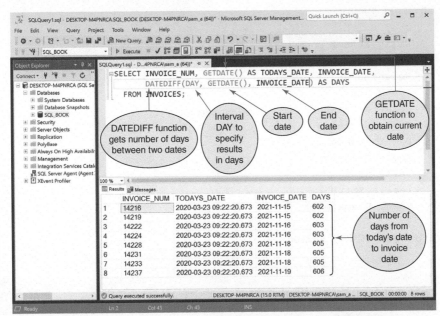

SQL SERVER FIGURE 8-2   Using GETDATE and DATEDIFF in SQL Server

CONCATENATING COLUMNS

Sometimes you need to **concatenate**, or combine, two or more character columns into a single expression when displaying them in a query; the process is called **concatenation**. To concatenate columns, you use the CONCAT() function as illustrated in Example 6.

EXAMPLE 6: List the number and name of each customer. Concatenate the FIRST_NAME and LAST_NAME columns into a single value, with a space separating the first and last names.

To concatenate the FIRST_NAME and LAST_NAME columns, use the CONCAT() function with character columns or strings separated by comma like the following expression: CONCAT(FIRST_NAME, ' '. LAST_NAME). See Figure 8-6.

```
SELECT CUST_ID, CONCAT (FIRST_NAME,'', LAST_NAME) AS FULL_NAME
            FROM CUSTOMER;
```

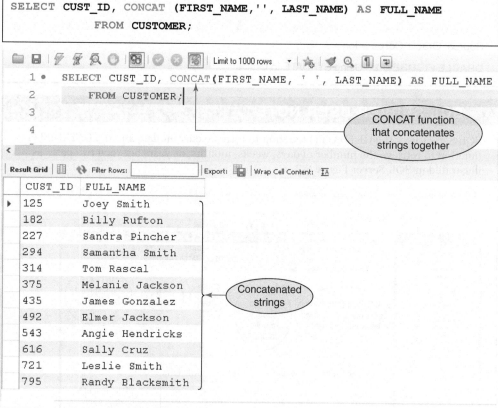

FIGURE 8-6   Using the CONCAT function

ORACLE USER NOTE

Oracle provides the CONCAT function; however, this function accepts only two string arguments to be concatenated.

▶ SQL SERVER USER NOTE

Similar to MySQL, the CONCAT function exists, and it can take more than two string arguments.

Q & A

Question: Why is it necessary to insert a single space character in single quotation marks in the query?
Answer: Without the space character, there would be no space between the first and last names. The name of customer 125, for example, would be displayed as "JoeySmith."

ORACLE USER NOTE

The CONCAT() function takes only two column strings or character strings. In a case where it is desired to concatenate three strings as in previous example: customer first name followed by a blank space and last name. It is required to use the CONCAT() function as an argument as shown in Oracle Figure 8-3.

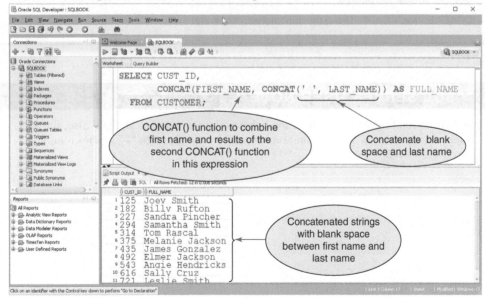

Source: Oracle Corporation

ORACLE FIGURE 8-3 Using the CONCAT() function in Oracle

(continued)

In addition, Oracle offers concatenation operator double vertical bars "||" to combine two or more character strings in one expression as shown in Oracle Figure 8-4.

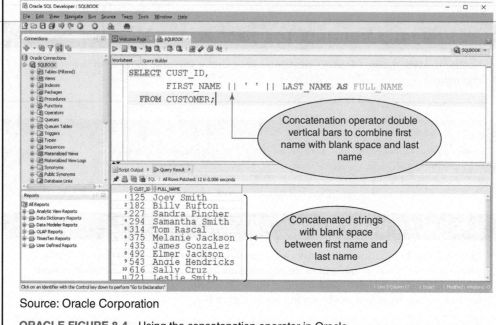

Source: Oracle Corporation

ORACLE FIGURE 8-4   Using the concatenation operator in Oracle

---

▶ SQL SERVER USER NOTE

In SQL Server, the CONCAT() function behaves the same way as MySQL. Also, the concatenation operator is available and represented by the plus sign "+" as shown in SQL Server Figure 8-3.

(continued)

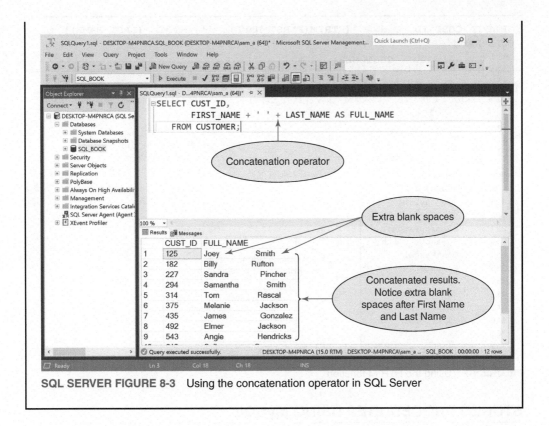

SQL SERVER FIGURE 8-3 Using the concatenation operator in SQL Server

When the first name doesn't include enough characters to fill the width of the column (as determined by the number of characters specified in the CREATE TABLE command), SQL inserts extra spaces. For example, when the FIRST_NAME column is 12 characters in length, the first name is Joey, and the last name is Smith, the concatenated expression FIRST_NAME and LAST_NAME is displayed as Joey, followed by eight spaces, and then Smith. To remove the extra spaces following the first name value, you use the **RTRIM** (right trim) function. When you apply this function to the value in a column, SQL displays the original value and removes any spaces inserted at the end of the value. Figure 8-7 shows the query and output with the extra spaces removed specifically if the column FIRST_NAME is created as a CHAR data type. For Customer 125, for example, this command trims the first name to "Joey," concatenates it with a single space, and then concatenates the last name "Smith."

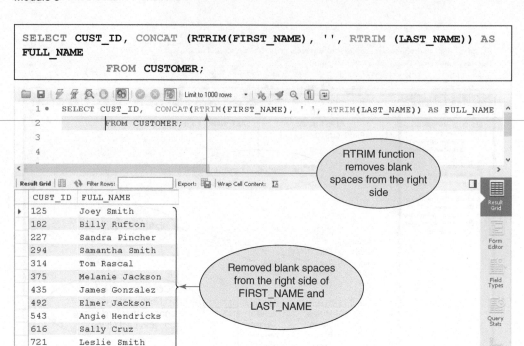

```
SELECT CUST_ID, CONCAT (RTRIM(FIRST_NAME), '', RTRIM (LAST_NAME)) AS
FULL_NAME
              FROM CUSTOMER;
```

FIGURE 8-7   Using the RTRIM function

STORED PROCEDURES USING MySQL

In a **client/server system**, the database is stored on a computer called the **server** and users access the database through clients. A **client** is a computer that is connected to a network and has access through the server to the database. Every time a user executes a query, the DBMS must determine the best way to process the query and provide the results. For example, the DBMS must determine which indexes are available and whether it can use those indexes to make the processing of the query more efficient.

When you anticipate running a particular query often, you can improve overall performance by saving the query in a file called a **stored procedure**. The stored procedure is placed on the server. The DBMS compiles the stored procedure (translating it into machine code) and creates an execution plan, which is the most efficient way of obtaining the results. From that point on, users execute the compiled, optimized code in the stored procedure.

Another reason for saving a query as a stored procedure, even when you are not working in a client/server system, is convenience. Rather than retyping the entire query each time you need it, you can use the stored procedure. For example, suppose you frequently execute a query that selects a customer ID with a given number and then displays the concatenation of the first name and last name of the customer. Instead of typing the query each time you want to display a customer's name, you can save the query in a stored procedure. You would then only need to run the stored procedure when you want to display a sales rep's name. In MySQL, you create stored procedures using a language called MySQL. You can create and save the procedures as script files.

Retrieving a Single Row and Column

Example 7 illustrates using a stored procedure to retrieve a single row and column from a table.

EXAMPLE 7: Write a MySQL procedure that takes a customer ID as input and displays the corresponding customer full name.

Figure 8-8 shows a procedure to find the name of the customer full name whose number is stored in the I_CUST_ID argument. Because the restriction involves the primary key, the query produces only one row of output. (You will see how to handle queries whose results can contain multiple rows later in this module.) The command shown in Figure 8-8 is stored in a script file and is displayed in the Script Editor. To create the procedure, you would run the script file. Assuming that the script file does not contain any errors, MySQL would then create the procedure and it would be available for use.

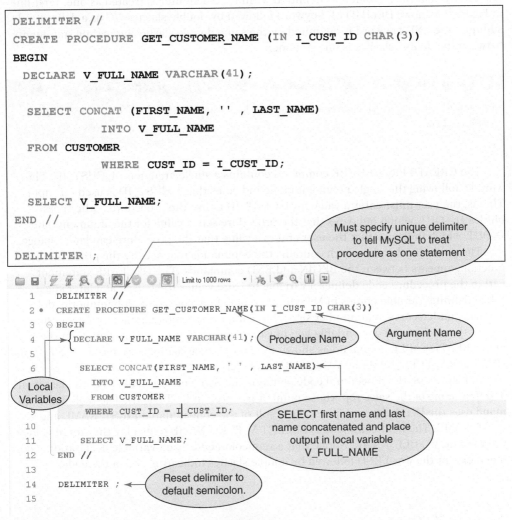

FIGURE 8-8 CREATE PROCEDURE using MySQL

The CREATE PROCEDURE command causes MySQL to create a procedure named GET_CUSTOMER_NAME. You must drop the procedure in case it was already created in the database previously by using the DROP PROCEDURE command.

Typically, MySQL Workbench uses a semicolon ";" as a delimiter to SQL commands and execute statements delimited by semicolon separately. When creating a procedure, it is necessary to write several statements using a semicolon to end each statement within the procedure. For this reason, the DELIMITER keyword is used to define characters that tell MySQL that the statements submitted within the delimiter is treated as one. First line in Figure 8-8 shows DELIMITER keyword followed by double slashes "//" as a delimiter. In addition, the END keyword is delimited by the same double slashes indicating statements between the double slashes is one statement.

The CREATE PROCEDURE command contains a single argument, I_CUST_ID. The word IN following the single argument name indicates that I_CUST_ID is used for input. That is, the user must enter a value for I_CUST_ID to use the procedure. Other possibilities are OUT, which indicates that the procedure sets a value for the argument, and INOUT, which indicates that the user enters a value that the procedure can later change.

The **procedural code**, which contains the commands that specify the procedure's function, appears between the BEGIN and END commands. The DECLARE statement within the procedure code defines a variable to store values to be used at a later stage. When defining variable names in MySQL, the name may consist of alphanumeric, dollar signs, underscores, and number signs, but cannot exceed 64 characters. In addition, part of the declaration of a variable you must assign a data type, just as you do in the SQL CREATE TABLE command as shown in Figure 8-8, assigning variables I_CUST_ID as CHAR and V_FULL_NAME as VARCHAR data type.

In Figure 8-8, the procedural code contains the SQL command to select the last name and first name of the sales rep whose number is stored in I_CUST_ID. The SQL command uses the INTO clause to place the result of the concatenated FIRST_NAME and LAST_NAME. The next command is SELECT V_FULL_NAME to display the stored value of the variable V_FULL_NAME. Notice that a semicolon ends each variable declaration, command except the word END followed by double slashes indicating end of the code.

HELPFUL HINT

To **execute** (or use) the procedure from the SQL Commands page, type the word CALL, followed by the name of the procedure including the desired value for the argument in parentheses, followed by a semi-colon on a separate line. To use the GET_CUSTOMER_NAME procedure to find the name of customer ID 125, for example, type the command shown in Figure 8-9.

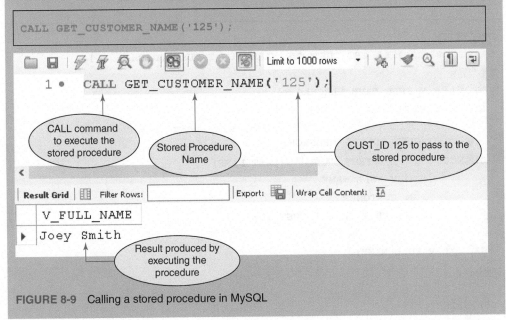

FIGURE 8-9   Calling a stored procedure in MySQL

ERROR HANDLING

Procedures must be able to handle conditions that can arise when accessing the database. For example, the user enters a customer ID and the GET_CUSTOMER_NAME procedure displays the corresponding customer's name. What happens when the user enters an invalid customer ID? This situation results with a NULL value as shown in Figure 8-10 because MySQL does not find any last name to display.

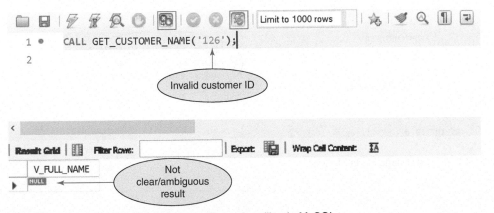

FIGURE 8-10   Results without the use of error handling in MySQL

You can include the "declare an exception" handler as shown in Figure 8-11 to handle processing an invalid customer ID. When a user enters a customer ID that does not match any customer in the CUSTOMER table, NOT FOUND condition is raised and the procedure displays the message proceeded by SELECT statement in the same line. The message 'No customer with this ID was found: ' followed by the invalid customer ID.

```
DELIMITER //
CREATE PROCEDURE GET_CUSTOMER_NAME (IN I_CUST_ID CHAR (3))
BEGIN
  DECLARE V_FULL_NAME VARCHAR (41);
  DECLARE EXIT HANDLER FOR NOT FOUND
        SELECT CONCAT ('No customer with this ID was found:',
        I_CUST_ID) AS MESSAGE;
  SELECT CONCAT (FIRST_NAME,'' , LAST_NAME)
        INTO V_FULL_NAME
        FROM CUSTOMER
        WHERE CUST_ID = I_CUST_ID;


  SELECT V_FULL_NAME;
END //


DELIMITER ;
```

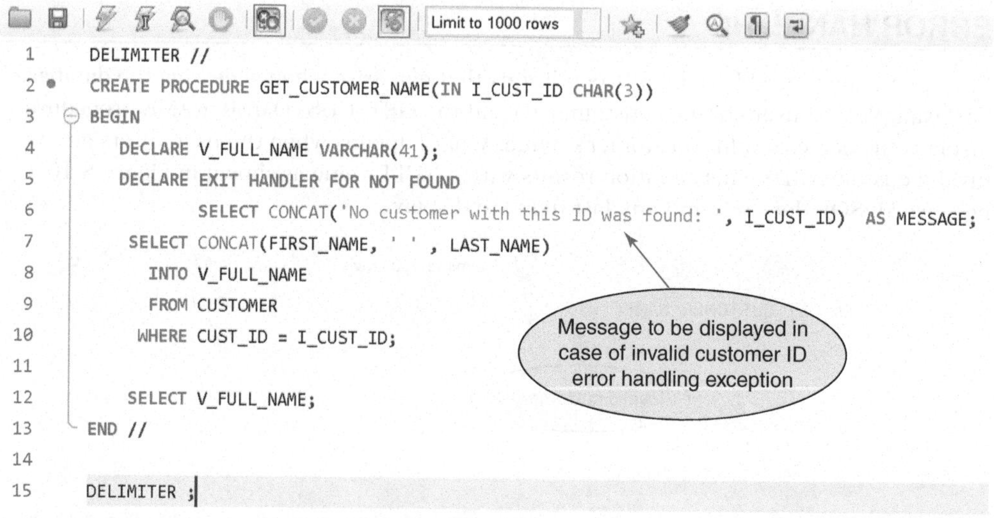

```
1      DELIMITER //
2  ●    CREATE PROCEDURE GET_CUSTOMER_NAME(IN I_CUST_ID CHAR(3))
3  ⊖    BEGIN
4          DECLARE V_FULL_NAME VARCHAR(41);
5          DECLARE EXIT HANDLER FOR NOT FOUND
6              SELECT CONCAT('No customer with this ID was found: ', I_CUST_ID)  AS MESSAGE;
7          SELECT CONCAT(FIRST_NAME, ' ' , LAST_NAME)
8            INTO V_FULL_NAME
9            FROM CUSTOMER
10           WHERE CUST_ID = I_CUST_ID;
11
12         SELECT V_FULL_NAME;
13   └   END //
14
15     DELIMITER ;|
```

Message to be displayed in case of invalid customer ID error handling exception

FIGURE 8-11   Error handling in MySQL

When you use this version of the procedure and enter an invalid rep number, you see the error message from the procedure (Figure 8-11) instead of a Null message (Figure 8-12).

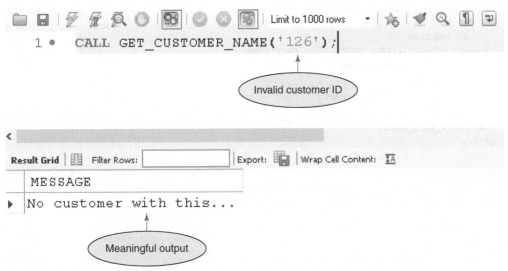

FIGURE 8-12   Results using error handling in MySQL

> ### HELPFUL HINT
>
> There are two options for error handling EXIT and CONTINUE. EXIT stops the execution of the code enclosed between BEGIN and END, while CONTINUE keeps executing the code proceeding the statement that caused the error.

The GET_CUSTOMER_NAME procedure handles an error that results when a user enters an invalid customer ID. There are other types of errors that procedures must handle, depending on the processing required. For example, a user might enter a commission rate in a procedure to find the name of the sales rep who has that commission rate. When the user enters the rate 0.04, the procedure displays an 1172 (stands for too many rows) error because Susan, Donna, and Daniel have this same commission rate—the procedure finds three rows instead of one. You can manage this error by trapping the error code 1172 in the error handling declaration statement as shown in Figure 8-13 and 8-14, respectively.

```
DELIMITER //
CREATE PROCEDURE GET_REP_NAME (IN I_RATE DECIMAL (4,2))
BEGIN
  DECLARE V_FULL_NAME VARCHAR (41);
  DECLARE EXIT HANDLER FOR 1172
      SELECT CONCAT ('There is more than one REP with RATE: ', I_RATE)
      AS MESSAGE;
  SELECT CONCAT (FIRST_NAME, '' , LAST_NAME)
          INTO V_FULL_NAME
  FROM SALES_REP
          WHERE RATE = I_RATE;

  SELECT V_FULL_NAME;
END//

DELIMITER ;
```

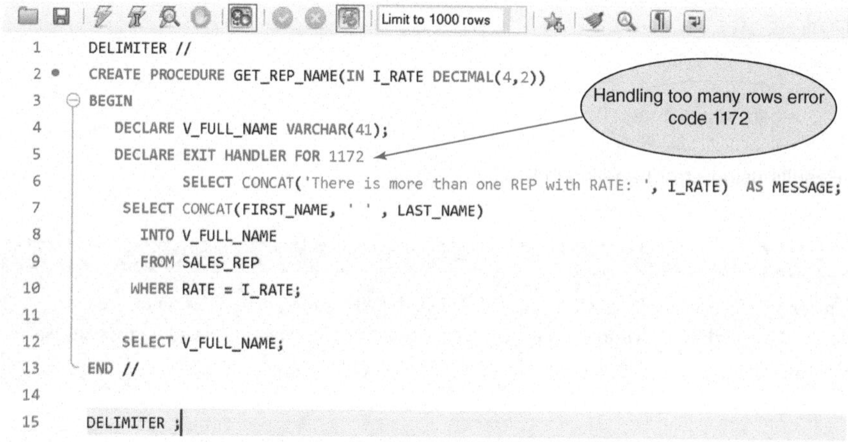

```
 1      DELIMITER //
 2 •    CREATE PROCEDURE GET_REP_NAME(IN I_RATE DECIMAL(4,2))
 3 ⊖   BEGIN
 4         DECLARE V_FULL_NAME VARCHAR(41);
 5         DECLARE EXIT HANDLER FOR 1172
 6             SELECT CONCAT('There is more than one REP with RATE: ', I_RATE)  AS MESSAGE;
 7        SELECT CONCAT(FIRST_NAME, ' ' , LAST_NAME)
 8           INTO V_FULL_NAME
 9           FROM SALES_REP
10          WHERE RATE = I_RATE;
11
12         SELECT V_FULL_NAME;
13        END //
14
15     DELIMITER ;
```

Handling too many rows error code 1172

FIGURE 8-13   Too many rows error handling in MySQL

```
 1 •   CALL GET_REP_NAME(0.04);
```

MESSAGE
There is more than one REP with RATE: 0.04

Message displayed resulted by handling too many rows error code 1172

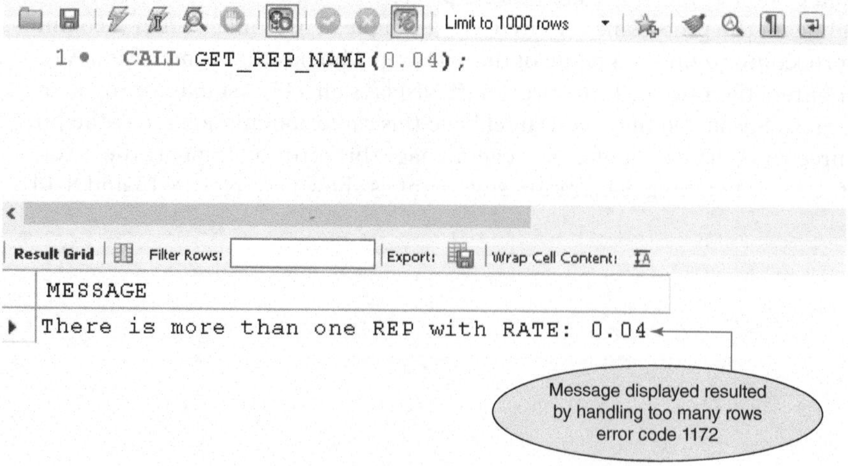

FIGURE 8-14   Results of too many rows error handling in MySQL

USING UPDATE PROCEDURES

In Module 6, you learned how to use SQL commands to update data. You can use the same commands within procedures. A procedure that updates data is called an **update procedure**.

Changing Data with a Procedure

You can use an update procedure to change a row in a table, as illustrated in Example 8.

EXAMPLE 8: Change the last name of the customer whose number is stored in I_CUST_ID to the value currently stored in I_NEW_NAME.

This procedure is similar to the procedures used in previous examples with two main differences: It uses an UPDATE command instead of a SELECT command, and there are two arguments, I_CUST_ID and I_NEW_NAME. The I_CUST_ID argument stores the customer ID to be updated and the I_NEW_NAME argument stores the new value for the customer last name. The procedure appears in Figure 8-15.

```
DELIMITER //

CREATE PROCEDURE CHG_CUSTOMER_LAST (IN I_CUST_ID CHAR (3),
IN I_NEW_NAME VARCHAR (20))
BEGIN
 DECLARE EXIT HANDLER FOR NOT FOUND
    SELECT CONCAT ('No customer with this ID was found: ', I_CUST_ID)
    AS MESSAGE;
 UPDATE CUSTOMER
   SET LAST_NAME = I_NEW_NAME
   WHERE CUST_ID = I_CUST_ID;


END //


DELIMITER ;
```

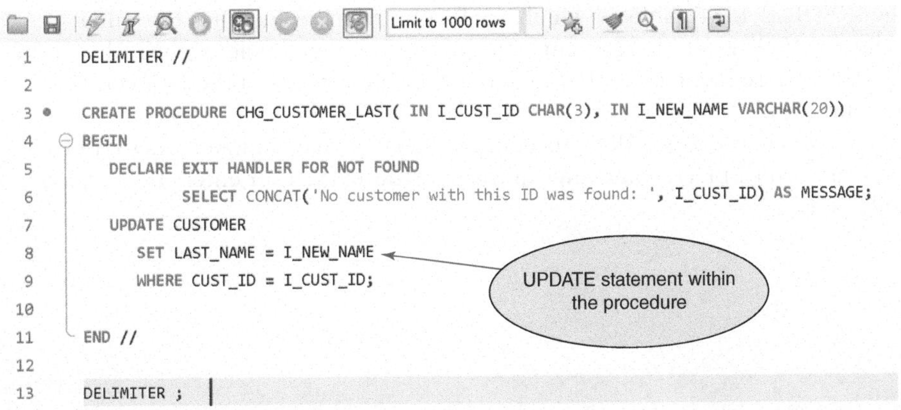

```
1    DELIMITER //
2
3 •  CREATE PROCEDURE CHG_CUSTOMER_LAST( IN I_CUST_ID CHAR(3), IN I_NEW_NAME VARCHAR(20))
4 ⊖  BEGIN
5       DECLARE EXIT HANDLER FOR NOT FOUND
6           SELECT CONCAT('No customer with this ID was found: ', I_CUST_ID) AS MESSAGE;
7       UPDATE CUSTOMER
8         SET LAST_NAME = I_NEW_NAME
9         WHERE CUST_ID = I_CUST_ID;
10
11    END //
12
13   DELIMITER ;
```

UPDATE statement within the procedure

FIGURE 8-15   Using UPDATE in a stored procedure in MySQL

When you run this procedure, you need to furnish values for two arguments. Figure 8-16 uses this procedure to change the name of customer 125 to Johnson.

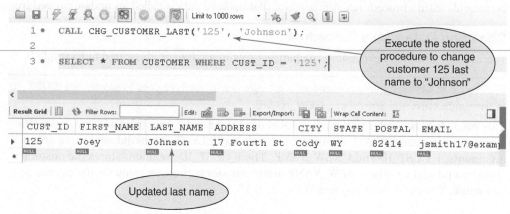

FIGURE 8-16   Execute a stored procedure in MySQL

Deleting Data with a Procedure

Just as you would expect, if you can use an update procedure to change a row in a table, you can also use one to delete a row from a table, as illustrated in Example 9.

EXAMPLE 9: Delete the invoice whose number is stored in I_INVOICE_NUM from the INVOICES table, and also delete each invoice line for the invoice whose invoice number is currently stored in the variable from the INVOICE_LINE table.

If you attempt to delete the invoice in the INVOICES table first, referential integrity will prevent the deletion because matching rows would still exist in the INVOICE_LINE table, so it is a good idea to delete the orders from the INVOICE_LINE table first. The procedure to delete an invoice and its related invoice lines appears in Figure 8-17. This procedure contains two DELETE commands. The first command deletes all invoice lines in the INVOICE_LINE table on which the invoice number matches the value stored in the I_INVOICE_NUM argument. The second command deletes the order in the INVOICES table whose invoice number matches the value stored in the I_INVOICE_NUM argument.

Figure 8-18 shows the use of this procedure to delete invoice number 14219. Even though there are two DELETE commands in the procedure, the user enters the invoice number only once.

```
DELIMITER //
CREATE PROCEDURE DEL_INVOICE (IN I_INVOICE_NUM CHAR (5))
BEGIN
  DELETE FROM INVOICE_LINES
          WHERE INVOICE_NUM = I_INVOICE_NUM;
  DELETE FROM INVOICES
          WHERE INVOICE_NUM = I_INVOICE_NUM;
END //

DELIMITER ;
```

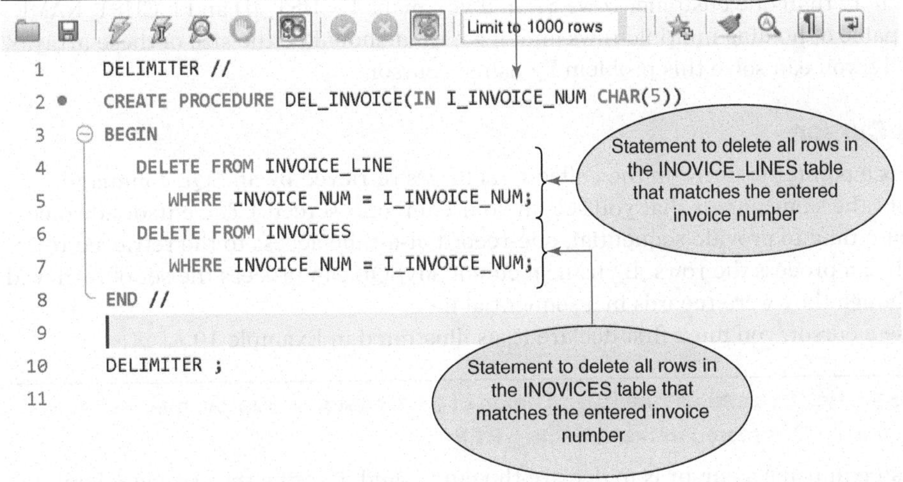

Argument that stores the invoice number to delete

```
1    DELIMITER //
2 •  CREATE PROCEDURE DEL_INVOICE(IN I_INVOICE_NUM CHAR(5))
3  ⊖ BEGIN
4      DELETE FROM INVOICE_LINE
5         WHERE INVOICE_NUM = I_INVOICE_NUM;
6      DELETE FROM INVOICES
7         WHERE INVOICE_NUM = I_INVOICE_NUM;
8    └ END //
9    |
10   DELIMITER ;
11
```

| Limit to 1000 rows |

Statement to delete all rows in the INOVICE_LINES table that matches the entered invoice number

Statement to delete all rows in the INOVICES table that matches the entered invoice number

FIGURE 8-17 Procedure to delete a row and its related rows from multiple tables in MySQL

```
CALL DEL_INVOICE ('14219');
```

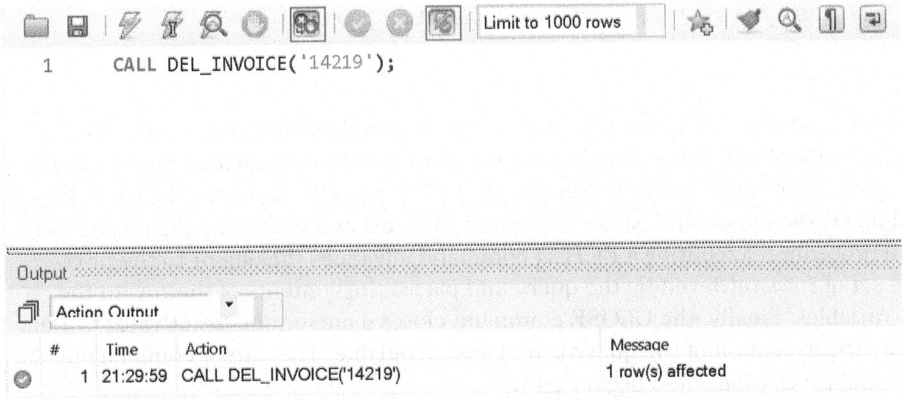

| Limit to 1000 rows |

```
1    CALL DEL_INVOICE('14219');
```

Output

Action Output ▾

#	Time	Action	Message
⊘ 1	21:29:59	CALL DEL_INVOICE('14219')	1 row(s) affected

FIGURE 8-18 Using the procedure to delete an invoice in MySQL

SELECTING MULTIPLE ROWS WITH A PROCEDURE

The procedures you have seen so far include commands that retrieve individual rows. You can use an UPDATE or a DELETE command in MySQL to update or delete multiple rows. The commands are executed and the updates or deletions occur. Then the procedure can move on to the next task.

What happens when a SELECT command in a procedure retrieves multiple rows? For example, suppose the SELECT command retrieves the ID and name of each customer represented by the sales rep whose ID is stored in I_REP_ID. There is a problem—MySQL can process only one record at a time, but this SQL command retrieves more than one row. Whose ID and name are placed in I_CUST_ID and I_CUST_NAME when the command retrieves more than one customer row? Should you make I_CUST_ID and I_CUST_NAME arrays capable of holding multiple rows and, if so, what should be the size of these arrays? Fortunately, you can solve this problem by using a cursor.

Using a Cursor

A **cursor** is a pointer to a row in the collection of rows retrieved by an SQL command. (This is *not* the same cursor that you see on your computer screen.) The cursor advances one row at a time to provide sequential, one-record-at-a-time access to the retrieved rows so MySQL can process the rows. By using a cursor, MySQL can process the set of retrieved rows as though they were records in a sequential file.

To use a cursor, you must first declare it, as illustrated in Example 10.

EXAMPLE 10: Retrieve and list the ID and name of each customer represented by the sales rep whose ID is stored in the variable I_REP_ID.

The first step in using a cursor is to declare the cursor and describe the associated query in the declaration section of the procedure. In this example, assuming the cursor is named CUSTGROUP, the command to declare the cursor is as follows:

```
DECLARE CUSTGROUP CURSOR FOR
SELECT CUST_ID,
  CONCAT(FIRST_NAME, ' ', LAST_NAME) AS CUST_NAME
FROM CUSTOMER
WHERE REP_ID = I_REP_ID;
```

This command does *not* cause the query to be executed at this time; it only declares a cursor named CUSTGROUP and associates the cursor with the indicated query. Using a cursor in a procedure involves three commands: OPEN, FETCH, and CLOSE. The **OPEN** command opens the cursor and causes the query to be executed, making the results available to the procedure. Executing a **FETCH** command advances the cursor to the next row in the set of rows retrieved by the query and places the contents of the row in the indicated variables. Finally, the **CLOSE** command closes a cursor and deactivates it. Data retrieved by the execution of the query is no longer available. The cursor could be opened again later and processing could begin again.

The OPEN, FETCH, and CLOSE commands used in processing a cursor are similar to the OPEN, READ, and CLOSE commands used in processing a sequential file.

Opening a Cursor

Prior to opening the cursor, there are no rows available to be fetched. In Figure 8-19, this is indicated by the absence of data in the CUSTGROUP portion of the figure. The right side of the figure illustrates the variables into which the data is placed (I_CUST_ID and I_CUST_NAME) and the value DONE set to FALSE. (DONE is a variable to be set to TRUE when an exception is raised indicating the cursor has no more rows.) Once the cursor has been opened and all the records have been fetched, the value of DONE is set to TRUE by an exception declared in the procedure. Procedures using the cursor can use this value to indicate when the fetching of rows is complete.

CUSTGROUP

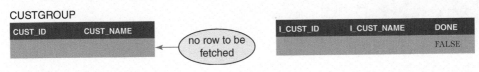

FIGURE 8-19   Before OPEN

The OPEN command is written as follows:

```
OPEN CUSTGROUP;
```

Figure 8-20 shows the result of opening the CUSTGROUP cursor. In the figure, assume that I_REP_ID is set to 15 before the OPEN command is executed; there are now three rows available to be fetched. No rows have yet been fetched, as indicated by the absence of values in I_CUST_NUM and I_CUST_NAME. DONE is still FALSE. The cursor is positioned at the first row; that is, the next FETCH command causes the contents of the first row to be placed in the indicated variables.

CUSTGROUP

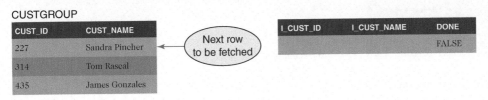

FIGURE 8-20   After OPEN, but before first FETCH

Fetching Rows from a Cursor

To fetch (get) the next row from a cursor, use the FETCH command. The FETCH command is written as follows:

```
FETCH CUSTGROUP INTO I_CUST_ID, I_CUST_NAME;
```

Note that the INTO clause is associated with the FETCH command itself and not with the query used in the cursor definition. The execution of this query could produce multiple rows. The execution of the FETCH command produces only a single row, so it is appropriate that the FETCH command causes data to be placed in the indicated variables.

Figures 8-21 through 8-24 show the result of four FETCH commands. The first three fetches are successful. In each case, the data from the appropriate row in the cursor is placed in the indicated variables and DONE is still FALSE. The fourth FETCH command is different, however, because there is no more data to fetch. In this case, the exception no more rows is raised and the contents of the variables are left untouched and DONE is set to TRUE.

CUSTGROUP

FIGURE 8-21   After first FETCH

CUSTGROUP

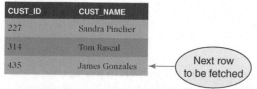

FIGURE 8-22   After second FETCH

CUSTGROUP

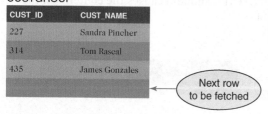

FIGURE 8-23   After third FETCH

CUSTGROUP

FIGURE 8-24   After attempting a fourth FETCH, DONE is set to TRUE

Closing a Cursor

The CLOSE command is written as follows:

```
CLOSE CUSTGROUP;
```

Figure 8-25 shows the result of closing the CUSTGROUP cursor. The data is no longer available.

CUSTGROUP

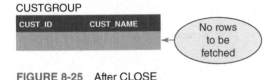

FIGURE 8-25   After CLOSE

Writing a Complete Procedure Using a Cursor

Figure 8-26 shows a complete procedure using a cursor. The declaration portion contains the CUSTGROUP cursor definition. The procedural portion begins with the command to open the CUSTGROUP cursor. The statements between the LOOP and END LOOP commands create a loop that begins by fetching the next row from the cursor and placing the results in I_CUST_ID and I_CUST_NAME. The LEAVE command exits the loop if the condition DONE is tested to be TRUE. If the condition is not true, the SELECT I_CUST_ID and I_CUST_NAME are displayed.

Using More Complex Cursors

The query formulation that defined the cursor in Example 10 was straightforward. Any SQL query is legitimate in a cursor definition. In fact, the more complicated the requirements for retrieval, the more numerous the benefits derived by the programmer who uses embedded SQL. Consider the query in Example 11.

EXAMPLE 11: For each invoice that contains an invoice line for the item whose item ID is stored in I_ITEM_ID, retrieve the invoice number, invoice date, customer ID, and the ID, last name, and first name of the sales rep who represents the customer.

Opening and closing the cursor is done exactly as shown in Example 10. The only difference in the FETCH command is that a different set of variables is used in the INTO clause. Thus, the only real difference is the cursor definition. The procedure shown in Figure 8-27 contains the appropriate cursor definition.

```
DELIMITER //
CREATE PROCEDURE DISP_REP_CUST (IN I_REP_ID CHAR (2))
BEGIN
  DECLARE DONE INT DEFAULT FALSE;
  DECLARE I_CUST_ID CHAR (3);
  DECLARE I_CUST_NAME CHAR(41);
  DECLARE CUSTGROUP CURSORFOR
     SELECT CUST_ID, CONCAT (FIRST_NAME, ' ', LAST_NAME) AS CUST_NAME
           FROM CUSTOMER
           WHERE REP_ID = I_REP_ID;
  DECLARE CONTINUE HANDLER FOR NOT FOUND SET DONE = TRUE;

  OPEN CUSTGROUP;
  READ_LOOP: LOOP
    FETCH CUSTGROUP INTO I_CUST_ID, I_CUST_NAME;
    IF DONE THEN
      LEAVE READ_LOOP;
    END IF;
    SELECT I_CUST_ID, I_CUST_NAME;
  END LOOP;
  CLOSE CUSTGROUP;
END //

DELIMITER ;
```

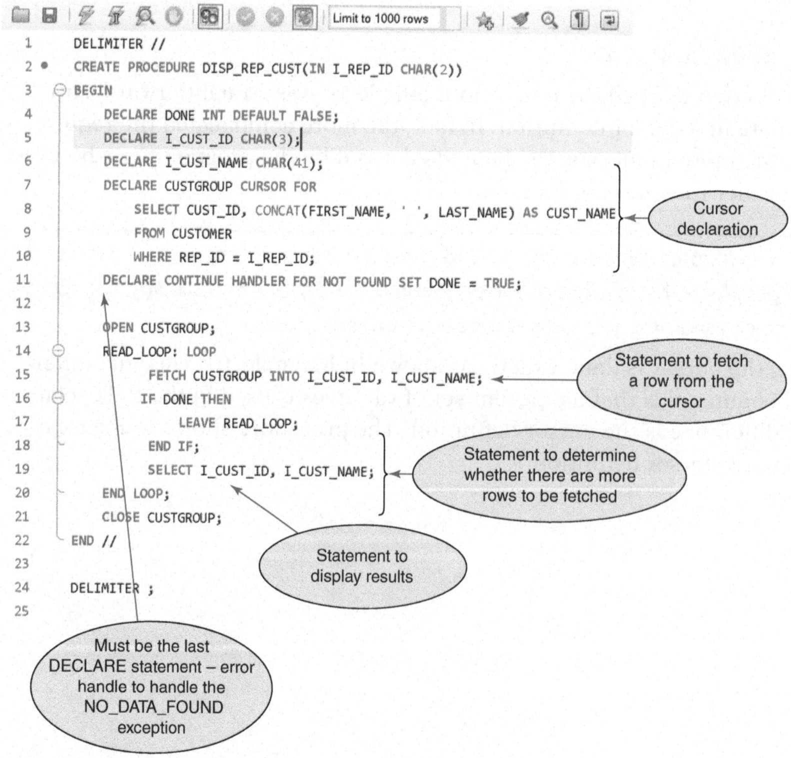

```
 1     DELIMITER //
 2 •   CREATE PROCEDURE DISP_REP_CUST(IN I_REP_ID CHAR(2))
 3   ⊖ BEGIN
 4         DECLARE DONE INT DEFAULT FALSE;
 5         DECLARE I_CUST_ID CHAR(3);
 6         DECLARE I_CUST_NAME CHAR(41);
 7         DECLARE CUSTGROUP CURSOR FOR
 8             SELECT CUST_ID, CONCAT(FIRST_NAME, ' ', LAST_NAME) AS CUST_NAME      Cursor
 9             FROM CUSTOMER                                                        declaration
10             WHERE REP_ID = I_REP_ID;
11         DECLARE CONTINUE HANDLER FOR NOT FOUND SET DONE = TRUE;
12
13         OPEN CUSTGROUP;
14   ⊖   READ_LOOP: LOOP
15             FETCH CUSTGROUP INTO I_CUST_ID, I_CUST_NAME;       Statement to fetch
16   ⊖       IF DONE THEN                                         a row from the
17                 LEAVE READ_LOOP;                               cursor
18             END IF;
19             SELECT I_CUST_ID, I_CUST_NAME;        Statement to determine
20         END LOOP;                                 whether there are more
21         CLOSE CUSTGROUP;                          rows to be fetched
22   END //
23
24     DELIMITER ;
25
```

Statement to display results

Must be the last DECLARE statement – error handle to handle the NO_DATA_FOUND exception

FIGURE 8-26   Procedure with a cursor in MySQL

```
DELIMITER //
CREATE PROCEDURE DISP_ITEM_INVOICES( IN I_ITEM_ID CHAR (4))
BEGIN
  DECLARE DONE INT DEFAULT FALSE;
  DECLARE V_INVOICE_NUM CHAR (5);
  DECLARE V_INVOICE_DATE DATE;
  DECLARE V_CUST_ID CHAR (3);
  DECLARE V_REP_ID CHAR (2);
  DECLARE V_REP_LAST CHAR (20);
  DECLARE V_REP_FIRST CHAR (20);
  DECLARE CUSTGROUP CURSOR FOR
  SELECT INVOICES.INVOICE_NUM, INVOICES.INVOICE_DATE,
  INVOICES.CUST_ID, CUSTOMER.REP_ID,
        SALES_REP.FIRST_NAME, SALES_REP.LAST_NAME
    FROM INVOICES, INVOICE_LINE, CUSTOMER, SALES_REP
   WHERE INVOICES.INVOICE_NUM = INVOICE_LINE.INVOICE_NUM
     AND INVOICES.CUST_ID = CUSTOMER.CUST_ID
     AND CUSTOMER.REP_ID = SALES_REP.REP_ID
     AND INVOICE_LINE.ITEM_ID = I_ITEM_ID;
  DECLARE CONTINUE HANDLER FOR NOT FOUND SET DONE = TRUE;
  OPEN CUSTGROUP;
  READ_LOOP: LOOP
  FETCH CUSTGROUP INTO V_INVOICE_NUM, V_INVOICE_DATE, V_CUST_ID,
  V_REP_ID, V_REP_LAST, V_REP_FIRST;
   IF DONE THEN
    LEAVE READ_LOOP;
   END IF;
   SELECT V_INVOICE_NUM, V_INVOICE_DATE, V_CUST_ID, V_REP_ID,
   V_REP_LAST, V_REP_FIRST;
  END LOOP;
  CLOSE CUSTGROUP;
END //
DELIMITER;
```

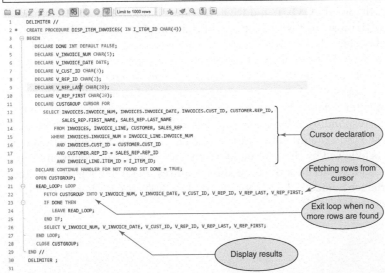

FIGURE 8-27   Procedure with a cursor that involves joining multiple tables in MySQL

Advantages of Cursors

The retrieval requirements in Example 11 are substantial. Beyond coding the preceding cursor definition, the programmer doesn't need to worry about the mechanics of obtaining the necessary data or placing it in the right order, because this happens automatically when the cursor is opened. To the programmer, it seems as if a sequential file already exists that contains the correct data, sorted in the right order. This assumption leads to three main advantages:

1. The coding in the procedure is greatly simplified.
2. Normally in a program, the programmer must determine the most efficient way to access the data. In a program or procedure using embedded SQL, the optimizer determines the best way to access the data. The programmer isn't concerned with the best way to retrieve the data. In addition, when an underlying structure changes (for example, an additional index is created), the optimizer determines the best way to execute the query with the new structure. The program or procedure does not have to change at all.
3. When the database structure changes in such a way that the necessary information is still obtainable using a different query, the only change required in the program or procedure is the cursor definition. The procedural code is not affected.

USING PL/SQL IN ORACLE

In PL/SQL procedural language the CREATE PROCEDURE command, like MySQL, tells Oracle to store the procedure in the database. By including the optional OR REPLACE clause in the CREATE PROCEDURE command, you can use the command to modify an existing procedure. If you omit the OR REPLACE clause, you would need to drop the procedure and then re-create it in order to change the procedure later.

Similar to MySQL, the word IN, OUT, and INOUT behave in the same way in Oracle. Variable names in PL/SQL must start with a letter and can contain letters, dollar signs, underscores, and number signs, but cannot exceed 30 characters. All declared variables must be assigned a data type. You can ensure that a variable has the same data type as a particular column in a table by using the %TYPE attribute. To do so, you include the name of the table, followed by a period and the name of the column, and then %TYPE. When you use %TYPE, you do not enter a data type because the variable is automatically assigned the same type as the corresponding column is written as CUSTOMER.CUST_ID%TYPE.

Oracle Figure 8-5 shows in the first line of the CREATE PROCEDURE command ends with the word AS and is followed by the commands in the procedure. The commands on lines 2 and 3 declare the local variables the procedure requires. In Oracle Figure 8-5, lines 2 and 3 create two variables named V_LAST_NAME and V_FIRST_NAME. Both variables are assigned data types using %TYPE.

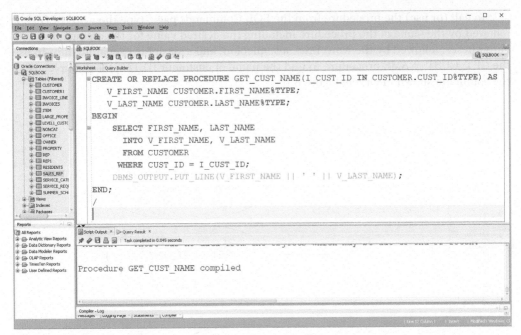

Source: Oracle Corporation

ORACLE FIGURE 8-5   Procedure to find a customer's name given the customer's ID in PL/SQL

In Oracle Figure 8-5, the procedural code begins with the SQL command to select the first name and last name of the sales rep whose number is stored in I_CUST_ID. Similar to MySQL, the SQL command uses the INTO clause to place the results in the V_FIRST_NAME and V_LAST_NAME variables. The next command uses the DBMS_OUTPUT.PUT_LINE procedure to display the concatenation of the V_FIRST_NAME and V_LAST_NAME variables. Notice that a semicolon ends each variable declaration, command, and the word END. The slash (/) at the end of the procedure appears on its own line. In some Oracle environments, the slash is optional. A good practice is to include the slash even when it's not necessary so your procedure always works correctly.

● ORACLE USER NOTE

DBMS_OUTPUT is a package that contains multiple procedures, including PUT_LINE. The SQL Commands page automatically displays the output produced by DBMS_OUTPUT. In the SQL Command Line environment, you first have to execute a SET SERVEROUTPUT ON command to display the output.

To **call** (or use) the procedure from the SQL Commands page, type the word BEGIN, followed by the name of the procedure including the desired value for the argument in parentheses, followed by the word END, a semicolon, and a slash on a separate line. To use the GET_CUST _NAME procedure to find the name of customer ID 125, for example, use the command shown in Oracle Figure 8-6.

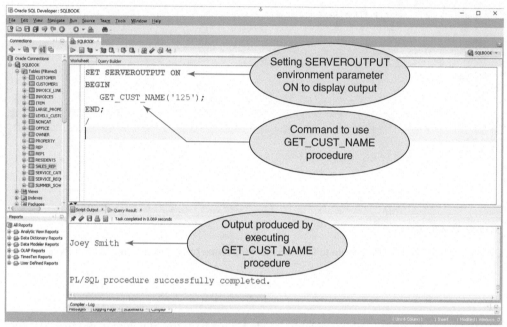

Source: Oracle Corporation

ORACLE FIGURE 8-6   Using the GET_CUST_NAME procedure within an SQL command in PL/SQL

Error Handling in PL/SQL

Similar to MySQL you can handle conditions that arise when accessing the database. You can include the EXCEPTION clause shown in Oracle Figure 8-7 to handle processing an invalid customer ID. In order to handle an exception error no data is found, you may use the NO_DATA_FOUND condition on line 11 as true. When the NO_DATA_FOUND condition is true, the procedure displays the "No customer with this ID: " message followed by the invalid customer ID.

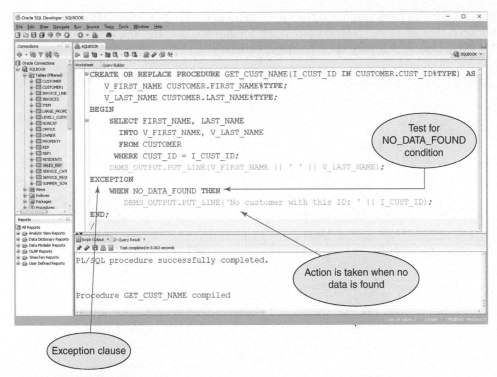

Source: Oracle Corporation

ORACLE FIGURE 8-7   Error handling in PL/SQL

Another common exception in PL/SQL is TOO_MANY_ROWS caused when the SELECT statement returns more than one row. You can manage this error by writing a WHEN clause that contains a TOO_MANY_ROWS condition, following the EXCEPTION clause in the procedure. You can write both WHEN clauses in the same procedure or in separate procedures. When adding both WHEN clauses to the same procedure, however, the EXCEPTION clause appears only once.

● ORACLE USER NOTE

Using UPDATE and DELETE statements in PL/SQL procedure is similar to MySQL with exception of differences in syntax.

Writing a Complete Procedure Using a Cursor in PL/SQL

Oracle Figure 8-8 shows a complete procedure using a cursor. The declaration portion contains the CUSTGROUP cursor definition. The procedural portion begins with the command to open the CUSTGROUP cursor. The statements between the LOOP and END LOOP commands create a loop that begins by fetching the next row from the cursor and placing the results in V_INVOICE_NUM, V_INVOICE_DATE, V_CUST_ID, V_REP_ID, V_REP_LAST,

V_REP_FIRST. The EXIT command tests the condition CUSTGROUP%NOTFOUND. If the condition is true, the loop is terminated. If the condition is not true, the DBMS_OUTPUT. PUT_LINE commands display the contents of variables.

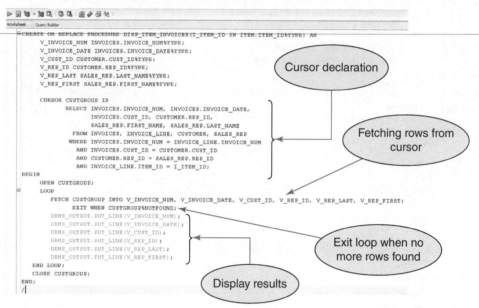

Source: Oracle Corporation

ORACLE FIGURE 8-8   Procedure with a cursor that involves joining multiple tables in PL/SQL

USING T-SQL IN SQL SERVER

SQL Server uses an extended version of SQL called T-SQL (Transact-SQL). You can use T-SQL to create stored procedures and use cursors. The reasons for creating and using stored procedures and cursors are identical to those discussed for PL/SQL. Only the command syntax is different.

Retrieving a Single Row and Column in T-SQL

In Example 7, you learned how to write a procedure in MySQL that takes a customer ID as input and displays the corresponding customer name. The following code shows how you would create the stored procedure in T-SQL:

```
CREATE PROCEDURE usp_GET_CUST_NAME
@custid char(3)
AS
SELECT RTRIM(FIRST_NAME)+' '+RTRIM(LAST_NAME)
FROM CUSTOMER
WHERE CUST_ID = @custid
GO
```

The CREATE PROCEDURE command in the stored procedure causes SQL Server to create a procedure named usp_GET_CUST_NAME. The usp_prefix identifies the procedure as a user-stored procedure. Although using the prefix is optional, it is an easy way to differentiate user-stored procedures from SQL Server system-stored procedures. The argument for this procedure is @custid. In T-SQL, you must assign a data type to parameters. All arguments start with the at (@) sign. Arguments should have the same data type and length as the particular column in a table that they represent. In the CUSTOMER table, CUST_ID was defined with a CHAR data type and a length of 2. The CREATE PROCEDURE command ends with the word AS followed by the SELECT command that comprises the procedure.

To call the procedure, use the EXEC command and include any arguments in single quotes. The procedure to find the name of customer ID 125 is as follows:

```
EXEC usp_DISP_REP_NAME '125'
```

Changing Data with a Stored Procedure in T-SQL

In Example 8, you learned how to write a procedure in MySQL that changes the name of a customer. The following commands show you how to create the stored procedure in T-SQL:

```
CREATE PROCEDURE usp_CHG_CUSTOMER_LAST
@custid char(3),
@newname char(20)
AS
UPDATE CUSTOMER
SET LAST_NAME = @newname
WHERE CUST_ID = @custid
GO
```

The procedure has two arguments, @custid and @newname, and uses an UPDATE command instead of a SELECT command. To execute a stored procedure with two arguments, separate the arguments with a comma as shown in the following command:

```
EXEC usp_CHG_CUST_NAME '125', 'Johnson'
```

Deleting Data with a Stored Procedure in T-SQL

In Example 9, you learned how to write a procedure in MySQL that deletes an invoice number from both the INVOICE_LINE table and the INVOICES table. The following commands show how to create the stored procedure in T-SQL:

```
CREATE PROCEDURE usp_DEL_INVOICE
@invoicenum char(5)
AS
DELETE
FROM INVOICE_LINE
WHERE INVOICE_NUM = @invoicenum
DELETE
FROM INVOICES
WHERE INVOICE_NUM = @invoicenum
GO
```

Using a Cursor in T-SQL

Cursors serve the same purpose in T-SQL as they do in MySQL and PL/SQL and work exactly the same way. You need to declare a cursor, open a cursor, fetch rows from a cursor, and close a cursor. The only difference is in the command syntax. The following T-SQL code performs exactly the same task as that shown in Example 10:

```
CREATE PROCEDURE usp_DISP_REP_CUST
@repid char(2)
AS
  DECLARE @custid char(3)
  DECLARE @custname char(41)
  DECLARE mycursor CURSOR READ_ONLY
      FOR SELECT CUST_ID, FIRST_NAME + ' ' + LAST_NAME AS CUST_NAME
      FROM CUSTOMER WHERE REP_ID = @repid

    OPEN mycursor
    FETCH NEXT FROM mycursor
     INTO @custid, @custname
    WHILE @@FETCH_STATUS = 0
    BEGIN
      PRINT @custid + ' ' + @custname
      FETCH NEXT FROM mycursor
       INTO @custid, @custname
    END
    CLOSE mycursor
    DEALLOCATE mycursor
  GO
```

The procedure uses one argument, @repid. It also uses two variables and each variable must be declared using a DECLARE statement. You also declare the cursor by giving it a name, describing its properties, and associating it with a SELECT statement. The cursor property, READ_ONLY, means that the cursor is used for retrieval purposes only. The OPEN, FETCH, and CLOSE commands perform the same tasks in T-SQL as they do in MySQL. The OPEN command opens the cursor and causes the query to be executed. The FETCH command advances the cursor to the next row and places the contents of the row in the indicated variables. The CLOSE command closes a cursor and the DEALLOCATE command flushes and the association to the cursor is removed. The DEALLOCATE command is not necessary, but it does enable the user to use the same cursor name with another procedure.

The WHILE loop repeats until the value of the system variable @@FETCH_STATUS is not zero. The PRINT command outputs the values stored in @custid and @custname variables.

Using More Complex Cursors in T-SQL

T-SQL also can handle more complex queries. The T-SQL code for Example 11 is shown below:

```
CREATE PROCEDURE usp_DISP_ITEM_INVOICES
@itemid char(4)
AS
DECLARE @invoicenum char(5)
DECLARE @invoicedate date
DECLARE @custid char(3)
DECLARE @repid char(2)
DECLARE @lastname char(15)
DECLARE @firstname char(15)
DECLARE mycursor CURSOR READ_ONLY
  FOR SELECT INVOICES.INVOICE_NUM, INVOICES.INVOICE_DATE,
INVOICES.CUST_ID, CUSTOMER.REP_ID,
     SALES_REP.FIRST_NAME, SALES_REP.LAST_NAME
  FROM INVOICES, INVOICE_LINE, CUSTOMER, SALES_REP
  WHERE INVOICES.INVOICE_NUM = INVOICE_LINE.INVOICE_NUM
  AND INVOICES.CUST_ID = CUSTOMER.CUST_ID
  AND CUSTOMER.REP_ID = SALES_REP.REP_ID
  AND INVOICE_LINE.ITEM_ID = @itemid
OPEN mycursor
FETCH NEXT FROM mycursor
INTO @invoicenum, @invoicedate, @custid, @repid, @lastname, @firstname
WHILE @@FETCH_STATUS = 0
BEGIN
PRINT @invoicenum
PRINT @invoicedate
PRINT @custid
PRINT @repid
PRINT @lastname
PRINT @firstname
FETCH NEXT FROM mycursor
INTO @invoicenum, @invoicedate, @custid, @repid, @lastname, @firstname
END
CLOSE mycursor
DEALLOCATE mycursor
GO
```

USING A TRIGGER

A **trigger** is a procedure that is executed automatically in response to an associated database operation, such as an INSERT, UPDATE, or DELETE command. Unlike a stored procedure, which is executed in response to a user request, a trigger is executed in response to a command that causes the associated database operation to occur.

The examples in this section assume there is a new column named ON_ORDER in the ITEM table. This column represents the number of units of an item currently on order. For example, if there are two separate invoice lines for an item and the number ordered on one invoice line is 3 and the number ordered on the other invoice line is 2, the ON_ORDER value for that item will be 5. Adding, changing, or deleting invoice lines affects the value in the ON_ORDER column for the item. To ensure that the value is updated appropriately, you can use a trigger.

If you created the ADD_INVOICE_LINE trigger in MySQL shown in Figure 8-28, the SQL command in the trigger would be executed when a user adds an invoice line. The trigger must update the ON_ORDER value for the corresponding item to reflect the invoice line. For example, if the value in the ON_ORDER column for item AD72 is 3 and the user adds an invoice line on which the item number is AD72 and the number of units ordered is 2, then 5 units of item AD72 will be on order. When a record is added to the ORDER_LINE table, the ADD_INVOICE_LINE trigger updates the ITEM table by adding the number of units ordered on the invoice line to the previous value in the ON_ORDER column.

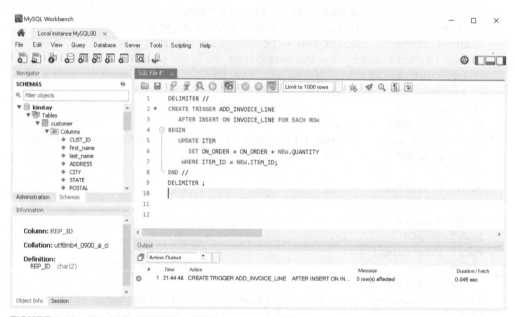

FIGURE 8-28   The ADD_INVOICE_LINE trigger in MySQL

● ORACLE USER NOTE

Oracle Figure 8-9 illustrates the creation of a trigger AFTER INSERT on the INVOICE_LINE table.

(continued)

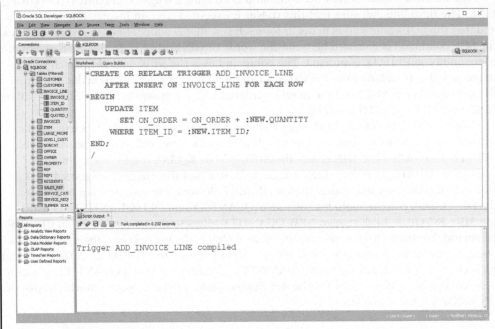

Source: Oracle Corporation

ORACLE FIGURE 8-9　　The ADD_INVOICE_LINE trigger in Oracle

▶ **SQL SERVER USER NOTE**

In SQL Server, you create triggers using T-SQL. The code to create the ADD_INVOICE_LINE trigger is as follows:

```
CREATE TRIGGER ADD_INVOICE_LINE
ON INVOICE_LINE
AFTER INSERT
AS
DECLARE @numbord decimal(3,0)
SELECT @numbord = (SELECT QUANTITY FROM INSERTED)
UPDATE ITEM
SET ON_ORDER = ON_ORDER + @numbord
```

This trigger uses one variable, @numbord, and the value placed in that variable is obtained from the SELECT statement. The INSERTED table is a temporary system table that contains a copy of the values that the last SQL command inserted. The column names are the same column names as in the INVOICE_LINE table. The INSERTED table holds the most recent value of the QUANTITY column, which is what you need to update the ITEM table.

The first line indicates that the command is creating a trigger named ADD_INVOICE_LINE. The third line indicates that this trigger is executed after an invoice line is inserted, and that the SQL command is to occur for each row that is added. Like stored procedures, the SQL command is enclosed between the words BEGIN and END. In this case, the SQL command is an UPDATE command. The command uses the NEW qualifier, which refers to the row that is added to the INVOICE_LINE table. If an invoice line is added on which the item number is AD72 and the number ordered is 2, for example, NEW.ITEM_ID will be AD72 and NEW.QUANTITY will be 2.

The UPDATE_INVOICE_LINE trigger shown in Figure 8-29 in MySQL is executed when a user attempts to update an invoice line. There are two differences between the UPDATE_INVOICE_LINE trigger and the ADD_INVOICE_LINE trigger. First, the third line of the UPDATE_INVOICE_LINE trigger indicates that this trigger is executed after an UPDATE of an invoice line rather than an INSERT. Second, the computation to update the ON_ORDER column includes both NEW.QUANTITY and OLD.QUANTITY. As with the ADD_INVOICE_LINE trigger, NEW.QUANTITY refers to the new value. In an UPDATE command, however, there is also an old value, which is the value before the update takes place. If an update changes the value for QUANTITY from 2 to 3, OLD.QUANTITY is 2 and NEW.QUANTITY is 3. Adding NEW.QUANTITY and subtracting OLD.QUANTITY results in a net change of an increase of 1. (The net change could also be negative, in which case the ON_ORDER value decreases.)

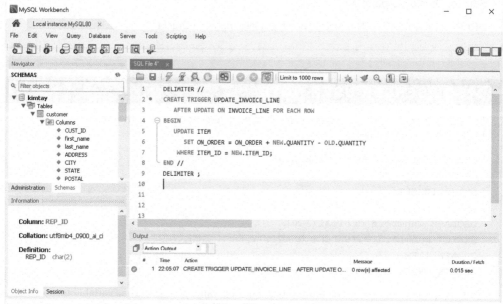

FIGURE 8-29   The UPDATE_INVOICE_LINE trigger in MySQL

● ORACLE USER NOTE

Oracle Figure 8-10 illustrates the creation of the UPDATE_INVOICE_LINE trigger, which executes AFTER UPDATE of the INOVICE_LINE table. Oracle uses a colon ":" as a prefix for OLD and NEW to indicate they are bind variables.

Source: Oracle Corporation

ORACLE FIGURE 8-10 The UPDATE_INVOICE_LINE trigger in Oracle

▶ SQL SERVER USER NOTE

The T-SQL trigger that executes after an UPDATE of an invoice line is as follows:

```
CREATE TRIGGER UPDATE_INVOICE_LINE
ON INVOICE_LINE
AFTER UPDATE
AS
DECLARE @newnumbord decimal(3,0)
DECLARE @oldnumbord decimal (3,0)
SELECT @newnumbord = (SELECT QUNATITY FROM INSERTED)
SELECT @oldnumbord = (SELECT QUNATITY FROM DELETED)
UPDATE ITEM
SET ON_ORDER = ON_ORDER + @newnumbord - @oldnumbord
```

This trigger uses the INSERTED table and the DELETED table. The DELETED table contains the previous value of the QUANTITY column, while the INSERTED column contains the updated value.

The DELETE_INVOICE_LINE trigger shown in Figure 8-30 in MySQL performs a function similar to the other two triggers. When an invoice line is deleted, the ON_ORDER value for the corresponding item is updated by subtracting OLD.QUANTITY from the current ON_ORDER value. (In a delete operation, there is no NEW.QUANTITY.)

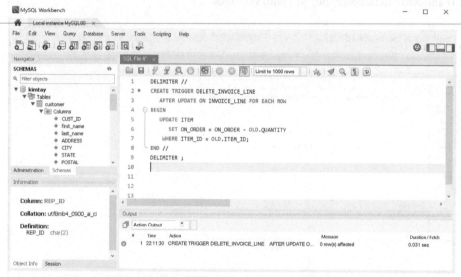

FIGURE 8-30   The DELETE_INVOICE_LINE trigger in MySQL

● ORACLE USER NOTE

Oracle Figure 8-11 illustrates the creation of the DELETE_INVOICE_LINE trigger, which executes AFTER DELETE of the INOVICE_LINE table.

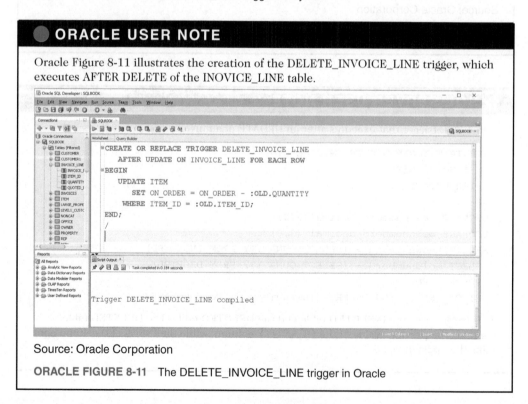

Source: Oracle Corporation

ORACLE FIGURE 8-11   The DELETE_INVOICE_LINE trigger in Oracle

▶ SQL SERVER USER NOTE

The DELETE_INVOICE_LINE trigger uses only the DELETED system table:

```
CREATE TRIGGER DELETE_INVOICE_LINE
ON INVOICE_LINE
AFTER DELETE
AS
DECLARE @numbord decimal (3,0)
SELECT @numbord = (SELECT QUANTITY FROM DELETED)
UPDATE ITEM
SET ON_ORDER = ON_ORDER - @numbord
```

Module Summary

- The results of some functions are based on the values in single records. UPPER and LOWER are two examples of functions that act on character data. UPPER displays each letter in the argument in uppercase. LOWER displays each letter in the argument in lowercase.

- ROUND and FLOOR are two examples of functions that act on numeric data. ROUND produces its result by rounding the value to the specified number of decimal places. FLOOR produces its result by truncating (removing) everything to the right of the decimal point.

- Use the DATE_ADD in MySQL to add days, months, or years to a date. Use the ADD_MONTHS function in Oracle to add a specific number of months to a date. In SQL Server, use the DATEADD function.

- To add a specific number of days to a date, use normal addition. You can also subtract one date from another to produce the number of days between two dates.

- To obtain today's date, use the CURDATE() in MySQL, SYSDATE function in Oracle, and the GETDATE() function in SQL Server.

- To concatenate values in character columns, use the CONCAT() function. In Oracle, separate the column names with two vertical lines (II). Use the RTRIM function to delete any extra spaces that follow the values. In SQL Server, use the + symbol to concatenate values. In Access, use the ampersand (&) symbol to concatenate values.

- A stored procedure is a query saved in a file that users can execute later.

- To create a stored procedure in MySQL, PL/SQL, or T-SQL, use the CREATE PROCEDURE command.

- Variables in MySQL procedures are declared after the word DECLARE. Assign variables as the same type as a column in the database. In Oracle, use the %TYPE attribute.

- Use the INTO clause in the SELECT command to place the results of a SELECT command in variables in MySQL and Oracle.

- You can use the INSERT, UPDATE, and DELETE commands in PL/SQL and T-SQL procedures, even when they affect more than one row.

- When a SELECT command is to retrieve more than one row in MySQL, PL/SQL, or T-SQL, it must be used to define a cursor that is used to select one row at a time.

- Use the OPEN command to activate a cursor and execute the query in the cursor definition.

- Use the FETCH command to select the next row in MySQL, PL/SQL, and T-SQL.

- Use the CLOSE command to deactivate a cursor. The rows initially retrieved will no longer be available to MySQL, PL/SQL, or T-SQL.

- A trigger is an action that occurs automatically in response to an associated database operation, such as an INSERT, UPDATE, or DELETE command. Like a stored procedure, a trigger is stored and compiled on the server. Unlike a stored procedure, which is executed in response to a user request, a trigger is executed in response to a command that causes the associated database operation to occur.

Key Terms

ADD_MONTHS	LOWER
argument	nonprocedural language
call	OPEN
client	PL/SQL
client/server system	procedural code
CLOSE	procedural language
concatenate	ROUND
concatenation	RTRIM
CONVERT	server
CURDATE()	stored procedure
cursor	SYSDATE
DATE_ADD	Transact-SQL
embed	trigger
execute	T-SQL
FETCH	update procedure
FLOOR	UPPER

Review Questions

Module Quiz

1. How do you display letters in uppercase in MySQL, Oracle, and SQL Server? How do you display letters in lowercase in MySQL, Oracle, and SQL Server?

2. How do you round a number to a specific number of decimal places in MySQL, Oracle, and SQL Server? How do you remove everything to the right of the decimal place in MySQL, Oracle, and SQL Server?

3. How do you add months to a date in MySQL, Oracle, and SQL Server? How do you add days to a date? How would you find the number of days between two dates?

4. How do you obtain today's date in MySQL, Oracle, and SQL Server?

5. How do you concatenate values in character columns in MySQL, Oracle, and SQL Server?

6. Which function deletes extra spaces at the end of a value?

7. What are stored procedures? What purpose do they serve?

8. In which portion of a MySQL and PL/SQL procedure do you embed SQL commands?

9. Where do you declare variables in MySQL and PL/SQL procedures?

10. In PL/SQL, how do you assign variables the same type as a column in the database?

11. How do you place the results of a SELECT command into variables in MySQL and PL/SQL?

12. Can you use the INSERT, UPDATE, or DELETE commands to affect more than one row in MySQL and PL/SQL procedures?

13. How do you use a SELECT command that retrieves more than one row in a procedure?

14. Which command activates a cursor?

15. Which command selects the next row in a cursor?

16. Which command deactivates a cursor?

17. What are triggers? What purpose do they serve?

18. What is the purpose of the INSERTED and DELETED tables in SQL Server?

Critical Thinking

1. When you run the following SQL command, the result is "no data found." You know that one record should be retrieved. Rewrite the SQL command using a function that retrieves the record.

```
SELECT ITEM_ID, DESCRIPTION, PRICE
FROM ITEM
WHERE DESCRIPTION = 'Dog Toy Gift Set';
```

Case Exercises

KimTay Pet Supplies

Use the KimTay Pet Supplies database (see Figure 1-2 in Module 1) to complete the following exercises. If directed to do so by your instructor, use the information provided with the Module 3 Exercises to print your output or save it to a file.

1. List the item ID and description for all items. The descriptions should appear in uppercase letters.

2. List the customer ID and first and last names for all customers located in the city of Cody. Your query should ignore case. For example, a customer with the city Cody should be included, as should customers whose city is CODY, cody, cOdY, and so on.

3. List the customer ID, first and last names, and balance for all customers. The balance should be rounded to the nearest dollar.

4. KimTay Pet Supplies is running a promotion that is valid for up to 20 days after an order is placed. List the invoice number, customer ID, customer first and last names, and the promotion date for each invoice. The promotion date is 20 days after the invoice was placed.

5. Write MySQL, PL/SQL, or T-SQL procedures to accomplish the following tasks:

    a. Obtain the name and credit limit of the customer whose ID currently is stored in I_CUST_ID. Place these values in the variables I_CUSTOMER_NAME and I_CREDIT_LIMIT, respectively. Output the contents of I_CUSTOMER_NAME and I_CREDIT_LIMIT.

    b. Obtain the invoice date, customer ID, and first and last names for the invoice whose number currently is stored in I_INVOICE_NUM. Place these values in the variables I_INVOICE_DATE, I_CUST_ID, and I_CUST_NAME, respectively. Output the contents of I_INVOICE_DATE, I_CUST_ID, and I_CUST_NAME.

    c. Add a row to the INVOICE table.

    d. Change the date of the invoice whose number is stored in I_INVOICE_NUM to the date currently found in I_INVOICE_DATE.

    e. Delete the invoice whose number is stored in I_INVOICE_NUM.

6. Write MySQL, PL/SQL, or T-SQL procedures to retrieve and output the item ID, description, location, and price of every item in the category stored in I_CATEGORY.

7. Write a stored procedure in MySQL, PL/SQL, or T-SQL that changes the price of an item with a given item ID. How would you use this stored procedure to change the price of item AD72 to $84.99?

8. Write the code for the following triggers in MySQL, PL/SQL, or T-SQL following the style shown in the text.

    a. When adding a customer, add the customer's balance multiplied by the sales rep's commission rate to the commission for the corresponding sales rep.

    b. When updating a customer, add the difference between the new balance and the old balance multiplied by the sales rep's commission rate to the commission for the corresponding sales rep.

    c. When deleting a customer, subtract the balance multiplied by the sales rep's commission rate from the commission for the corresponding sales rep.

Critical Thinking

1. Oracle SQL includes several date and time functions. Two of these functions are CURRENT_DATE and MONTHS_BETWEEN. Use the Internet to research these functions. How does the CURRENT_DATE function differ from the SYSDATE function? Are the functions available in MySQL and SQL Server? Write a paragraph that discusses what the functions do and any differences and/or similarities between the functions in MySQL, Oracle, and SQL Server. Then perform the following task:

    KimTay Pet Supplies would like to know the number of months between the current date and the invoice date of an invoice. Write an SQL statement in MySQL and Oracle that displays the invoice number and the number of months between the current date and the invoice date. The number of months should display as an integer. (*Hint:* You can nest one function within another function.)

StayWell Student Accommodation

Use the StayWell Accommodation Database (see Figures 1-4 through 1-9 in Module 1) to complete the following exercises. If directed to do so by your instructor, use the information provided with the Module 3 Exercises to print your output or save it to a file.

1. List the owner number, first name, and last name for all owners. The first name should appear in uppercase letters and the last name should appear in lowercase letters.

2. List the owner number and last name for all owners located in the city of Seattle. Your query should ignore case. For example, a customer with the city Seattle should be included, as should customers whose city is SEATTLE, SEAttle, SeAttle, and so on.

3. StayWell is offering a monthly discount for residents who pay their rent on a quarterly basis. The discount is 1.75 percent of the monthly fee. For each property, list the office number, address, owner number, owner's last name, monthly rent, and discount. The discount should be rounded to the nearest dollar.

4. Write PL/SQL or T-SQL procedures to accomplish the following tasks:

    a. Obtain the first name and last name of the owner whose number currently is stored in I_OWNER_NUM. Place these values in the variables I_FIRST_NAME and I_LAST_NAME. Output the contents of I_OWNER_NUM, I_FIRST_NAME, and I_LAST_NAME.

    b. Obtain the office number, address, owner number, owner first name, and owner last name for the property whose property ID is currently stored in I_PROPERTY_ID. Place these values in the variables I_LOCATION_NUM, I_ADDRESS, I_OWNER_NUM, I_FIRST_NAME, and I_LAST_NAME, respectively. Output the contents of I_PROPERTY_ID, I_ADDRESS, I_OWNER_NUM, I_FIRST_NAME, and I_LAST_NAME.

    c. Add a row to the OWNER table.

    d. Change the last name of the owner whose number is stored in I_OWNER_NUM to the value currently found in I_LAST_NAME.

    e. Delete the owner whose number is stored in I_OWNER_NUM.

5. Write PL/SQL or T-SQL procedures to retrieve and output the office number, address, monthly rent, and owner number for every property whose square footage is equal to the square footage stored in I_SQR_FT.

6. Write MySQL functions to accomplish the following tasks:

    a. Delete the owner whose number is stored in I_OWNER_NUM.

    b. Change the last name of the owner whose number is stored in I_OWNER_NUM to the value currently found in I_LAST_NAME.

    c. Retrieve and output the location number, address, monthly rent, and owner number for every property whose square footage is equal to the square footage stored in I_SQR_FT.

7. Write a stored procedure in PL/SQL or T-SQL that changes the monthly rent of a property with a given address and office number. How would you use this stored procedure to change the monthly rent for the property with the address "782 Queen Ln." and office number 1 to $1,100?

8. Assume the OWNER table contains a column named TOTAL_RENT_INCOME that represents the total monthly rent income for all properties owned by that owner. Write the code in PL/SQL or T-SQL for the following triggers following the style shown in the text.

   a. When inserting a row in the PROPERTY table, add the monthly rent to the total rent income for the appropriate owner.

   b. When updating a row in the PROPERTY table, add the difference between the new monthly rent and the old monthly rent to the total rent income for the appropriate owner.

   c. When deleting a row in the PROPERTY table, subtract the monthly rent from the total rent income for the appropriate owner.

Critical Thinking

1. SQL includes many numerical functions. Two of these functions are FLOOR and CEIL. Use the Internet to research these functions. Are the functions available in MySQL, Oracle, and SQL Server? Write a paragraph that discusses what the functions do and any differences and/or similarities between the functions in MySQL, Oracle, and SQL Server. Then perform the following tasks:

   a. StayWell would like to know the impact of discounting monthly rents by 3 percent. Write an SQL statement in Oracle that displays the property ID, address, discounted monthly rent, discounted monthly rent with the CEIL function, and discounted monthly rent with the FLOOR function.

   b. Based on your research, will the values in the three columns vary? If so, how? Use the property with the ID of 6 to explain your answer. Be sure to cite your references.

SQL REFERENCE

You can use this appendix to obtain details concerning important components and syntax of the SQL language. Items are arranged alphabetically. Each item contains a description and a reference to where the item is covered in the text. When appropriate, an example and a description of the query results are given. Some SQL commands also include a description of the clauses associated with them. For each clause, there is a brief description and an indication of whether the clause is required or optional.

ALIASES (PAGES 108, 145–148)

You can specify an alias (alternative name) for each table in a query. You can use the alias in the rest of the command by following the name of the table with a space and the alias name.

The following command creates an alias named R for the SALES_REP table and an alias named C for the CUSTOMER table:

```
SELECT S.REP_ID, S.LAST_NAME, S.FIRST_NAME, C.CUST_ID,
    C.FIRST_NAME, C.LAST_NAME
    FROM SALES_REP S, CUSTOMER C
    WHERE S.REP_ID = C.REP_ID;
```

ALTER TABLE (PAGES 189–190)

Use the ALTER TABLE command to change a table's structure. As shown in Figure A-1, you type the ALTER TABLE command, followed by the table name, and then the alteration to perform.

CLAUSE	DESCRIPTION	REQUIRED?
ALTER TABLE *table name*	Indicates name of table to be altered.	Yes
alteration	Indicates type of alteration to be performed.	Yes

FIGURE A-1 ALTER TABLE command

The following command alters the CUSTOMER table by adding a new CUSTOMER_TYPE column:

```
ALTER TABLE CUSTOMER
ADD CUSTOMER_TYPE CHAR(1);
```

The following command changes the CITY column in the CUSTOMER table so that it cannot accept nulls:

```
ALTER TABLE CUSTOMER
MODIFY CITY NOT NULL;
```

Note: In SQL Server, you must use the ALTER COLUMN clause and completely define the column as follows:

```
ALTER TABLE CUSTOMER
ALTER COLUMN CITY CHAR(15) NOT NULL
```

COLUMN OR EXPRESSION LIST (SELECT CLAUSE) (PAGES 97–99)

To select columns, use the SELECT clause followed by the list of columns, separated by commas.

The following SELECT clause selects the CUST_ID, FIRST_NAME, LAST_NAME, and BALANCE columns:

```
SELECT CUST_ID, FIRST_NAME, LAST_NAME, BALANCE
```

Use an asterisk in a SELECT clause to select all columns in a table. The following SELECT clause selects all columns:

```
SELECT *
```

Computed Columns (Pages 107–108)

You can use a computation in place of a column by typing the computation. For readability, you can type the computation in parentheses, although it is not necessary to do so.

The following SELECT clause selects the CUST_ID, FIRST_NAME, and LAST_NAME columns as well as the results of subtracting the BALANCE column from the CREDIT_LIMIT column:

```
SELECT CUST_ID, FIRST_NAME, LAST_NAME,  (CREDIT_LIMIT - BALANCE)
```

The DISTINCT Operator (Pages 117–119)

To avoid selecting duplicate values in a command, use the DISTINCT operator. When you omit the DISTINCT operator from the command and the same value appears on multiple rows in the table, that value appears on multiple rows in the query results.

The following query selects all customer numbers from the INVOICES table, but lists each customer number only once in the results:

```
SELECT DISTINCT(CUST_ID)
FROM INVOICES;
```

Functions (Pages 113–119)

You can use functions in a SELECT clause. The most commonly used functions are AVG (to calculate an average), COUNT (to count the number of rows), MAX (to determine the maximum value), MIN (to determine the minimum value), and SUM (to calculate a total).

The following SELECT clause calculates the average balance:

```
SELECT AVG(BALANCE)
```

COMMIT (PAGES 180–183)

Use the COMMIT command to make permanent any updates made since the last command. If no previous COMMIT command has been executed, the COMMIT command makes all the updates during the current work session permanent immediately. All updates become permanent automatically when you exit SQL. Figure A-2 describes the COMMIT command.

CLAUSE	DESCRIPTION	REQUIRED?
COMMIT	Indicates that a COMMIT is to be performed.	Yes

FIGURE A-2   COMMIT command

The following command makes all updates since the most recent COMMIT command permanent:

```
COMMIT;
```

Note: In SQL Server, the following command makes all updates since the most recent COMMIT command:

```
COMMIT TRANSACTION
```

CONDITIONS (PAGES 97–113)

A condition is an expression that can be evaluated as either true or false. When you use a condition in a WHERE clause, the results of the query contain those rows for which the condition is true. You can create simple conditions and compound conditions using the BETWEEN, LIKE, IN, EXISTS, ALL, and ANY operators, as described in the following sections.

Simple Conditions (Pages 97–102)

A simple condition has the form column name, comparison operator, and then either another column name or a value. The available comparison operators are = (equal to), < (less than), > (greater than), <= (less than or equal to), >= (greater than or equal to), and <> (not equal to).

The following WHERE clause uses a condition to select rows where the balance is greater than the credit limit:

```
WHERE BALANCE > CREDIT_LIMIT
```

Compound Conditions (Pages 102–105)

Compound conditions are formed by connecting two or more simple conditions using the AND, OR, and NOT operators. When simple conditions are connected by the AND operator, all the simple conditions must be true in order for the compound condition to be true. When simple conditions are connected by the OR operator, the compound condition is true whenever any one of the simple conditions is true. Preceding a condition by the NOT operator reverses the truth of the original condition.

The following WHERE clause is true if the location is equal to B *or* the units on hand is greater than 15, *or* both:

```
WHERE (LOCATION = 'B') OR (ON_HAND > 15)
```

The following WHERE clause is true if the location is equal to B *and* the units on hand is greater than 15:

```
WHERE (LOCATION = 'B') AND (ON_HAND > 15)
```

The following WHERE clause is true if the location is *not* equal to B:

```
WHERE NOT (LOCATION = 'B')
```

BETWEEN Conditions (Pages 105–107)

You can use the BETWEEN operator to determine if a value is within a range of values. The following WHERE clause is true if the balance is between 500 and 1,000:

```
WHERE BALANCE BETWEEN 500 AND 1000
```

LIKE Conditions (Pages 109–110)

LIKE conditions use wildcards to select rows. Use the percent (%) wildcard to represent any collection of characters. The condition LIKE '%Rock%' is true for data consisting of any character or characters, followed by the letters "Rock," followed by any other character or characters. Another wildcard symbol is the underscore (_), which represents any individual character. For example, "T_m" represents the letter "T," followed by any single character, followed by the letter "m," and would be true for a collection of characters such as Tim, Tom, or T3m.

The following WHERE clause is true if the value in the ADDRESS column is Rock, Rocky, or any other value that contains "Rock":

```
WHERE ADDRESS LIKE '%ROCK%'
```

IN Conditions (Pages 111, 139–140)

You can use IN to determine whether a value is in some specific collection of values. The following WHERE clause is true if the credit limit is 500, 750, or 1,000:

```
WHERE CREDIT_LIMIT IN (500, 750, 1000)
```

The following WHERE clause is true if the item ID is in the collection of item IDs associated with invoice number 14228:

```
WHERE ITEM_ID IN
(SELECT ITEM_ID
FROM INVOICE_LINE
WHERE ITEM_ID = '14228')
```

EXISTS Conditions (Pages 140–142)

You can use EXISTS to determine whether the results of a subquery contain at least one row. The following WHERE clause is true if the results of the subquery contain at least one row that has at least one invoice line with the desired invoice number and on which the item number is FS42:

```
WHERE EXISTS
(SELECT *
FROM INVOICE_LINE
WHERE INVOICES.INVOICE_NUM = INVOICE_LINE.INVOICE_NUM
AND INVOICE_LINE.ITEM_ID = 'FS42')
```

ALL and ANY (Pages 159–162)

You can use ALL or ANY with subqueries. If you precede the subquery by ALL, the condition is true only if it is satisfied for all values produced by the subquery. If you precede the subquery by ANY, the condition is true if it is satisfied for any value (one or more) produced by the subquery.

The following WHERE clause is true if the balance is greater than every balance contained in the results of the subquery:

```
WHERE BALANCE > ALL
(SELECT BALANCE
FROM CUSTOMER
WHERE REP_ID= '20')
```

The following WHERE clause is true if the balance is greater than at least one balance contained in the results of the subquery:

```
WHERE BALANCE > ANY
(SELECT BALANCE
FROM CUSTOMER
WHERE REP_ID = '20')
```

CREATE INDEX (PAGES 219–223)

Use the CREATE INDEX command to create an index for a table. Figure A-3 describes the CREATE INDEX command.

CLAUSE	DESCRIPTION	REQUIRED?
CREATE INDEX *index name*	Indicates the name of the index.	Yes
ON *table name*	Indicates the table for which the index is to be created.	Yes
column list	Indicates the column(s) on which the index is to be based.	Yes

FIGURE A-3   CREATE INDEX command

The following CREATE INDEX command creates an index named REP_NAME for the SALES_REP table on the combination of the LAST_NAME and FIRST_NAME columns:

```
CREATE INDEX REP_NAME ON SALES_ REP (LAST_NAME, FIRST_NAME);
```

CREATE TABLE (PAGES 60–65)

Use the CREATE TABLE command to define the structure of a new table. Figure A-4 describes the CREATE TABLE command.

CLAUSE	DESCRIPTION	REQUIRED?
CREATE TABLE *table name*	Indicates the name of the table to be created.	Yes
(column and data type list)	Indicates the columns that comprise the table along with their corresponding data types (see Data Types section).	Yes

FIGURE A-4   CREATE TABLE command

The following CREATE TABLE command creates the SALES_REP table and its associated columns and data types. REP_ID is the table's primary key.

```
CREATE TABLE SALES_REP
(REP_ID CHAR(2) PRIMARY KEY,
FIRST_NAME CHAR(15),
LAST_NAME CHAR(15),
ADDRESS CHAR(15),
CITY CHAR(15),
STATE CHAR(2),
POSTAL CHAR(5),
COMMISSION DECIMAL(7,2),
RATE DECIMAL(3,2) );
```

CREATE VIEW (PAGES 201–210)

Use the CREATE VIEW command to create a view. Figure A-5 describes the CREATE VIEW command.

CLAUSE	DESCRIPTION	REQUIRED?
CREATE VIEW *view name* AS	Indicates the name of the view to be created.	Yes
query	Indicates the defining query for the view.	Yes

FIGURE A-5   CREATE VIEW command

The following CREATE VIEW command creates a view named DOGS, which consists of the item ID, item description, units on hand, and unit price for all rows in the ITEM table on which the category is DOG:

```
CREATE VIEW DOGS AS
SELECT ITEM_ID, DESCRIPTION, ON_HAND, PRICE
FROM ITEM
WHERE CATEGORY = 'DOG';
```

DATA TYPES (PAGES 67–68)

Figure A-6 describes the data types that you can use in a CREATE TABLE command.

DATA TYPE	DESCRIPTION
CHAR(n)	Stores a character string n characters long. You use the CHAR data type for columns that contain letters and special characters and for columns containing numbers that are not used in any calculations. Because neither sales rep ID numbers nor customer ID numbers are used in any calculations, for example, the REP_ID and CUST_ID columns are both assigned the CHAR data type.
VARCHAR(n)	An alternative to CHAR that stores a character string up to n characters long. Unlike CHAR, only the actual character string is stored. If a character string 20 characters long is stored in a CHAR(30) column, for example, it will occupy 30 characters (20 characters plus 10 blank spaces). If it is stored in a VARCHAR(30) column, it will only occupy 20 spaces. In general, tables that use VARCHAR instead of CHAR occupy less space, but the DBMS does not process them as rapidly during queries and updates. However, both are legitimate choices. This text uses CHAR, but VARCHAR works equally well.
DATE	Stores date data. The specific format in which dates are stored varies from one SQL implementation to another. In MySQL and SQL Server, dates are enclosed in single quotation marks and have the format YYYY-MM-DD (for example, '2020-10-23' is October 23, 2020). In Oracle, dates are enclosed in single quotation marks and have the format DD-MON-YYYY (for example, '23-OCT-2020' is October 23, 2020).
DECIMAL(p,q)	Stores a decimal number p digits long with q of the digits being decimal places to the right of the decimal point. For example, the data type DECIMAL(5,2) represents a number with three places to the left and two places to the right of the decimal (for example, 123.45). You can use the contents of DECIMAL columns in calculations. You also can use the NUMERIC(p,q) data type in MySQL to store a decimal number. Oracle and SQL Server also use NUMBER(p,q) to store a decimal number.
INT	Stores integers, which are numbers without a decimal part. The valid range is –2147483648 to 2147483647. You can use the contents of INT columns in calculations. If you follow the word INT with AUTO_INCREMENT, you create a column for which SQL will automatically generate a new sequence number each time you add a new row. This would be the appropriate choice, for example, when you want the DBMS to generate a value for a primary key.
SMALLINT	Stores integers but uses less space than the INT data type. The valid range is –32768 to 32767. SMALLINT is a better choice than INT when you are certain that the column will store numbers within the indicated range. You can use the contents of SMALLINT columns in calculations.

FIGURE A-6   Data types

DELETE ROWS (PAGES 78, 184–185)

Use the DELETE command to delete one or more rows from a table. Figure A-7 describes the DELETE command.

CLAUSE	DESCRIPTION	REQUIRED?
DELETE *table name*	Indicates the table from which the row(s) are to be deleted.	Yes
WHERE *condition*	Indicates a condition. Those rows for which the condition is true are retrieved and deleted.	No (If you omit the WHERE clause, all rows are deleted.)

FIGURE A-7   DELETE command

The following DELETE command deletes any row from the LEVEL1_CUSTOMER table on which the customer ID is 227:

```
DELETE LEVEL1_CUSTOMER
WHERE CUST_ID = '227';
```

DESCRIBE (PAGES 88–91)

In Oracle, you can use the DESCRIBE command to list all the columns in a table and their properties. The following command describes the SALES_REP table:

```
DESCRIBE SALES_REP;
```

Note: In SQL Server, execute the sp_columns command to list all the columns in a table. The following command lists all the columns in the SALES_REP table (note that you may omit command EXEC):

```
exec sp_columns SALES_REP
```

DROP INDEX (PAGES 223–224)

Use the DROP INDEX command to delete an index, as shown in Figure A-8.

CLAUSE	DESCRIPTION	REQUIRED?
DROP INDEX *index name*	Indicates the name of the index to be dropped.	Yes

FIGURE A-8   DROP INDEX command

The following DROP INDEX command deletes the index named CRED_NAME:

```
DROP INDEX CRED_NAME;
```

Note: In SQL Server, you must qualify the index name with table name as follows:

```
DROP INDEX CUSTOMER.CRED_NAME
```

DROP TABLE (PAGES 66–67, 196)

Use the DROP TABLE command to delete a table, as shown in Figure A-9.

CLAUSE	DESCRIPTION	REQUIRED?
DROP TABLE *table name*	Indicates name of the table to be dropped.	Yes

FIGURE A-9   DROP TABLE command

The following DROP TABLE command deletes the table named LEVEL1_CUSTOMER:

```
DROP TABLE LEVEL1_CUSTOMER;
```

DROP VIEW (PAGE 216)

Use the DROP VIEW command to delete a view, as shown in Figure A-10.

CLAUSE	DESCRIPTION	REQUIRED?
DROP VIEW *view name*	Indicates the name of the view to be dropped.	Yes

FIGURE A-10   DROP VIEW command

The following DROP VIEW command deletes the view named DOGS:

```
DROP VIEW DOGS;
```

GRANT (PAGES 217–219)

Use the GRANT command to grant privileges to a user. Figure A-11 describes the GRANT command.

CLAUSE	DESCRIPTION	REQUIRED?
GRANT *privilege*	Indicates the type of privilege(s) to be granted.	Yes
ON *database object*	Indicates the database object(s) to which the privilege(s) pertain.	Yes
TO *user name*	Indicates the user(s) to whom the privilege(s) are to be granted. To grant the privilege(s) to all users, use the TO PUBLIC clause.	Yes

FIGURE A-11   GRANT command

The following GRANT command grants the user named Johnson the privilege of selecting rows from the SALES_REP table:

```
GRANT SELECT
ON SALES_REP
TO Johnson;
```

INSERT INTO (QUERY) (PAGES 174–175)

Use the INSERT INTO command with a query to insert the rows retrieved by a query into a table. As shown in Figure A-12, you must indicate the name of the table into which the row(s) is inserted and the query whose results are inserted into the named table.

Clause	DESCRIPTION	Required?
INSERT INTO *table name*	Indicates the name of the table into which the row(s) is inserted.	Yes
query	Indicates the query whose results are inserted into the table.	Yes

FIGURE A-12   INSERT INTO (query) command

The following INSERT INTO command inserts rows selected by a query into the LEVEL1_CUSTOMER table:

```
INSERT INTO LEVEL1_CUSTOMER
SELECT CUST_ID, FIRST_NAME, LAST_NAME, BALANCE, CREDIT_LIMIT, REP_ID
FROM CUSTOMER
WHERE CREDIT_LIMIT = 500;
```

INSERT INTO (VALUES) (PAGES 69–73)

Use the INSERT INTO command and the VALUES clause to insert a row into a table by specifying the values for each of the columns. As shown in Figure A-13, you must indicate the table into which to insert the values and then list the values to insert in parentheses.

Clause	DESCRIPTION	Required?
INSERT INTO *table name*	Indicates the name of the table into which the row is inserted.	Yes
VALUES *(values list)*	Indicates the values for each of the columns on the new row.	Yes

FIGURE A-13   INSERT INTO (values) command

The following INSERT INTO command inserts the values shown in parentheses as a new row in the SALES_REP table:

```
INSERT INTO SALES_REP
VALUES
('25', 'Campos', 'Rafael', '724 Vinca Dr. ', 'Grove', 'WY', '90092',
'305-555-1234', 23457.50, 0.06);
```

INTEGRITY (PAGES 229–232)

You can use the ALTER TABLE command with an appropriate ADD CHECK, ADD PRIMARY KEY, or ADD FOREIGN KEY clause to specify integrity. Figure A-14 describes the ALTER TABLE command for specifying integrity.

Clause	DESCRIPTION	Required?
ALTER TABLE *table name*	Indicates the table for which integrity is being specified.	Yes
integrity clause	ADD CHECK, ADD PRIMARY KEY, or ADD FOREIGN KEY	Yes

FIGURE A-14   Integrity options

The following ALTER TABLE command changes the ITEM table so the only legal values for the CATEGORY column are BRD, FSH, DOG, CAT, and HOR:

```
ALTER TABLE ITEM
ADD CHECK (CATEGORY IN ('BRD', 'FSH ', 'DOG ','CAT', 'HOR') );
```

The following ALTER TABLE command changes the SALES_REP table so the REP_ID column is the table's primary key:

```
ALTER TABLE SALES_REP
ADD PRIMARY KEY(REP_ID);
```

The following ALTER TABLE command changes the CUSTOMER table so that the REP_ID column in the CUSTOMER table is a foreign key referencing the primary key of the SALES_REP table:

```
ALTER TABLE CUSTOMER
ADD FOREIGN KEY(REP_ID) REFERENCES SALES_REP;
```

REVOKE (PAGES 218–219)

Use the REVOKE command to revoke privileges from a user. Figure A-15 describes the REVOKE command.

CLAUSE	DESCRIPTION	REQUIRED?
REVOKE *privilege*	Indicates the type of the privilege(s) to be revoked.	Yes
ON *database object*	Indicates the database object(s) to which the privilege pertains.	Yes
FROM *user name*	Indicates the user name(s) from whom the privilege(s) are to be revoked.	Yes

FIGURE A-15   REVOKE command

The following REVOKE command revokes the SELECT privilege for the SALES_REP table from the user named Johnson:

```
REVOKE SELECT
ON SALES_REP
FROM Johnson;
```

ROLLBACK (PAGES 186–187)

Use the ROLLBACK command to reverse (undo) all updates since the execution of the previous COMMIT command. If no COMMIT command has been executed, the command will undo all changes made during the current work session. Figure A-16 describes the ROLLBACK command.

CLAUSE	DESCRIPTION	REQUIRED?
ROLLBACK	Indicates that a rollback is to be performed.	Yes

FIGURE A-16   ROLLBACK command

The following command reverses all updates made since the time of the last COMMIT command:

```
ROLLBACK;
```

Note: In SQL Server, the following command reverses all updates made since the time of the last COMMIT command:

```
ROLLBACK TRANSACTION
```

SELECT (PAGES 74–76, 97–129)

Use the SELECT command to retrieve data from a table or from multiple tables. Figure A-17 describes the SELECT command.

CLAUSE	DESCRIPTION	REQUIRED?
SELECT *column or expression list*	Indicates the column(s) and/or expression(s) to be retrieved.	Yes
FROM *table list*	Indicates the table(s) required for the query.	Yes
WHERE *condition*	Indicates one or more conditions. Only the rows for which the condition(s) are true are retrieved.	No (If you omit the WHERE clause, all rows are retrieved.)
GROUP BY *column list*	Indicates column(s) on which rows are to be grouped.	No (If you omit the GROUP BY clause, no grouping occurs.)
HAVING *condition involving groups*	Indicates a condition for groups. Only groups for which the condition is true is included in query results. Use the HAVING clause only if the query output is grouped.	No (If you omit the HAVING clause, all groups are included.)
ORDER BY *column or expression list*	Indicates column(s) on which the query output is to be sorted.	No (If you omit the ORDER BY clause, no sorting occurs.)

FIGURE A-17   SELECT command

The following SELECT command joins the INVOICES and INVOICE_LINE tables. The command selects the customer ID, invoice number, invoice date, and the sum of the product of the number ordered and unit price, renamed as INVOICE_TOTAL. Records are grouped by invoice number, customer ID, and date. Only groups on which the invoice total is greater than 250 are included. Groups are ordered by invoice number.

```
SELECT INVOICES.CUST_ID, INVOICES.INVOICE_NUM, INVOICE_DATE,
SUM(QUANTITY * QUOTED_PRICE) AS INVOICE_TOTAL
FROM INVOICES, INVOICE_LINE
WHERE INVOICES.INVOICE_NUM = INVOICE_LINE.INVOICE_NUM
  GROUP BY INVOICES.INVOICE_NUM, CUST_ID, INVOICE_DATE
  HAVING SUM(QUANTITY * QUOTED_PRICE) > 250
ORDER BY INVOICES.INVOICE_NUM;
```

SUBQUERIES (PAGES 121–123, 142–144)

You can use one query within another. The inner query is called a subquery and it is evaluated first. The outer query is evaluated next, producing the item description for each item whose item ID is in the list.

The following command contains a subquery that produces a list of item IDs included in invoice number 14216:

```
SELECT DESCRIPTION
FROM ITEM
WHERE ITEM_ID IN
(SELECT ITEM_ID
FROM INVOICE_LINE
WHERE INVOICE_NUM = '14216');
```

UNION, INTERSECT, AND MINUS (PAGES 153–158)

Connecting two SELECT commands with the UNION operator produces all the rows that are in the results of the first query, the second query, or both queries. Connecting two SELECT commands with the INTERSECT operator produces all the rows that are in the results of both queries. Connecting two SELECT commands with the MINUS operator produces all the rows that are in the results of the first query, but *not* in the results of the second query. Figure A-18 describes the UNION, INTERSECT, and MINUS operators.

CLAUSE	DESCRIPTION
UNION	Produces all the rows that are in the results of the first query, the second query, or both queries.
INTERSECT	Produces all the rows that are in the results of both queries.
MINUS	Produces all the rows that are in the results of the first query but not in the results of the second query.

FIGURE A-18   UNION, INTERSECT, and MINUS operators

Note: SQL Server supports the UNION and INTERSECT operations; however, SQL Server does not support the MINUS operator.

The following query displays the customer ID and customer name of all customers that are represented by sales rep 15, *or* that have orders, *or* both:

```
SELECT CUST_ID, FIRST_NAME, LAST_NAME
FROM CUSTOMER
WHERE REP_ID = '15'
UNION
SELECT CUSTOMER.CUST_ID, FIRST_NAME, LAST_NAME
FROM CUSTOMER, INVOICES
WHERE CUSTOMER.CUST_ID = INVOICES.CUST_ID;
```

The following query displays the customer ID and customer name of all customers that are represented by sales rep 15 *and* that have orders:

```
SELECT CUST_ID, FIRST_NAME, LAST_NAME
FROM CUSTOMER
WHERE REP_ID = '15'
INTERSECT
SELECT CUSTOMER.CUST_ID, FIRST_NAME, LAST_NAME
FROM CUSTOMER, INVOICES
WHERE CUSTOMER.CUST_ID = INVOICES.CUST_ID;
```

The following query displays the customer ID and customer name of all customers that are represented by sales rep 15 but that do *not* have orders:

```
SELECT CUST_ID, FIRST_NAME, LAST_NAME
FROM CUSTOMER
WHERE REP_ID = '15'
MINUS
SELECT CUSTOMER.CUST_ID, FIRST_NAME, LAST_NAME
FROM CUSTOMER, INVOICES
WHERE CUSTOMER.CUST_ID = INVOICES.CUST_ID;
```

UPDATE (PAGES 76–77, 176–179, 184–185)

Use the UPDATE command to change the contents of one or more rows in a table. Figure A-19 describes the UPDATE command.

CLAUSE	DESCRIPTION	REQUIRED?
UPDATE *table name*	Indicates the table whose contents are changed.	Yes
SET *column = expression*	Indicates the column to be changed, along with an expression that provides the new value.	Yes
WHERE *condition*	Indicates a condition. The change occurs only on those rows for which the condition is true.	No (If you omit the WHERE clause, all rows are updated.)

FIGURE A-19 UPDATE command

The following UPDATE command changes the customer name on the row in LEVEL1_CUSTOMER on which the customer ID is 227:

```
UPDATE LEVEL1_CUSTOMER
SET FIRST_NAME = 'Janet'
WHERE CUST_ID = '227';
```

HOW DO I REFERENCE

This appendix answers frequently asked questions about how to accomplish a variety of tasks using SQL. Use the second column to locate the correct section in Appendix A that answers your question.

How Do I	Review the Named Section(s) in Appendix A
Add columns to an existing table?	ALTER TABLE
Add rows or insert rows?	INSERT INTO (Values)
Calculate a statistic (sum, average, maximum, minimum, or count)?	1. SELECT 2. Column or Expression List (SELECT Clause) (Use the appropriate function in the query.)
Change rows?	UPDATE
Create data type for a column?	1. CREATE TABLE 2. Data Types
Create a table?	CREATE TABLE
Create a view?	CREATE VIEW
Create an index?	CREATE INDEX
Delete a table?	DROP TABLE
Delete a view?	DROP VIEW
Delete an index?	DROP INDEX
Delete rows?	DELETE Rows
Describe a table's layout?	DESCRIBE
Drop a table?	DROP TABLE
Drop a view?	DROP VIEW
Drop an index?	DROP INDEX
Grant a privilege?	GRANT
Group data in a query?	SELECT (Use a GROUP BY clause.)
Insert rows?	INSERT INTO (Values)
Insert rows using a query?	INSERT INTO (Query)
Join tables?	Conditions (Include a WHERE clause to relate the tables.)
Make updates permanent?	COMMIT
Order query results?	SELECT (Use the ORDER BY clause.)
Prohibit nulls?	1. CREATE TABLE 2. ALTER TABLE (Include the NOT NULL clause in a CREATE TABLE or ALTER TABLE command.)
Remove a privilege?	REVOKE
Remove rows?	DELETE Rows
Retrieve all columns?	1. SELECT 2. Column or Expression List (SELECT Clause) (Type * in the SELECT clause.)

FIGURE B-1   How Do I reference

How Do I	Review the Named Section(s) in Appendix A
Retrieve all rows?	SELECT (Omit the WHERE clause.)
Retrieve only certain columns?	1. SELECT 2. Column or Expression List (SELECT Clause) (Type the list of columns in the SELECT clause.)
Select all columns?	1. SELECT 2. Column or Expression List (SELECT Clause) (Type * in the SELECT clause.)
Select all rows?	SELECT (Omit the WHERE clause.)
Select only certain columns?	1. SELECT 2. Column or Expression List (SELECT Clause) (Type the list of columns in the SELECT clause.)
Select only certain rows?	1. SELECT 2. Conditions (Use a WHERE clause.)
Sort query results?	SELECT (Use an ORDER BY clause.)
Specify a foreign key?	Integrity (Use the ADD FOREIGN KEY clause in an ALTER TABLE command.)
Specify a primary key?	Integrity (Use the ADD PRIMARY KEY clause in an ALTER TABLE command.)
Specify a privilege?	GRANT
Specify integrity?	Integrity (Use an ADD CHECK, ADD PRIMARY KEY, and/or ADD FOREIGN KEY clause in an ALTER TABLE command.)
Specify legal values?	Integrity (Use an ADD CHECK clause in an ALTER TABLE command.)
Undo updates?	ROLLBACK
Update rows?	UPDATE
Use a calculated field?	1. SELECT 2. Column or Expression List (SELECT Clause) (Enter a calculation in the query.)
Use a compound condition?	1. SELECT 2. Conditions (Use simple conditions connected by AND, OR, or NOT in a WHERE clause.)
Use a compound condition in a query?	Conditions

FIGURE B-1 How Do I reference (Continued)

How Do I	Review the Named Section(s) in Appendix A
Use a condition in a query?	1. SELECT 2. Conditions (Use a WHERE clause.)
Use a subquery?	Subqueries
Use a wildcard?	1. SELECT 2. Conditions (Use LIKE and a wildcard in a WHERE clause.)
Use an alias?	Aliases (Enter an alias after the name of each table in the FROM clause.)
Use set operations (union, intersection, difference)?	UNION, INTERSECT, and MINUS (Connect two SELECT commands with UNION, INTERSECT, or MINUS.)

FIGURE B-1   How Do I reference (Continued)

THE 10 COMMANDMENTS OF WRITING QUERIES

1. Always select the columns or any derived column you want to display. These columns are part of SELECT.
2. In the FROM clause, list all the tables where columns or derived columns belong. Add all tables required to complete the join.
3. If you have more than one table in the FROM clause, you must join them using the WHERE clause.
4. Use the WHERE clause if you want to restrict (filter) rows from the result set.
5. You must use the GROUP BY clause when one of the columns listed in the SELECT clause is part of a group function (aggregate function or multiple-row function) and other columns listed in the SELECT clause are not. You must list all columns that are not part of the group function in GROUP BY.
6. Use the HAVING clause when you need to restrict (filter) groups from the result set.
7. ORDER BY is always the last clause in the SELECT statement.
8. Use a subquery when you need a piece of data to answer a question.
9. Columns in the outer query are visible to the inner query but not vice versa.
10. An outer join is when you want rows to return from table A even though there is no match in table B.

INDEX